WITHDRAWN

# The
# Reading/Writing
# Connection

**Cynthia B. Earle**
*St. Petersburg College*

**Christine Zimmermann**
*Southern New Hampshire University*

D0024330

Longman

New York • San Francisco • Boston
London • Toronto • Sydney • Tokyo • Singapore • Madrid
Mexico City • Munich • Paris • Cape Town • Hong Kong • Montreal

Vice President and Publisher: Joseph Terry
Senior Acquisitions Editor: Steven Rigolosi
Senior Marketing Manager: Melanie Craig
Supplements Editor: Donna Campion
Production Manager: Joseph Vella
Project Coordination, Photo Research, Text Design,
 and Electronic Page Makeup: Thompson Steele, Inc.
Cover Design Manager: John Callahan
Cover Designer: Joan O'Connor
Cover Illustration: Artville
Manufacturing Buyer: Roy Pickering
Printer and Binder: Hamilton Printing
Cover Printer: Phoenix Color Corp.

For permission to use copyrighted material, grateful acknowledgment is made to the copyright holders on pp. 251–254, which are hereby made part of this copyright page.

**Library of Congress Cataloging-in-Publication Data**

Earle, Cynthia B.
 The reading/writing connection / Cynthia B. Earle, Christine Zimmermann.
  p. ; cm.
 Includes bibliographical references and index.
 ISBN 0-321-08950-2 (pbk. : alk. paper).
  1. English language--Rhetoric. 2. English language--Grammar--Handbooks,
manuals, etc. 3. Reading comprehension. 4. Report writing. I. Zimmermann,
Christine. II. Title.

PE1408.E24 2002
808'.0427--dc21

                                                    2002276819

Copyright © 2003 by Addison Wesley Longman, Inc.

All rights reserved. No part of this publication may be reproduced, stored in a retrieval system, or transmitted, in any form or by any means, electronic, mechanical, photo-copying, recording, or otherwise, without the prior written permission of the publisher. Printed in the United States.

Please visit our website at http://www.ablongman.com

ISBN 0-321-08950-2

1 2 3 4 5 6 7 8 9 10—HT—05 04 03 02

*Dedicated to our college students,
past, present, and future, from
whom we have learned so much*

# Brief Contents

# Contents

# Preface

*The Reading/Writing Connection* combines a reading and writing text and a grammar handbook and emphasizes the connection between receptive and expressive language. The text, designed to assist students in acquiring the basic reading and writing skills essential for success in college and beyond, combines the dual sides of the literacy coin: reading and writing. But, unlike most writing texts, this book begins with a crash course in reading. We introduce students to the five levels of reading: the literal, interpretive, analytical, critical, and creative. Before receiving intensive instruction and practice in the reading and writing of short essays, students study and practice identifying the basic components of the literal and interpretive levels—topic, main idea, thesis statement, minor details, purpose, style, and tone. Next we introduce the writing process. Students study the rhetorical modes as tools to help them with both reading and writing. As they learn the analytical, critical, and creative levels of reading and writing, they study the ideas and issues found in selected readings and respond to them in carefully organized and clearly written essays of their own, thereby combining reading skills with composing strategies.

In addition to many reading and writing exercises, *The Reading/Writing Connection* offers a basic review of the most frequent grammatical errors made by college students. We believe that acquiring these skills, combined with improved reading and composing strategies, will allow students to meet the writing expectations of the academic community as well as those of future employers.

## CONTENT OVERVIEW

Part I introduces the combined reading/writing process and examines the common features of the two. We illustrate this process with two examples of model essays written by students, showing the methods these students used to reach their final products.

Part II explores the act of reading. We define reading and explain the components of active reading. We then detail the literal and interpretive levels of reading before probing how to improve, acquire, and respond to reading. In all instances, we offer exercises to aid understanding of these concepts.

Part III discusses the act of writing. We define writing and then introduce and explain the writing process. Prewriting draws a parallel to the third level of reading, the analytical level, when we compare the techniques used to read analytically with those techniques used to write—including active reading, brainstorming, clustering or mapping, outlining, and journal writing. A chapter on writing paragraphs leads to the rhetorical modes that we believe students need to know in order to recognize reading and writing patterns. Responding to text corresponds to the critical and creative levels of reading; we explain summary, paraphrase, quotation, and we give examples of written responses that analyze essays. A chapter explaining revision and editing (and the differences between them) ends the writing part of the text.

Finally, the handbook in Part IV reviews the most common grammar errors we see in college writing: form and function of parts of speech, sentence patterns, pronoun problems, punctuation problems, and sentence problems.

# FEATURES

*The Reading/Writing Connection* offers many features designed to help students become better readers and writers.

- Varied and high-interest student essays as well as professionally written models by multicultural authors
- Focus on academic reading and writing skills
- Emphasis on active reading at literal, interpretive, analytical, critical, and creative levels paralleled by writing skills
- Exercises that aid skills comprehension
- Contextual grammar exercises that use the student's own work
- Glossary of unfamiliar terms
- List of homonyms and other commonly confused words
- Study skills integrated through the text
- An awareness of ESL concerns

You will note that we have not included vocabulary study. Although we strongly recommend continual attention to vocabulary building, we believe students should be responsible for their personal vocabulary lists; we do not think text authors should provide those lists.

You will also note that we have not stressed computer information. This text is a reading and writing text, not an introduction to computers. We have, though, occasionally suggested ways in which the computer can help us all as we strive to become better writers.

# THE TEACHING AND LEARNING PACKAGE

A complete **instructor's manual** to accompany *The Reading/Writing Connection* is available (ISBN 0-321-08949-9). Prepared by the author, the instructor's manual for *The Reading/Writing Connection* serves as a companion to instructors using this text. It provides instructors with an awareness of the skills college freshmen need to master as they progress through the text. The body of the manual follows the order of chapters in the text and consists of a four-part structure for each chapter: learning objectives, an abstract for each chapter, teaching suggestions, and answers to selected exercises. It also introduces some additional writing exercises.

Students who purchase a new copy of this text can receive a free subscription to **The Longman Writer's Warehouse**, an all-inclusive multimedia Website for developing writers. The innovative and exciting online supplement is the perfect accompaniment to any developmental writing course. Developed by developmental English instructors especially for developing writers, The Writer's Warehouse covers every part of the writing process. Also included are electronic journaling capabilities, multimedia activities, diagnostic tests, an interactive handbook, and a complete instructor's manual. The Writer's Warehouse requires no space on your school's server; rather, students complete and store their work on the Longman server, and are able to access it, revise it, and continue working at any time. For more details about how to shrinkwrap a free subscription to The Writer's Warehouse with this text, please consult your Longman sales representative. For a free guided tour of the site, visit **http://longmanwriterswarehouse.com.**

In addition, a series of other skills-based supplements is available for both instructors and students. All of these supplements are available either free or at greatly reduced prices.

## For Additional Reading and Reference

**The Dictionary Deal**    Two dictionaries can be shrinkwrapped with *The Reading/Writing Connection* at a nominal fee. *The New American Webster Handy College Dictionary* is a paperback reference text with more than 100,000 entries. *Merriam Webster's Collegiate Dictionary*, tenth edition, is a hardback reference with a citation file of more than 14.5 million examples of English words drawn from actual use. For more information on how to shrinkwrap a dictionary with your text, please contact your Longman sales representative.

**Penguin Quality Paperback Titles**    A series of Penguin paperbacks is available at a significant discount when shrinkwrapped with this text. Some titles available are Toni Morrison's *Beloved*, Julia Alvarez's *How the Garcia Girls Lost Their Accents*, Mark Twain's *Huckleberry Finn, Narrative of the Life of*

*Frederick Douglass*, Harriet Beecher Stowe's *Uncle Tom's Cabin*, Dr. Martin Luther King, Jr.'s *Why We Can't Wait*, and plays by Shakespeare, Miller, and Albee. For a complete list of titles or more information, please contact your Longman sales consultant.

***100 Things to Write About***    This 100-page book contains 100 individual assignments for writing on a variety of topics and in a wide range of formats, from expressive to analytical. Ask your Longman sales representative for a sample copy. 0-673-98239-4

**Newsweek Alliance**    Instructors may choose to shrinkwrap a 12-week subscription to *Newsweek* with any Longman text. The price of the subscription is 57 cents per issue (a total of $6.84 for the subscription). Available with the subscription is a free "Interactive Guide to *Newsweek*"—a workbook for students who are using the text. In addition, Newsweek provides a wide variety of instructor supplements free to teachers, including maps, Skills Builders, and weekly quizzes. For more information on the Newsweek program, please contact your Longman sales representative.

## Electronic and Online Offerings

**The Writer's ToolKit Plus**    This CD-ROM offers a wealth of tutorial, exercise, and reference material for writers. It is compatible with either a PC or Macintosh platform, and is flexible enough to be used either occasionally for practice or regularly in class lab sessions. For information on how to bundle this CD-ROM FREE with your text, please contact your Longman sales representative.

**The Longman English Pages Web Site**    Both students and instructors can visit our free content-rich Web site for additional reading selections and writing exercises. From the Longman English pages, visitors can conduct a simulated Web search, learn how to write a resume and cover letter, or try their hand at poetry writing. Stop by and visit us at
**http://www.ablongman.com/englishpages.**

**The Longman Electronic Newsletter**    Twice a month during the spring and fall, instructors who have subscribed receive a free copy of the Longman Developmental English Newsletter in their e-mailbox. Written by experienced classroom instructors, the newsletter offers teaching tips, classroom activities, book reviews, and more. To subscribe, visit the Longman Developmental English Web site at **http://www.ablongman.com/basicskills**, or send an e-mail to **Basic Skills@ablongman.com.**

## For Instructors

**[NEW] Electronic Test Bank for Writing**   This electronic test bank features more than 5,000 questions in all areas of writing, from grammar to paragraphing, through essay writing, research, and documentation. With this easy-to-use CD-ROM, instructors simply choose questions from the electronic test bank, then print out the completed test for distribution. CD-ROM: 0-321-08117-X Print version: 0-321-08486-1

**Competency Profile Test Bank, Second Edition**   This series of 60 objective tests covers ten general areas of English competency, including fragments; comma splices and run-ons; pronouns; commas; and capitalization. Each test is available in remedial, standard, and advanced versions. Available as reproducible sheets or in computerized versions. Free to instructors. Paper version: 0-321-02224-6; Computerized IBM: 0-321-02633-0; Computerized Mac: 0-321-02632-2

**Diagnostic and Editing Tests, and Exercises, Fourth Edition**   This collection of diagnostic tests helps instructors assess students' competence in Standard Written English for purpose of placement or to gauge progress. Available as reproducible sheets or in computerized versions, and free to instructors. Paper: 0-321-10022-0; CD-ROM: 0-321-10499-4

**ESL Worksheets, Third Edition**   These reproducible worksheets provide ESL students with extra practice in areas they find the most troublesome. A diagnostic test and post-test are provided, along with answer keys and suggested topics for writing. Free to adopters. 0-321-07765-2

**Longman Editing Exercises**   54 pages of paragraph editing exercises give students extra practice using grammar skills in the context of longer passages. Free when packaged with any Longman title. 0-205-31792-8

**80 Practices**   A collection of reproducible, ten-item exercises that provide additional practices for specific grammatical usage problems, such as comma splices, capitalization, and pronouns. Includes an answer key, and free to adopters. 0-673-53422-7

**CLAST Test Package, Fourth Edition**   These two 40-item objective tests evaluate students' readiness for the CLAST exams. Strategies for teaching CLAST preparedness are included. Free with any Longman English title. Reproducible sheets: 0-321-01950-4 Computerized IBM version: 0-321-01982-2 Computerized Mac version: 0-321-01983-0

**TASP Test Package, Third Edition**   These 12 practice pre-tests and post-tests assess the same reading and writing skills covered in the TASP examination. Free with any Longman English title. Reproducible sheets: 0-321-01959-8 Computerized IBM version: 0-321-01985-7 Computerized Mac version: 0-321-01984-9

*Teaching Online: Internet Research, Conversation, and Composition,* **Second Edition**   Ideal for instructors who have never surfed the Net, this easy-to-follow guide offers basic definitions, numerous examples, and step-by-step information about finding and using Internet sources. Free to adopters. 0-321-01957-1

*Teaching Writing to the Non-Native Speaker*   This booklet examines the issues that arise when non-native speakers enter the developmental classroom. Free to instructors, it includes profiles of international and permanent ESL students, factors influencing second-language acquisition, and tips on managing a multicultural classroom. 0-673-97452-9

## For Students

**[NEW] The Longman Writer's Journal**   This journal for writers, free with *The Reading/Writing Connection*, offers students a place to think, write, and react. For an examination copy, contact your Longman sales consultant. 0-321-08639-2

**[NEW] The Longman Researcher's Journal**   This journal for writers and researchers, free with this text, helps students plan, schedule, write, and revise their research project. An all-in-one resource for first-time researchers, the journal guides students gently through the research process. 0-321-09530-8

**[NEW] The Longman Writer's Portfolio**   This unique supplement provides students with a space to plan, think about, and present their work. The portfolio includes an assessing/organizing area (including a grammar diagnostic test, a spelling quiz, and project planning worksheets), a before and during writing area (including peer review sheets, editing checklists, writing self-evaluations, and a personal editing profile), and an after-writing area (including a progress chart, a final table of contents, and a final assessment). Ask your Longman sales representative for ISBN 0-321-10765-9

*Researching Online,* **Sixth Edition**   A perfect companion for a new age, this indispensable new supplement helps students navigate the Internet. Adapted from *Teaching Online,* the instructor's Internet guide, *Researching*

*Online* speaks directly to students, giving them detailed, step-by-step instructions for performing electronic searches. Available free when shrink-wrapped with this text. 0-321-11733-6

***Learning Together: An Introduction to Collaborative Theory***  This brief guide to the fundamentals of collaborative learning teaches students how to work effectively in groups, how to revise with peer response, and how to co-author a paper or report. Shrinkwrapped free with any Longman Basic Skills text. 0-673-46848-8

***A Guide for Peer Response,*** **Second Edition**  This guide offers students forms for peer critiques, including general guidelines and specific forms for different stages in the writing process. Also appropriate for freshman-level course. Free to adopters. 0-321-01948-2

**[FOR FLORIDA ADOPTIONS]** ***Thinking Through the Test,*** **by D.J. Henry**  This workbook, prepared especially for students in Florida, offers ample skill and practice exercises to help students prep for the Florida State Exit Exam. To shrinkwrap this workbook free with your textbook, please contact your Longman sales representative. Available in two versions: with and without answers. Also available: two laminated grids (one for reading, one for writing) that can serve as handy references for students preparing for the Florida State Exit Exam.

# ACKNOWLEDGMENTS

We would like to thank the following students and friends for their assistance with this book: Robert Begiebing, professor of English, for his contribution of the "Active Reader's Outline" and for his positive comments on our very first draft that encouraged us to continue on to final publication; Helen Berthiaume, accounting manager, for her continuing faith and encouragement; Lois Bradt, lecturer in English, for her rhetorical modes writing exercise; Jeannine Chasse, for her essay on alcohol and heredity; Melissa J. Downs, for her writing exercise based on "Why Isn't Pete Rose in the Baseball Hall of Fame?"; Eleanor Freiburger, professor of ethics, for "Analyzing Essays" and "Critical Reading Worksheet;" Robert Fleeson, professor of English, for his submission of the essay about alcohol and heredity; Clifford D. Guilfoyle, for his fall 1997 English exam; Margaret Murphy, lecturer in English, for her grammar exercise suggestions and for just "being there;" Danielle Vander Voort, for her fall 1997 English exam; Susan Youngs, assistant professor, for her essay, "A Civility Lesson for Students;" and Walter Zimmermann, professor of psychology, for his hours of encouragement.

We would also like to thank the following reviewers: James Allen, College of DuPage; Joseph Booker, Palo Alto College; Rafael Castillo, Palo Alto College; Charles Grogg, Santa Barbara City College; Adam C. Hartman, California State University, San Bernadino; and Will Zhang, Des Moines Area Community College.

And finally, we wish to thank Steven Rigolosi, senior editor at Longman Publishers, for his patience, his humor, and his brilliance. Without his encouragement, right from the start, this book would never have come to fruition.

*Cynthia B. Earle*
*Christine Zimmermann*

# Introduction to Students

*The Reading/Writing Connection* is designed to help you acquire the basic reading and writing skills essential for success in college and beyond by combining the dual sides of the literacy coin: reading and writing. The book provides intensive instruction and practice in the reading and writing of short essays. You will study the ideas and issues found in selected readings and respond to them in carefully organized and clearly written essays of your own. You will examine the texts of other writers and prepare essays, thereby combining reading skills with composing strategies.

In addition, you will review the most frequent grammatical errors made by college students. The handbook for writers will help you learn to edit your own errors to ensure a high level of correctness and clarity in your prose. Acquiring these skills, combined with improving reading and composing strategies, will allow you to meet the writing expectations of the academic community as well as those of future employers.

Few can deny the critical importance of reading and writing skills in academic and employment circles. Unfortunately, not all students enter college with proficiency in these vital areas. We want you to succeed in your new academic environment, and we are convinced that written expression often determines whether or not you will achieve your educational objectives. As a result, we are fully committed to helping you acquire the reading and writing skills that will allow you to perform effectively in your classrooms, in your professions, and in your respective communities. This text will help you read more effectively and produce acceptable if not exemplary essays if you follow its advice—and if you practice sufficiently.

# The Reading/Writing Connection

# PART I
# Introduction

# CHAPTER 1

# The Reading/Writing Process

You may be wondering why you need a course in basic writing. Here is our response: Communication is the number one skill needed in the workplace. It ranks above all technical expertise, including an understanding of computers. Very simply stated, it does not matter how much you know about any subject if you are unable to communicate that knowledge to others.

The actual process of communication involves four components: listening, speaking, reading, and writing. Learning these skills occurs in this order when we are children and first acquire language. As we develop our language ability, these four components continually interact with one another. Most of your college courses will help you develop listening and speaking skills, and many of them will also require generous quantities of reading and writing to develop the last two.

But this course is singularly devoted to the reading/writing connection. It is probably the most important course you will take in college because success in all of your other courses will depend on how well you can read and write. And these two processes are inseparable as we create meaning from our reading and as we express our own ideas on paper. When we read and when we write, we create a text based on our memories and past experiences. We plan, compose, reflect, and edit with both reading and writing. These stages overlap and repeat, sometimes occurring at the same time. The use of questions forms another connecting link between these two processes. **Critical thinking**, necessary for college success, comes from questioning. The acts of reading and writing continually merge as we ask questions and answer them to construct meaning (McKusick et al. 30).

# COMMON FEATURES
# OF READING AND WRITING

What are some of the common features of these two forms of communication? During the planning stages for both reading and writing, we determine a **topic**, consider background experience (prior knowledge), set purposes, and make predictions. The composing or drafting step, although traditionally applied to writing, also describes steps in the act of reading. We need to reflect on our understanding, expand our vocabularies, and decide on major and minor ideas. This revising step calls for us to reconsider meaning of the author's or our own words, and to reread or rewrite (Chamblee 533).

So when we read and write, we go through a series of comparable steps. But why do we need to engage in both processes simultaneously? These two forms of communication enhance one another continually in college course work.

As we read, we constantly mark the text and take notes; in other words, we write in response to the meaning we derive from the printed pages to assure our understanding of the material. We often ask and answer specific questions and write a summary upon completion as well.

When we write, we pause at various points to read and reflect on what we have written. In the prewriting stage, we might brainstorm or map our ideas and then step back to review what we have assembled. As we draft a piece, we might read that draft and then reread sentences, paragraphs, or entire sections—and, of course, we reread the completed draft. With each time through, we gain further insight and continue to revise beyond the original text.

# TWO SUCCESSFUL ESSAYS

In order to demonstrate the reading/writing connection and the process involved in writing an essay in response to a reading, we present two students' essays, exactly as they wrote them (complete with errors). You will also see two copies of the assigned essay (one as the students first saw it, and one marked up by a student after she completed her second reading). Next you will see these students' rough drafts (one with an accompanying outline), followed by their final drafts. Throughout the entire preparation time, these students used the combined literacy skills of reading and writing interchangeably. These examples serve as models of the kind of reading and writing you will be able to produce when you finish this course successfully.

# Turn Off the TV Before It Ruins Us

## David Nyhan

1    I'm not a doctor, but I play one when I'm talking about TV.

2    And the American Medical Association and I agree: Television is bad for kids.

3    Young people not only would kill to watch TV; they do kill from staring goggle-eyed at the box, a truly infernal machine that delivers two hundred thousand acts of violence to the typical youngster's brain pan before he's old enough to drive.

4    Every kid in America, on average, witnesses sixteen thousand murders on TV before reaching the ripe old age of eighteen. And you wonder why they throw candy wrappers on the sidewalk or refuse to give an old lady a seat on a crowded bus? Geddoudda here, witch, or I'll blow you away!

5    Four hours a day is what the average kid watches. That twenty-eight hours a week, over the year, is more time than he spends in school (less than one-fourth of the day for less than 180 days).

6    The AMA has studied the phenomena of self-hypnotic television consumption and concluded: Aaaaarrrrrrgh!!!

7    Did you know that wherever television-watching is introduced, homicide rates double within a decade and a half? The babies born to households where TV was just coming in grow up (if they're lucky) to be fifteen-year-olds in communities with twice as many homicides.

8    Little kids who OD on TV kick and punch and bite much more frequently than the little monsters who do not have their sensitivities dulled by the repetitive and mindless violence of the cathode ray projector.

9    How bad does it get for a teenager who watches a lot of TV? He or she is fatter, sicker, more likely to drink and smoke and drug, and more likely to engage in premature sexual conduct that can be harmful to him or the kid he's messing with.

10    TV is an open sewer running into the minds of the impressionable, and progressively desensitized, young. It is a conveyor belt of cynicism, of self-gratification, of violence-inducing behavior, of role modeling gone wrong, of tasteless drivel. The more meretricious the content, the more successful the sale of same. TV is repackaged dross on video for the ages, syndication rights reserved.

11    It is ruining the country. Our society's rot owes more to television than any other single cause. As the dominant medium, it overwhelms the periodic, valiant, and ultimately futile appeals to a higher morality and a more inspirational way of dealing with the rest of humanity.

12    Television makes everyone cynical, more convinced that no one is honest, no one pure, no one even admirable. All the politicians are crooks, the athletes

crooks, the journalists cynics, the businessmen greedheads, the clergy corrupt, the movie stars perverse.

13    Six out of ten family meals take place under the baleful glare of a working TV set. More than half of America's kids have TV sets in their bedrooms, where they can pig out on whatever vile fare is lowest common denominator of the day.

14    We already have 1.6 million Americans behind bars. That's almost 2 percent of our total employment rate. Most of them are young, most are uneducated, and most are coming out, eventually, to a community near you. They watched too much TV when they were kids, raised in single-parent, often violence-racked households where they got cuffed around when they weren't staring at some stupid television program.

15    Does it get any better if we shut off the tube and ask them to listen to music? Not much. Three out of four of the top-selling CDs of 1995 use cuss words and exalt guns, rape, or murder, according to a *Providence Journal-Bulletin* report.

16    Between grades seven to twelve, teenagers drain in 10,500 hours of rock music—that's more hours than they spent in class in all the years between second grade and graduating from high school.

17    The impact on our kids of electronic media—ranging from the soporific to the truly horrific—is the single biggest problem our society faces. It's a much bigger deal than the deficit or taxes or "job-loss anxiety" labels tossed about in the election campaigns.

18    The degrading of our human capital by the corrosive moral erosion of television and the related video-audio industries is a challenge of immense significance. The politicians nibble around the edges for slivers of political advantage.

19    But the dumbing-down of a generation, the deadening of moral sensitivity in millions of youngsters, is a much greater threat than anything rumbling in the Middle East. Our real problem is the Middle West, and the rest of Middle America. Our kids are bathed in filth, in trivia, in meaningless violence, in false happy endings, in cynical nattering from false media gods.

20    It's a disease. It requires prevention. And vaccination. And, occasionally, something drastic, like amputation. In my family we still talk about one Super Bowl eve when my sister got so mad at the stupefied gazes on the faces of her four kids that she lugged the TV set into her car, drove to the reservoir, and tossed it in, leaving it sitting cockeyed and unplugged on the ice she forgot to take into account.

21    The AMA is on the right side on this one. Our future is rotting, one channel at a time.

## Response: Danielle

### *Nyhan's Marked-Up Essay*

## TURN OFF THE TV BEFORE IT RUINS US
### The Boston Globe/September 16, 1996

I'm not a doctor, but I play one when I'm talking about TV.

And the American Medical Association and I agree: <u>Television is bad for kids.</u>

**Nyhan's thesis**

**influences kids into doing bad acts**

Young people not only would kill to watch TV; <u>they do kill from staring goggle-eyed at the box, a truly infernal machine that delivers two hundred thousand acts of violence to the typical youngster's brain pan before he's old enough to drive.</u>

**connection between TV violence and real violence**

Every kid in America, on average, <u>witnesses sixteen thousand murders on TV before reaching the ripe old age of eighteen.</u> And you wonder why they throw candy wrappers on the sidewalk or refuse to give an old lady a seat on a crowded bus? Geddoudda here, witch, or I'll blow you away!

Four hours a day is what the average kid watches. That twenty-eight hours a week, over the year, is more time than he spends in school (less than one-fourth of the day for less than 180 days).

The AMA has studied the phenomena of self-hypnotic television consumption and concluded: Aaaaarrrrrrgh!!!

**¶ of supporting facts**

Did you know that wherever television-watching is introduced, homicide rates double within a decade and a half? The babies born to households where TV was just coming in grow up (if they're lucky) to be fifteen-year-olds in communities with twice as many homicides.

Little kids who OD on TV kick and punch and bite much more frequently than the little monsters who do not have their sensitivities dulled by the repetitive and mindless violence of the cathode ray projector.

How bad does it get for a teenager who watches a lot of TV? He or she is fatter, sicker, more likely to drink and smoke and drug, and more likely to

*Kids who watch TV are more likely to do things that will hurt them and others.*

engage in premature sexual conduct that can be harmful to him or the kid he's messing with.

TV is an open sewer running into the minds of the impressionable, and progressively desensitized, young. It is a conveyor belt of cynicism, of self-gratification, of violence-inducing behavior, of <u>role modeling gone wrong</u>, of

*feels it has to do w/bad role models*

tasteless drivel. The more meretricious the content, the more successful the sale of same. TV is repackaged dross on video for the ages, syndication rights reserved.

It is ruining the country. Our society's rot owes more to television than any other single cause. As the dominant medium, it overwhelms the periodic, valiant, and ultimately futile appeals to a higher morality and a more inspirational way of dealing with the rest of humanity.

Television makes everyone cynical, more convinced that no one is honest, no one pure, no one even admirable. <u>All the politicians are crooks, the athletes</u>

*TV gives us a bad impression of people.*

<u>crooks, the journalists cynics, the businessmen greedheads, the clergy corrupt, the movie stars perverse.</u>

Six out of ten family meals take place under the baleful glare of a working TV set. More than half of America's kids have TV sets in their bedrooms, where they can pig out on whatever vile fare is lowest common denominator of the day.

We already have 1.6 million Americans behind bars. That's almost 2 percent of our total employment rate. Most of them are young, most are uneducated, and most are coming out, eventually, to a community near you. <u>They</u>

*Is this the common characteristics of a felon?*

<u>watched too much TV when they were kids, raised in single-parent, often violence-racked households where they got cuffed around when they weren't staring at some stupid television program.</u>

Does it get any better if we shut off the tube and ask them to listen to music? Not much. <u>Three out of four of the top-selling CDs of 1995 use cuss</u>

*Music is just as bad.*

<u>words and exalt guns, rape, or murder, according to a *Providence Journal-Bulletin* report.</u>

Between grades seven to twelve, teenagers drain in 10,500 hours of rock music—that's more hours than they spent in class in all the years between second grade and graduating from high school.

The impact on our kids of electronic media—ranging from the soporific to the truly horrific—is the single biggest problem our society faces. It's a much bigger deal than the deficit or taxes or "job-loss anxiety" labels tossed about in the election campaigns.

The degrading of our human capital by the corrosive moral erosion of television and the related video-audio industries is a challenge of immense significance. The politicians nibble around the edges for slivers of political advantage.

*The television is more devastating to our youngsters than any problems we may have in the Middle East.*

But the dumbing-down of a generation, the deadening of moral sensitivity in millions of youngsters, is a much greater threat than anything rumbling in the Middle East. Our real problem is the Middle West, and the rest of Middle America. Our kids are bathed in filth, in trivia, in meaningless violence, in false happy endings, in cynical nattering from false media gods.

*moral*

It's a disease. It requires prevention. And vaccination. And, occasionally, something drastic, like amputation. In my family we still talk about one Super Bowl eve when my sister got so mad at the stupefied gazes on the faces of her four kids that she lugged the TV set into her car, drove to the reservoir, and tossed it in, leaving it sitting cockeyed and unplugged on the ice she forgot to take into account.

The AMA is on the right side on this one. Our future is rotting, one channel at a time.

### Danielle's Outline

#### Outline

I. Opening Paragraph
   Interesting Opening
   Author
   Thesis
   Supporting facts

II.  TV Influence: Violence (Music too!)

III. TV Influence: Harmful to kids

IV. TV Influence: Bad impression on leaders

V.  My Personal Experience

   Summarization agree, but not w/felons

   Ways to change

VI. Conclusion: Restate Thesis

### Danielle's First Draft

## TAKE ME TO YOUR LEADER

*? OK*

Every once in awhile a movie that has been (recently) released from the theaters is shown on TV. In the hopes that some sort of violence will be displayed, children rush to the television with drooling mouths and oggling eyes most of the time they will be disappointed with the "modified to fit your television" version, but it is sad to see how anxious they are to see a person's head blown to pieces. Television has become a leader to the youngsters of America. It influences them into committing ~~hanous~~ *heinous* acts of violences and gives them a bad impression *100* of our nation's superior people. David Nyhan, a columnist and an associate editor for the Boston Globes, relates this idea ~~xxxxxxxxxxxx~~ in his essay, "Turn Off the TV ~~xxxxx~~ *before* It Ruins Us." ~~Nyhan states, "Television is bad for kids . . . they would kill to watch ??? it."~~ *Nyhan states that the violence shown on T.V. influences young people to go out and kill.* He supports his thesis with facts such as, "wherever television-watching is introduced, homicide rates double within a decade and a half." What is our world coming to when kids ~~find~~ *see* a box plugged into a wall, *as* a good role model? Nyhan asks ~~that very same~~ *xxxx* *that very same* question in his article.

*(O.K.)*

*200*

Nyhan examines the effects television has on youngsters. Kids ~~watch more television~~ *spend more time* watching television than they do learning in school. Television ~~teacher~~ *has become the*. Children learn that it is ~~xxx~~ all right to have an aggressive attitude and that violence will solve any problems. Nyhan can't understand the ignorance that has developed among people. Parents have to monitor what their children watch ~~or else~~ *before* it ~~may turn~~ *escalates* into something they can't control. Nyhan brings ~~in~~ *also up* the fact that most Americans who are in jail, were ~~often~~ raised in single-parent homes

and they were taught that what they saw on television was reality based.
Television  $_3$00
~~It~~ convinced these children that committing crimes would give them the good

life, but all it got them was a set of solid, metal bars.
                                    negative
    Another aspect of television, that Nyhan introduces is the presence of
                                                        He states that,
drugs, alcohol and premature sex on the "box". He states that, "Kids who sit

around, all day watching television become fat, sick and are more likely to drink,
                                                Then
smoke, drug and engage in premature sex." People wonder why AIDS is spreading
              Television, which
so rapidly. ~~Thia~~                   kids see as a role model, is emptying garbage into
              heads                              4$00$                       new
their young ~~minds~~. Each day that television is allowed to corrupt the ~~younger~~
                                                              allowed to
generation's minds, is just another day that our country is deterior~~ating~~.

    Nyhan also examines the way television makes people cynical. It causes chil-

dren, as well as adults, to believe that ~~no one can be trusted and that~~ no one is
                                                                  being
honest. When this happens this country is no longer connected; it is teared

apart. With politicians, athletes, journalists, businessmen, clergymen and movie

stars, children get the impression that ~~All~~ these superior figures are corrupt

and can't be trusted.

    Television has become a parent to our children. It teaches them bad ethics
                                                          5$00$
and morals, and shows them that the sports heros and award-winning media
they used to admire
~~is~~ are not so great after all. Nyhan wants the television turned off because if it

continues to stay on, it will ruin our country.
                              about
    I agree with Nyhan and his ideas ~~on~~ television's negative influence. I feel that

there is too much violence on television and it causes our young people to think

incorrectly about the real world. When I was younger I was introduced to MTV,

music television. I use to watch it morning, noon and night so that I wouldn't
                                      I viewed involved        6$00$
miss anything. The music videos that ~~they showed~~ sex, drugs and acts of

violence. I remember one time in particular; I was watching Madonna's video

"Just Like A Prayer." It told a story of a woman getting killed and a black man

~~go~~ being blamed. While Madonna was singing, burning crosses were aflame in the
                                              horrible
background. When I asked my mother why these ~~hara~~ things were being shown

on television, she quickly shut it off. She explained to me that what I saw wasn't

real ~~and~~ that I wasn't allowed to watch ~~the show~~ MTV ever again. I realize now that she wasn't

punishing me, she was just preventing me from growing up [100] with the belief that

black people were always bad and that it was alright to burn crosses. How can

~~our~~ society allow television to lead our children? Can't ~~they~~ our nation see that ~~it~~ television is corrupting

them, both physically and mentally.

~~Nyhan also~~ Another effect, that Nyhan ~~giv~~ brings up is music. Today's singers

and rappers can't produce ~~a~~ single song without the use of ~~a~~ cuss curse words ~~and~~ or

violent attacks on other people. ~~I took a CD~~ I own from the artists, The Outhere

Bros., ~~and~~ [800] The lyrics consisted of words that ~~degraded~~ women and no verse

was complete without a swear. [850]

*Not Impressive Danielle Too Many Words*

## Danielle's Final Draft

# TAKE ME TO YOUR LEADER

Every once in awhile a movie that has been recently released from the theaters is shown on T.V. In the hopes that some sort of violence will be displayed, children rush to the television with drooling mouth and oggling eyes. Most of the time they are disappointed with the "modified to fit your T.V." version, but it is sad to see how anxious they are to see a person's head blown to pieces. Television has become a leader to the youngsters of America. It influences them into committing heinous acts of violence and gives them a bad impression of our nation's superior people. David Nyhan, a columnist for the Boston Globe, relates this idea in his essay. "Turn Off the T.V. before It Ruins Us." Nyhan states that the violence shown on T.V. influences young people to kill. He supports his thesis with facts such as, "wherever television-watching is introduced, homicide rates double within a decade and a half." What is our world coming to when kids see a box plugged into a wall, as a good role model? Nyhan asks that very same question in his article.

Nyhan examines the effects television has on youngsters. Kids spend more time watching television than they do learning in school. Television has become the teacher. Children learn that it is all right to have an aggressive attitude and that violence will solve any problem. Nyhan can't understand the ignorance that has developed among people. Parents have to monitor what their children watch before it escalates into something they can't control. Nyhan also brings up the fact that most Americans who are in jail, were raised in a single-parent home and they were taught that what they saw on television was reality based. Television convinced these children that committing crimes would give them the good life, but all it got them was a set of solid, metal bars.

Another negative aspect of television, that Nyhan introduces is the presence of drugs, alcohol, and premature sex on the "box." Kids who sit around, all day watching television become fat, sick and are more likely to drink, smoke drug and engage in premature sex. Then people wonder why AIDS is spreading so rapidly. Television is emptying garbage into kids' young heads. Each day that television is allowed to corrupt the new generation's minds, is another day that our country is allowed to deteriorate.

Nyhan also examines the way television makes children cynical. It causes them to believe that no one is honest. When this happens, then our country is no longer connected; it is teared apart. With politicians, athletes, journalists, businessmen and movie stars, children get the impression that these superior figures are corrupt and can't be trusted. Television has become a parent to these children. It teaches them bad ethics and morals, and shows them that the sports heros and award-winning media they use to admire, are not so great after all. Nyhan wants the television turned off because if it continues to stay on, it will ruin our country.

I agree with Nyhan and his ideas about television's negative influence. I think that there is too much violence on television and it causes our young people to think incorrectly about the real world. When I was younger I use to watch MW music television. I would watch it morning noon and night The music videos that I viewed involved sex drugs and acts of violence. I remember one time in particular; I was watching Madonna's video, "Just Like A Prayer." It told a story of a woman getting killed and a black man getting blamed for the crime. While Madonna was singing, a burning cross was aflame in the background. When I asked my mother why these horrible things were being shown on television, she quickly shut it off. She explained to me that what I saw wasn't real and that I was not allowed to watch MTV ever again. I realize now that she wasn't punishing me; she was just preventing me from growing up with the belief that black people were always evil and that it was alright to burn a cross. How can our society allow television to lead our children? Can't our nation see that television is corrupting them, both physically and mentally. Television has to be limited. I think the idea of a chip used to control and limit the amount of violence a child watches is an excellent idea. Still, I believe the parents should be the ones to peel their children's eyes off of the screen. If kids were made to go outside and get some fresh air, the television would lose its leadership role, but the parents need to take the first step.

David Nyhan relates his feelings strongly. With good word usage and supporting facts, he relates his views on television's negative affects on children quite well. He says that television is causing our young people to become violent and gives them a bad impression of people, whom should be looked up to. The younger generation will someday be running the Country and I'd hate to have a Magnivox for a president.

## Response: Cliff

### *Cliff's First Draft*

In his <u>Boston Globe</u> article, "Turn Off the TV Before It Ruins Us," David Nyhan comes down hard on ~~can~~ television. He sides with the American Medical Association with his thesis statement: television is bad for kids. He believes that children are exposed to ~~tremendous~~ tremendous amounts of negative images of ~~violence~~ our society.

~~David Nyhan's ~~~~~~~~ article in the Boston Globe, "Turn Off the TV Before It Ruins Us," is one of the most negative pieces of writing.~~

To support his thesis, Nyhan uses ^plenty of^ figures. ~~~~~~~~~~~~~~~~ He states that children will see two hundred thousand acts of violence, and sixteen thousand murders on television before their ~~~~~~ eighteenth birthday. Nyhan says that kids ~~~~~~ spend more time watching TV than they do in school. He believes that this makes kids violent.

Nyhan cites data that concludes that television watching has had an effect on ^raising^ homicide rates. He states that, "Little kids who O.D. on TV kick and punch and bite much more". He says that teenagers who watch a lot of TV are going to be "fatter, sicker, more likely to drink and smoke and drug."

The author believes that TV is just a big purveyor of the worst that society has to offer. "It is a conveyor belt of cynicism, of self-gratification, of violence-inducing behavior, of role modeling gone wrong of tasteless drivel." He believes that TV is the biggest contributor to our society's rot; more so than any other factor.

Nyhan is definitely down on TV, but he doesn't stop there. He states that music isn't any better. He thinks kids ~~today~~ spend too much time listening to music; as a result, they are bombarded with cuss words and lyrics that exalt guns, rape and murder.

The author concludes that one whole electronic media is responsible for bathing our youngsters "in filth, in trivia, in meaningless violence, in false happy endings, in cynical nattering from false media gods." He ends with his secondary thesis, unplug the tube.

I have read many articles in the Globe ~~that~~ that were written by David Nyhan, and I usually agree with his point of view; however, in this case I must disagree. I would tell Nyhan to get up, walk over to the television and change the channel. There is a variety of progra~~mm~~ming on TV. Take a look at the positive side of the issue. Take a good look at what one electronic media has done on the positive side, by educating our young. Take a look at the educational informational, and news channels. Look at the internet and all the information it has brought to our fingertips. ~~that~~ For Nyhan to brush off all electronic media as a negative experience is very foolish of him.

I will agree that there is a lot of trash on television, but there is a lot of everything on television. There is a little something for everybody; something to suit your every mood or craving. It is up to the viewer to determine what he or she selects to watch. That selection is based on the value system of the viewer, a ~~whole~~ set of values we acquire from ~~other~~ sources other than television.

I believe children are a little smarter than Nyhan gives them credit for being. I believe that they can sort fact from fiction, good from evil, and worthless from worthwhile on the television screen.

I can remember when I was young, and there was very little TV, only a couple of hours a day. I can remember watching the news and being better able to understand ~~understand~~ the things my parents discussed. I still will watch the news on TV as many times a day as I can.

I have watched youngsters in my family grow up with television, a lot of television. In general they have all turned out to be intelligent productive members of society. I believe their television viewing made them more well rounded individuals they were exposed to a lot of things, good and bad, that they wouldn't have been without TV. I think they were better off because of television.

My advice to David Nyhan is to give kids a little credit. They know where the channel selection knob is, and how to use it. Mr. Nyhan should try the same.

### *Cliff's Final Draft*

In his *Boston Globe* article, "Turn Off the TV before It Ruins Us," David Nyhan comes down very hard on television and television programming. He sides with the American Medical Association in his thesis statement: Television is bad for kids. Nyhan believes that children are exposed to tremendous amounts of violence and negative images on TV, as it is broadcast currently.

In support of his thesis, Nyhan uses plenty of figures. He states that children will see two hundred thousand acts of violence, and sixteen thousand murders, on television, before their eighteenth birthday. Nyhan says that kids spend more time watching TV than they do in school. He believes that this makes kids violent, and prone to acting out a violent manner.

Nyhan cites data that concludes that television has had an effect on raising homicide rates. He states, "Kids who OD on TV kick and punch and bite much more." He says that teenagers who watch a lot of TV are going to be "fatter, sicker, more likely to drink and smoke and drug."

The author believes that TV is just a big purveyor of the worst that society has to offer, "It is a conveyor belt of cynicism, of self-gratification, of violence-inducing behavior, of role modeling gone wrong, of tasteless drivel." He believes that TV is the biggest downfall to our society; more so than any other factor.

Nyhan is definitely down on TV, but he doesn't stop there. He thinks that music isn't any better. He says that kids spend too much time listening to music; as a result, they are bombarded with cuss words and lyrics that exalt guns, rape, and murder.

The author concludes that the whole electronic media is responsible for bathing our youngsters "in filth, in trivia, in meaningless violence, in false happy endings, in cynical nattering from false media gods." He ends with his solution that we should unplug the tube.

I have read many articles trashing TV as a negative experience, but I say turn the channel and look at the positive. There is a variety of programming on TV. Take a good look at the educational, informational, and cultural aspects of television. Look at all the resources the electronic media has placed at our fingertips. For Nyhan to brush off electronic media as a negative experience is very foolish of him.

I will agree that there is a lot of trash on TV, but there is a lot of everything on TV. There is something to suit our every mood or craving. It is up to the viewer to decide what he or she wants to watch. It's a value judgment, one that kids are able to make also.

I believe children are a little smarter than Nyhan gives them credit for being. I believe that they are good at sorting fact from fiction, good from evil, and worthless from worthwhile on the television screen.

I have watched youngsters in my family grow up with TV, a lot of TV? In general, they have all turned out to be intelligent, productive, members of society I believe their television viewing made them well rounded and better educated individuals. They were exposed to many things, both good and bad, that they would not have been without TV. I think they were all better off because of television that they would have been without it. Believe me, they watched their share of violence and smut TV.

My advice to David Nyhan is to give kids a little more credit. They know where the channel selection button is, and they know how to use it. Mr. Nyhan should do the same, and see some of the positive aspects of electronic media. I wonder how Nyhan deals with the Internet.

## Review

As you can see from these models, the students engaged in the reading/ writing process continually as they developed their responses to the essay. The students read the assigned essay by Nyhan twice. They read the essay once for an overview; during the second reading they looked up any unfamiliar words and marked up Nyhan's essay by identifying the **thesis** (the author's main point), the major supporting points, and the minor details they thought they might use in their review of the essay. This **text marking** is where the reading and writing processes connect.

Danielle's next step was to form an outline; Cliff made a "mental outline" but put nothing on paper, feeling confident without this step. All of Cliff and Danielle's reading and writing completed up to this point fit into the category of prewriting.

The writing stage came next. Cliff wrote his discovery draft without a printed outline. Using her outline, Danielle completed her initial draft. Along the way both students probably stopped a number of times during their writing to read portions of what they had written and to reread parts of the assigned essay, once again connecting the reading and writing processes throughout their drafts. Having finished the entire drafts, they reread and edited them, possibly repeating this process two or three times. Then the students again returned to the act of reading, this time in the form of proofreading for omissions and errors in spelling, punctuation, and sentence structure.

## Conclusion

The student writers of these successful essays used their reading and writing skills throughout the process of completing the assignment. In most of your college work, you will find that these two communication processes merge. Because they are so closely intertwined, sometimes it is difficult to tell where one leaves off and the other begins. To become proficient in both, as we stated earlier, you need to practice. In the following chapters you will complete exercises to help you learn what these acts really entail.

# PART II
# The Act of Reading

# CHAPTER 2

# Components of Reading

What is reading? Some of you might define it as recognizing words on a page, a process you have been engaged in since you were six or seven. Others of you might say it is pronouncing printed words. Both of these definitions are too simplistic because decoding (saying the word) does not mean you understand the meaning of the combinations of letters. Each of you might read groups of letters the same way as you look at identical passages, but, because you have each had different life experiences, you attach individual meanings to those words and, therefore, interpret the same text differently.

Reading is actually an extremely complex process of making sense of a printed passage based on vocabulary recognition, background knowledge and experience, and the ability to predict what is coming. Reading requires a combination of seeing and hearing. It involves strategies that call for active, not passive, behavior. And it is hard work.

Although most standardized reading tests measure reading ability in three ways—wide vocabulary development, comprehension, and rate—our focus in this book is primarily on the act of comprehension. Your vocabulary and rate will improve as by-products as you practice. To develop your comprehension, you will learn about the five professionally recognized reading levels: *literal*, *interpretive*, *analytical*, *critical*, and *creative*. We cover the first two of these levels in depth in this chapter and save the other three for later in the text.

## LITERAL LEVEL

The **literal level** deals with what an author says. When we apply the word *literal* to the act of reading, we mean comprehending the message on the page—being able to identify the general topic and the author's thesis or main idea.

Understanding a work at the literal level also means being able to recognize the major points that support the thesis and the important minor details for each of those major points. We cover the skill of summarizing, which is also a literal-level skill, later when you learn the difference between summary and analysis.

## Identifying the Topic

The **topic,** or general subject of a passage, can usually be stated in a single word or simple phrase. A topic never requires an entire sentence. For a better understanding of the word *topic*, let's examine some groups of words and the general topics, or categories, under which they fall:

| | |
|---|---|
| Red Sox | Collies |
| Indians | Golden retrievers |
| Blue Jays | Fox terriers |
| Devil Rays | Poodles |
| **Topic:** American League Teams | **Topic:** Breeds of dogs |

Notice that these topics are not entire sentences, but only phrases.

Here are two groups of words that should have relevance for you:

| | |
|---|---|
| Drama club | Massachusetts |
| Cheerleading squad | Maine |
| Soccer team | Vermont |
| Student Government Association | New Hampshire |
| **Topic:** _____ | **Topic:** _____ |

Now let's move to stating a topic for a paragraph. Next is a paragraph with a stated topic following it. Read the paragraph to see if you agree with the topic we've identified. You might think of an alternate topic, but this paragraph is general enough so we think you will accept the topic we've selected as well.

### Confessions of a Former Smoker

Americans can be divided into three groups—smokers, nonsmokers, and that expanding pack of us who have quit. Those who have never smoked don't know what they're missing, but former smokers, ex-smokers, reformed smokers can never forget. We are veterans of a personal war, linked by that watershed experience of ceasing to smoke and by the temptation to have just one more cigarette. For almost all of us ex-smokers, smoking continues to play an important part in our lives. And now that it is being restricted in restaurants around the country and will be banned in almost all indoor public places in New York state starting next month, it is vital that everyone understand the different emotional states cessation of smoking can cause. I have observed four of them; and in the interest of science have classified them as those of the zealot, the evangelist, the elect, and the serene. Each day, each category gains new recruits.

Franklin E. Zimring, "Confessions of a Former Smoker"

**Topic:** Types of Former Smokers

Now try one on your own.

### The Fashionable Body

One of the boldest ways to interfere with human anatomy is to mold the skull. Among tribes who practice this art, it is part and parcel of a child's upbringing. It calls for special skills and has traditionally been a mother's duty and, we may presume, pleasure. The first provocation for a mother's pinching and kneading her baby's skull was perhaps its yielding softness. Playful handling developed into more conscious efforts to deform, and racial and aesthetic concepts were added later. Thus, broad heads were broadened, flat noses flattened closer to the face, a tapering occiput sharpened to a point—a shape mostly associated today with humanoids from outer space. These spectacular forms were achieved with the aid of contraptions no more ingenious than a common mousetrap.

Bernard Rudolfsky, "The Fashionable Body"

**Topic:** _____

## Identifying the Main Idea

The next step in reading at the literal level is to identify the main idea or topic sentence. You can construct a paragraph with the topic sentence in five different locations. Some texts on reading say as often as 85 percent of the time the topic sentence is located at the beginning of a paragraph—the very first sentence (see Figure 2.1, A., p. 22). Textbooks frequently follow this pattern, called **deduction**, making it easy for you to skim a chapter and catch the gist of its content even if you do not have time before a class to read all of the supporting details. (Of course, you will go back to your room after class and read those details.) To demonstrate this familiar pattern, here is a paragraph with its topic sentence underlined:

### Women and Men

<u>When the women I met at college thought about the joys and privileges of men, they did not carry in their minds the sort of men I had known in my childhood.</u> They thought of their fathers, who were bankers, physicians, architects, stockbrokers, the big wheels of the big cities. These fathers rode the train to work or drove cars that cost more than any of my

childhood houses. They were attended from morning to night by female helpers, wives and nurses and secretaries. They were never laid off, never short of cash at month's end, never lined up for welfare. These fathers made decisions that mattered. They ran the world.

Scott Russell Sanders, "Women and Men"

Sometimes, in a pattern called **induction,** the details come first, followed by the topic sentence at the end (see Figure 2.1, B., p. 22):

### Role Models, Bogus and Real

Why then the constant "role model" morality play? Partly it's the archaic notion that athletes need to be paragons of virtue and temperance, exempt from moral flaw. Beyond that, I think, lies a deeper and more unfortunate presumption: that only stars can affect children's lives for the better, that the mere mortals among us are powerless to guide, shape, or enlighten. The sadness here is that the reverse is true. <u>The only legitimate "role model" is the person whom children can see, feel, and interact with in their daily lives.</u>

Brent Staples, "Role Models, Bogus and Real"

At still other times an author combines these two patterns, stating a general sentence at the beginning of the paragraph (the original topic sentence) and then summing up the paragraph at the end after including the details (see Figure 2.1, C., p. 22). The two sentences do not say exactly the same thing; however, both serve as a summary sentence for the paragraph. Here's an example of this pattern:

### Rationality About the Mentally Ill

<u>Legislation such as the conditional release being sponsored this year by state Senator William Keating of Sharon should be passed when the Legislature next convenes.</u> It should not be confused with "outpatient commitment" initiatives, which propose a form of civil commitment that mental health advocates reasonably fear could lead to further stigmatization and coercion of patients who pose little threat to others. The MacArthur study made clear that discharged mental patients are not a "homogeneous class" and that public fear of violence is "misdirected." <u>Strong measures, like conditional release, should be targeted carefully to the criminally insane and steer clear of the majority of patients whose illnesses produce bouts of loneliness and aloofness, not violence.</u>

"Rationality About the Mentally Ill," Boston Globe editorial

A fourth type of paragraph structure, called a *split pattern,* occurs when the topic sentence comes somewhere in the middle of a paragraph. It might be the second sentence after a brief introduction by the author, or it may

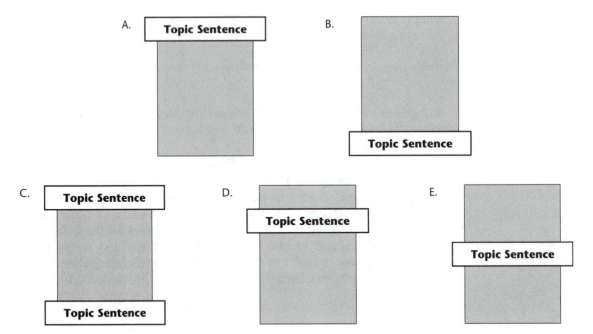

**Figure 2.1**    The Five Different Locations of Topic Sentences

occur in the middle of the details, perhaps between two parallel examples (see Figure 2.1, D and E). Here is an example:

### Street Smart

I grew up in a big city, so I suppose you could say I was practically born street smart. I learned the hard way how to act and what to do, and so did my friends. <u>To us, being street smart meant having common sense.</u> We wanted to be cool, but we needed to be safe, too. Now I go to college in a big city, and I realize that not everyone here grew up the way I did. Lots of students are from suburbs or rural areas, and they are either terrified of the city or totally ignorant of city life. The few suburban or rural kids who are willing to venture downtown all have one thing in common: They are not street smart.

Kristin Whitehead, "Street Smart" (college essay)

One final type is the paragraph with *no stated topic sentence.* Some authors do not include a general sentence in every paragraph. An author might include one general statement for two or three subsequent paragraphs rather than for just one paragraph, or she might just imply the main idea and keep going.

### I Know Why the Caged Bird Sings

<u>In Stamps the custom was to can everything that could possibly be preserved</u>. During the killing season, after the first frost, all neighbors helped each other to slaughter hogs and even the quiet, big-eyed cows if they had stopped giving milk.

The missionary ladies of the Christian Methodist Episcopal Church helped Momma prepare the pork for sausage. They squeezed their fat arms elbow deep in the ground meat, mixed it with gray nose-opening sage, pepper and salt, and made tasty little samples for all obedient children who brought wood for the slick black stove. The men chopped off the larger pieces of meat and laid them in the smokehouse to begin the curing process. They opened the knuckle of the hams with their deadly-looking knives, took out a certain round harmless bone ("it could make the meat go bad") and rubbed salt, coarse brown salt that looked like fine gravel, into the flesh, and the blood popped to the surface.

Maya Angelou, I Know Why the Caged Bird Sings

Now comes a chance to practice. Select the topic sentences of the paragraphs from the following essay, an op-ed column in the *Boston Globe* (July 20, 1998). The paragraph structure for each will be one of the five just covered. When you have located the most general sentence in each paragraph, the umbrella under which all of the other sentences in that paragraph can fit, underline it. If a topic sentence is only implied, state it in the margin.

## KENNEDY'S DESTRUCTIVE HATE CRIMES BILL

### Jeff Jacoby

1    In 1998, Congress passed the Hate Crimes Statistics Act. In 1994, it passed the Hate Crimes Sentencing Enhancement Act and the Violence Against Women Act. In 1996, it passed the Church Arson Prevention Act. Now, saying that Congress must do still more, Senator Edward Kennedy proposed yet another federal statute, the Hate Crimes Prevention Act of 1998.

2    Kennedy's bill would expand federal criminal jurisdiction to a degree never before contemplated. It would overlap with hate-crimes laws already in force in 41 states. It would give US attorneys the authority to prosecute violent crimes—from simple assault to murder—which have always been illegal in *every* state. It would stretch the definition of "hate crime" far beyond what

most Americans understand that term to mean; for example, it would turn every rape into a federal "hate crime" against women.

3     And why is so tremendous an increase in federal power necessary? Two words, says Kennedy: Jasper, Texas. The sickening murder there last month "shocked the conscience of the country," he told the Judiciary Committee a few days ago. "A strong response is clearly needed." To drive home his point, the daughter of James Byrd Jr.—the black man butchered so monstrously in Jasper—was brought to Washington to testify in favor of Kennedy's bill.

4     But there is nothing a new federal hate crime law can supply that isn't already in the Texas criminal code. "A strong response"? Prosecutors in the Jasper case will seek the death penalty if the men charged with killing Byrd are convicted. How much stronger a response did Kennedy have in mind? There is no state in the union where prosecutors would ignore so stomach-churning a hate crime, or fail to demand the harshest punishment available. Far from proving that a vast expansion of federal prosecutorial powers is urgently needed, the horror in Jasper demonstrates that it isn't.

5     What minorities have to fear most is not white-supremacist hate crimes going unpunished. It is "ordinary" violent crime, the great bulk of which is black-on-black. One of the nation's leading scholars of crime and race, Harvard Law professor Randall Kennedy, writes: "It makes sense to suppose that local law enforcement officials will probably allocate more of their scarce resources to the crime that is a Page 1 cause célèbre than to the crime that never makes it past the back pages of the local press."

6     But that's not a problem Ted Kennedy cares about. Liberal politicians of his stripe find it a lot sexier to denounce hate crimes that cross racial, ethnic, religious, or sexual lines than to deal seriously with punishing violent crime in general. Even though it is violent crime in general that causes most of the bloodshed and mayhem in America. Of the roughly 20,000 homicides, 30,000 rapes, 150,000 robberies, and half a million aggravated assaults for which police will make arrests this year, only a tiny fraction would qualify as hate

crimes. What do we gain by shining a spotlight on that fraction and eclipsing the rest?

7    The recent rash of hate crime laws would be understandable if crime motivated by bigotry and racism were out of control. It isn't. A few years back, the Minnesota Department of Public Safety reported that there had been 425 bias crimes statewide the year before, a finding that led the district attorney in St. Paul to decry the "massive increase in hate crimes." Yet those 425 criminal attacks accounted for just two-tenths of 1 percent of all the violent crimes reported in Minnesota that year. Check the numbers for the other states; the results will be the same.

8    The blood of bias-crime victims is no redder than that of "ordinary" victims. The daughter of a man murdered because he was black sheds tears just as hot as the daughter of a man murdered because he had $20 in his pocket. By singling out hate crimes for special statistical and prosecutorial attention lawmakers in effect declare some victims—and some victims grieving loved ones—more equal than others.

9    In an age when Americans are under constant pressure to splinter into groups—to see themselves first and foremost as members of an aggrieved race, class, or gender—the last thing they need are more laws emphasizing their differences and calling inordinate attention to bias and hatred. Kennedy's bill furthers a deeply destructive trend: an insistence on casting violent offenders not merely as criminals who threaten society's well-being, but as various kinds of bigots—racists, sexists, gay-bashers, Jew-haters. This is profoundly wrong. The purpose of criminal codes is not to protect blacks from whites, Jews from skinheads, women from misogynists, gays from straights, or immigrants from nativists. It is to protect all of us from lawbreakers.

10    Every single crime that would be covered by Kennedy's legislation is already a crime. Each one can already be prosecuted. Each can already be punished. "Hate Crimes Prevention" has a fine ring to it, but this bill would prevent nothing except unity. What it would promote is balkanization, class

**Responding to Essays**

Following each of the essays you will be reading in this text are writing prompts you will answer in a formal essay of your own. Your audience members are readers who have not read the essay to which you are responding. Thus in your opening paragraph, be sure to cite the author, the title of the essay, and any other contextual material that will help your readers.

Carefully and accurately summarize the reading. Be certain to identify the author's thesis and the examples used in its support. In addition, prepare a thoughtful and well-developed response to the issues raised in the reading. Include a thesis of your own that either agrees with or challenges the author's views, and support it with personal experiences and/or observations. Consider the prompts as you plan your response.

warfare, and identity politics. Of all the ways to memorialize James Byrd, that has to be the worst.

## WRITING PROMPTS

1. What is Jacoby's opinion about the need for a new federal hate crime law?
2. What terrible Texas case prompted the action of Senator Edward Kennedy suggesting such a law?
3. What kinds of support does Jacoby include to prove his side?
4. What recent cases can you think of—either locally or nationally—that would be considered hate crimes?
5. From your reading and research, do you think a new federal hate crimes law should be on the books? Why or why not?

The next step in learning to locate the main idea is to study longer selections. Now instead of searching for a topic sentence in a paragraph, you'll be working with a short essay and hunting for the *thesis*, the main idea of the essay. The thesis statement is to an essay what a topic sentence is to a paragraph. The thesis statement directs the essay; it tells the reader what the essay will be about.

Read the following essay and see if you can discover the sentence that summarizes the author's main point.

# POVERTY

### George Orwell

1    It is altogether curious, your first contact with poverty. You have thought so much about poverty—it is the thing you have feared all your life, the thing you knew would happen to you sooner or later; and it is all so utterly and prosaically different. You thought it would be quite simple; it is extraordinarily complicated. You thought it would be terrible; it is merely squalid and boring. It is the peculiar *lowness* of poverty that you discover first; the shifts that it puts you to, the complicated meanness, the crust-wiping.

2    You discover, for instance, the secrecy attaching to poverty. At a sudden stroke you have been reduced to an income of six francs a day. But of course you dare not admit it—you have got to pretend that you are living quite as usual. From the start it tangles you in a net of lies, and even with the lies you can hardly manage it. You stop sending clothes to the laundry, and the laundress catches you in the street and asks you why; you mumble something, and she, thinking you are sending the clothes elsewhere, is your enemy for life. The tobacconist keeps asking why you have cut down your smoking. There are letters you want to answer, and cannot, because stamps are too expensive. And then there are your meals—meals are the worst difficulty of all. Every day at meal-times you go out, ostensibly to a restaurant, and loaf an hour in the Luxembourg Gardens, watching the pigeons. Afterwards you smuggle your food home in your pockets. Your food is bread and margarine, or bread and wine and even the nature of the food is governed by lies. You have to buy rye bread instead of household bread, because the rye loaves, though dearer, are round and can be smuggled in your pockets. This wastes you a franc a day. Sometimes, to keep up appearances, you have to spend sixty centimes on a drink, and go correspondingly short of food. Your linen gets filthy, and you run out of soap and razor-blades. Your hair wants cutting, and you try to cut it yourself, with such fearful results that you have to go to the barber after all, and spend the equivalent of a day's food. All day you are telling lies, and expensive lies.

3    You discover the extreme precariousness of your six francs a day. Mean disasters can happen and rob you of food. You have spent your last eighty centimes on half a litre of milk, and are boiling it over the spirit lamp. While it boils a bug runs down your forearm; you give the bug a flick with your nail, and it falls, plop! Straight into the milk. There is nothing for it but to throw the milk away and go foodless.

4    You go to the baker's to buy a pound of bread, and you wait while the girl cuts a pound for another customer. She is clumsy, and cuts more than a pound. *"Pardon, monsieur,"* she says, "I suppose you don't mind paying two sous extra?" Bread is a franc a pound, and you have exactly a franc. When you think that you too might be asked to pay two sous extra, and would have to confess that you could not, you bolt in panic. It is hours before you dare venture into a baker's shop again.

5    You go to the greengrocer's to spend a franc on a kilogram of potatoes. But one of the pieces that make up the franc is a Belgium piece, and the shopman refuses it. You slink out of the shop, and can never go there again.

6    You have strayed into a respectable quarter, and you see a prosperous friend coming. To avoid him you dodge into the nearest café. Once in the café you must buy something, so you spend your last fifty centimes on a glass of black coffee with a dead fly in it. One could multiply these disasters by the hundred. They are part of the process of being hard up.

7    You discover what it is like to be hungry. With bread and margarine in your belly, you go out and look into the shop windows. Everywhere there is food insulting you in huge, wasteful piles; whole dead pigs, baskets of hot loaves, great yellow blocks of butter, strings of sausages, mountains of potatoes, vast Gruyere cheeses like grindstones. A snivelling self-pity comes over you at the sight of so much food. You plan to grab a loaf and run, swallowing it before they catch you; and you refrain, from pure funk.

8    You discover the *boredom* which is inseparable from poverty; the times when you have nothing to do and, being underfed, can interest yourself in nothing. For half a day at a time you lie on your bed, feeling like the *jeune squelette* in Baudelaire's poem. Only food could rouse you. You discover that a man who has gone even a week on bread and margarine is not a man any longer, only a belly with a few accessory organs.

9    This—one could describe it further, but it is all in the same style—is life on six francs a day. Thousands of people in Paris live it—struggling artists and students, prostitutes when their luck is out, out-of-work people of all kinds. It is the suburbs, as it were, of poverty.

## WRITING PROMPTS

1. How does Orwell define poverty?
2. According to Orwell, what are the five characteristics of living a poor existence?
3. Why does Orwell say boredom and poverty are inseparable?
4. How do you define poverty, and what do you see as its causes? Its consequences?
5. Have you ever had to cut back on your spending? What were the effects of these cutbacks on your physical, spiritual, and emotional wellness?

## Identifying the Major Support

The next literal-level skill is identifying the major supporting details for a topic sentence or thesis statement and the important minor details for those supporting examples. Every paragraph and essay include at least one supporting detail. Usually paragraphs contain anywhere from one to three or more examples; essays are apt to contain many more. Of course, with some essays, especially personal narratives, there may be only one extended example to support the thesis. See how Rose Del Castillo Guilbault, in an essay called "Americanization Is Tough on 'Macho'," includes one supporting example for her topic sentence. She describes the nonassertive un-macho behavior of her father.

### Americanization Is Tough on 'Macho'

Americans regarded my father as decidedly un-macho. His character was interpreted as nonassertive, his loyalty, nonambition, and his quietness, ignorance. I once overheard the boss's son blame him for plowing crooked rows in a field. My father merely smiled at the lie, knowing the boy had done it, but didn't refute it, confident his good work was well-known. But the boss instead ridiculed him for being "stupid" and letting a kid get away with a lie. Seeing my embarrassment, my father dismissed the incident, saying "They're the dumb ones. Imagine, me fighting with a kid."

Rose Del Castillo Guilbault, "Americanization Is Tough on 'Macho'"

Do you see how this example forwards the main point? The passage met the writing requirement of completeness with just one clear example; however, sometimes one supporting point is not enough to make a definite statement. The following paragraph, describing the physical condition of a boy with Down's syndrome and a heart defect, contains multiple supporting points:

### The Case of Phillip Becker

He has Down's syndrome (Mongolism), a chromosomal defect that involves varying degrees of retardation and physical abnormalities. He has a common heart defect, correctable by standard surgery. Uncorrected, it probably will kill him by 30. The pattern is progressive debilitation, until reduced to a torturous bed-to-chair existence, with headaches, chest pains and fainting spells during which the sufferer turns a terrifying blue-black. Already Phillip suffers attacks of weakness and bluishness. His heart must work three times harder than a normal heart. Blood is pumped into his lungs under dangerously high pressure, damaging the lungs' thin vessels. Already he may have passed the threshold of dangerous harm; soon his condition may be inoperable, his decline irreversible.

George F. Will, "The Case of Phillip Becker"

The first two sentences in this paragraph serve as "the topic sentence." Then Will includes examples of Phillip's symptoms and the danger of letting those symptoms progress. He tells his reader that Phillip is already weak and deteriorating and will probably die by the time he is thirty. Will goes on to say that Phillip's heart must work three times harder than it should, that the blood vessels of his lungs are in danger, and that it may already be too late to operate.

The next paragraph has nothing marked. Underline the topic sentence and number the major supporting details.

### Equal Before the Law

As a beginning public defender, I litigate mostly misdemeanors. Their maximum jail sentence cannot exceed one year. My clients have been accused of such heinous crimes as possessing a spiny lobster out of season (a case that actually went to a jury trial), surfing in a swim zone and collecting trash without a permit (a homeless man was cited for taking cans from the garbage for recycling). Of course, I've also handled more serious offenses: rape, child molestation and vehicular manslaughter.

Tamara Rice Lave, "Equal Before the Law"

## Locating the Minor Details

After you recognize the topic, locate the topic sentence or thesis statement (or understand an implied one), and find the major supporting points, your final task in reading at the literal level is to locate the significant minor details. These details might take the form of facts, reasons, statistics, examples, or testimony. As a model, let's return to a paragraph we have already included—paragraph 2 from "The Case of Phillip Becker." The minor details are few because it is a short paragraph with a number of major supporting points; however, there are some details. Phillip will experience a horrible and painful existence confined to a chair or bed; he will suffer from headaches, chest pains, and fainting spells and turn dark blue if he doesn't have the surgery. There is far too much pressure under which blood is pumped into his lungs, and his condition, if nothing is done, may be "irreversible."

Here in the following paragraph, underline the topic sentence(s) and number the major supporting points. Then identify by letter the kinds of minor details, the filler, the author uses to develop his major points, which, in turn, forward the thesis.

### The Three New Yorks

There are roughly three New Yorks. There is, first, the New York of the man or woman who was born here, who takes the city for granted and accepts its size and its turbulence as natural and inevitable. Second, there is the New York of the commuter—the city that is devoured by locusts each day and spat out each night. Third, there is the New York of the person who was born somewhere else and came to New York in quest of something. Of these three trembling cities the greatest is the last—the city of final destination, the city that is a goal. It is this third city that accounts for New York's high-strung disposition, its poetical deportment, its dedication to the arts, and its incomparable achievements. Commuters give the city its tidal restlessness, natives give it solidarity and continuity, but the settlers give it passion. And whether it is a farmer arriving from Italy to set up a small grocery store in a slum, or a young girl arriving from a small town in Mississippi to escape the indignity of being observed by her neighbors, or a boy arriving from the Corn Belt with a manuscript in his suitcase and a pain in his heart, it makes no difference: each embraces New York with the intense excitement of first love, each absorbs New York with the fresh eyes of an adventurer, each generates heat and light to dwarf the Consolidated Edison Company.

E. B. White, "The Three New Yorks"

# INTERPRETIVE LEVEL

The **interpretive level** involves understanding what an author really means. It includes the skills of recognizing an author's *purpose*, *style*, and *tone*.

## Understanding Purpose

Do you always mean what you say? On first thought, you might answer, "Yes, of course. I'm basically an honest person." If you are reporting something objectively with the intent of informing another, you will try to be as accurate as possible in your description of the event. But suppose you want to entertain that other person—or persuade him to take some course of action. Do you think then you might exaggerate parts of your story and ignore or at least downplay others? We use language, oral and written, for three purposes: to inform, to entertain, and to persuade. And writers, to be effective, do omit some details and embellish others. This action is all a part of their style and tone, which help them accomplish their purpose with each writing assignment. The authors of the following three paragraphs demonstrate these purposes. Can you identify each author's purpose?

### Seventy-Five Years of Underestimating Calvin Coolidge

The attorney general urged Coolidge to take the oath of office without delay. He "went across the street to the general store and telephoned Secretary of State [Charles Evans] Hughes, who informed him the oath could be administered by a notary. Coolidge told Hughes his father was a notary. Coolidge returned home, and in the downstairs sitting room John Coolidge, using the family Bible, swore his son in as president. The time was 2:47 A.M."

Jeff Jacoby, "Seventy-Five Years of Underestimating Calvin Coolidge"

### Self-Serving Society

BOSTON—It is 8:30 in the morning and I am standing at a gas station in a silk suit with an unusual fashion accessory dangling from my right hand. This metal and rubber accouterment looks exactly like a gasoline hose. In fact it is a gasoline hose.

Ellen Goodman, "Self-Serving Society"

### Save the Cape from Overdevelopment

But even that won't be enough. Even that won't stop the chain saws and bulldozers. A land bank can be a cornerstone of an effort to save Cape Cod, but it won't do the whole job. Saving the Cape will require stricter zoning, caps on building permits and other measures to curb development.

Tim White, "Save the Cape from Overdevelopment"

You were accurate if you kept the order of the three purposes as we presented it. Jeff Jacoby, the conservative author of "75 Years of Underestimating Calvin Coolidge," writes with *objectivity* in order to inform his readers of an event. Although his purpose in the entire essay is to persuade those readers that Coolidge was an excellent president, in this paragraph his purpose is to inform them of the way in which Coolidge was sworn in

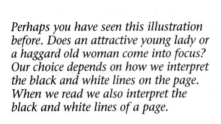

*Perhaps you have seen this illustration before. Does an attractive young lady or a haggard old woman come into focus? Our choice depends on how we interpret the black and white lines on the page. When we read we also interpret the black and white lines of a page.*

as president. Ellen Goodman's purpose in "Self-Serving Society" is to *entertain* in this particular paragraph, although like Jacoby the overall purpose of her entire essay is mildly persuasive. Finally, in the paragraph from "Save the Cape from Overdevelopment," author Tim White demonstrates his purpose of *persuasion* in both this paragraph and the entire column.

## Understanding Style

**Style** refers to the words an author chooses (her **diction**) and the way she arranges those words in sentences and paragraphs. Through her style, this writer presents her voice. In order to illustrate our definition, let's examine the two very different styles of two columnists whose purpose is the same—to persuade. Through diverse styles and tones, Bob Greene and Ellen Goodman attempt to convince their readers. Bob Greene's essay, "It Took This Night to Make Us Know," gains its serious tone through its subject matter; however, he adds to the somber mood by his repetition of the opening words in many of his paragraphs: "It is not supposed to be very strong in us." This repetition sounds almost like the tolling of a bell, a funeral bell.

Notice how Greene uses a straightforward approach and serious tone to fit his subject. He discusses the issue of prejudice against the Jews with clear diction and complete sentences. His argument is straightforward and serious in tone.

In stark contrast to Greene as a writer is Ellen Goodman. Typically, she is a liberal, a feminist who champions women's causes, especially those of underprivileged women. But she sometimes strays from her usual subject matter when she feels a need to vent, when she has "an itch."

One of these columns is "Flying into Air Rage." Like most of her work, it contains a mixture of humor and outright sarcasm, references to current events, personal experience, and sentence structure variety, including the careful and conscious use of fragments. (It is acceptable to break a rule on occasion when you have also demonstrated repeatedly that you know that rule.) If you have ever been left waiting at an airport, you will appreciate Goodman's caustic humor.

## It Took This Night to Make Us Know

### Bob Greene

1    It is not supposed to be very strong in us, for we cannot remember. We are the young Jews, born after Hitler, and we have never considered the fact that we are Jewish to be a large part of our identity. A lot of us have not been near a temple in ten years, and we laugh along with the Jewish jokes to show that we are very cool about the whole thing. We are Americans, we have told ourselves, we do not go around calling ourselves Jews: that is for the elderly men

with the tortured faces, the old Jews we feel a little embarrassed to be around. Let them recall the centuries of hurt, we think; it is over now, so let them recall those years while we live our good todays.

2    It is not supposed to be very strong in us, and yet I am sitting at a typewriter in a hotel room hundreds of miles from home trying to write a story about a presidential campaign, and I cannot do it. For the television has just got done telling the story, the story of how once again people who hate the Jews have knocked on a door in the middle of the night and done their killing, and I can think of nothing else. Now the lesson is being taught all over again; it is not up to us to decide how to treat our Jewishness. That was decided for us centuries ago.

3    It is not supposed to be very strong in us, because all the barriers are down now, and a hotel will not turn us away or a restaurant will not deny us a table if our name does not sound right. And yet when the killings began, they thought to get a young man named Mark Spitz out of Germany, because he may be the best swimmer in the world, but first of all he is a Jew, and no one wanted to think what might happen to him. Many of the people who thrilled as he won his gold medals were very surprised to find out now that Spitz is a Jew. Later they will say that of course it doesn't matter what his religion is. But Spitz knew that it mattered; we all knew that it mattered, and that it would be smarter for him to go.

4    It is not supposed to be very strong in us and we have heard the term "six million Jews are dead" so often that it is just an abstraction to us. And yet if the Dachau concentration camp, just a few miles from the Olympic site, was not enough to remind us, the killers in the Munich darkness made sure that we remembered. There is a hate for us that goes back centuries, and every time it seems to have weakened with the years there is another band of men ready to show us that the hate is still strong enough to make them kill in the night.

5    When the news was certain, when there was no question but that the young Jewish men were dead, I called some friends and we talked about it. They were thinking the same way I was. For all these years we have acted bored with the Jewish traditions, smirked at the ancient, detailed ceremonies, patronized the old ones who insisted on showing their link with the past.

6    And for us, it took this one night to make us know that maybe it will never go away. We are all Jews who were born into a world where money and education and parents who speak with no accent were part of the package, and that can fool you. But this is the oldest hate the world has ever seen, and 25 years of Jewish prosperity in the United States is hardly enough to erase it from the earth.

7    It is nothing that we young ones have ever talked much about, and there are not many words to tell it now. Words cannot tell it as well as the look we have seen for years in the faces of the oldest Jews, the look of deepest sorrow that has been there for as many centuries as the hate.

8    This time the look is there because of a group of Arab terrorists. But it goes so far beyond Middle Eastern politics; the look was there in this same

Germany 30 years ago, it was there in Egypt centuries ago, it has been there in every place there have ever been Jews who were not wanted because they were Jews. And because there have been so many of these places, the look has been reborn and reborn and reborn.

9    There are young men who are dead this week who should be alive, and it would be a horrible thing no matter who they were. But of course they were Jews; the reason that they are dead is because they were Jews, and that is why on this night there are so many of us starting to realize for the first time what that means.

10    It is not supposed to be very strong in us, for we cannot remember. We grew up laughing at the solemn old Jewish phrases that sounded so mournful and outmoded and out of date in the second half of the twentieth century. Ancient, outmoded phrases from the temples, phrases like "Let my people go." Phrases that we chose to let mean nothing, because it is not supposed to be very strong in us.

## WRITING PROMPTS

1. What event occurred that changed Greene's attitude toward his heritage?

2. What historical references does Greene make about this heritage?

3. Repetition of words, phrases, or sentences can be very effective in persuasion. What repetitions do you notice in this essay? Do you think they help convince Greene's readers?

4. Based on more recent attacks with which you may be more familiar, how do you think we can prevent such deaths at public events (including the Olympic games)?

5. Have you ever experienced an event that caused you to change your views of your own ethnic background or that of older relatives?

## FLYING INTO AIR RAGE
### Ellen Goodman

1    Ever since it was discovered that Russell Weston Jr., the man charged with the Capitol murders, had a cabin in Rimini, Mont., we have been subject to yet another round of stories titled, loosely: "There's something about Montana."

2    What is it about the "last best place" that breeds, attracts, or harbors the Freeman, the Kehoes, the Unabomber and the Westons? Psycho- and socio-babblers have all weighed in with theories about the isolation, the altitude, the power of myth.

3    But I have come up with a much simpler and more logical explanation. What is it about Montana that drives people over the edge? Northwest Airlines.

4    I have concluded from my own personal research that Northwest is largely responsible for the fact that anybody who actually makes it into Montana by

the available air corridors will arrive in a state of paranoia and helpless rage, harboring violent fantasies toward unseen authority figures who control their lives from computer banks if not molars in their mouths.

5    Allow me to share my research. One sunny summer evening, I innocently set off for a long family weekend.

6    Phase One: After boarding, and with no warning, I am held prisoner on the runway long enough to make virtually certain that anyone Montana-bound will miss the last connection.

7    That, to paraphrase Dustin Hoffman in "Wag the Dog," was nothing.

8    Phase Two: After arriving at the Northwest holding station and purgatory located in Minneapolis, I race to the next gate and discover that—Hurrah!—my plane is still there. However, having been locked into one plane, I am now locked out of another.

9    That was nothing.

10    Phase Three: The beleaguered ticket agent says that I am rescheduled! Why, I am all set to leave Minneapolis late the next afternoon and go to Montana via Minsk—excuse me—Seattle. I reply in my best Ted Kaczynski tone that this is "unacceptable." She nervously discovers two morning flights on two other airlines that reach Montana via Denver.

11    That was nothing.

12    Phase Four: After a few sleepless hours in a voucher-paid hotel room previously occupied by a chain-smoker who broke the phone, I return to the airport to discover that, yes, I can get to Denver! The Northwest agent, however, neglected to mention that the seat out of Denver on an overbooked flight is unconfirmed. An itsy-bitsy piece of deception. I decide to chance it and book a backup flight via Minsk—excuse me—Seattle.

13    As luck would have it—and I do mean luck—I make the overbooked flight and reach Montana grasping the silver masking tape that holds my armrest together. I make the whole trip in slightly less time and worse shape than Lewis and Clark.

14    Take me to my cabin.

15    Now, I generally don't take out my grudges in print. Lord knows, as an all-too-frequent flier I would suffer in silence, but for the sake of national security and mental health. Of course, it is not just Montana. Nor is it just Northwest, although as of May, Northwest won the ribbon as worst-ranked carrier in the government's Air Travel Consumer Report. This is an airline that handles 9 percent of the fliers and gets 23 percent of the complaints. Yet for reasons that escape me, the pilots and not the customers are planning to strike.

16    But the true scandal of this vastly overbooked and screwed up summer of air-travel discontent is not a safety disaster but a civility disaster. With the system bulging at over 70 percent capacity, with the number of airline employees shrinking faster than the size of the seats, we have an epidemic of air rage.

17    Remember back in June when beleaguered flight attendants testified in Congress about scuffles in the skyways? Remember the stores of passengers jammed in spaces fit for 12-year-olds fighting for Lebensraum in the overhead

bin? The bumped, the canceled, the overbooked, the under-oxygenated travelers living on a diet of pretzels and peanuts and false promises have finally snapped.

18    Air rage over mistreatment and deception has become so routine that this summer the American Society of Travel Agents compiled a "Consumers' Bill of Rights." It includes fantasies like the right to "timely, complete and truthful information regarding delays, cancellations, and equipment changes."

19    In fairness, Northwest has its good points. It has a charming tap-dancing video they play to the prisoners: "We'll feed you / Proceed you / Wherever life leads you / Northwest will take you there."

20    Right. Oh, did I tell you about the flight home? They canceled it.

## WRITING PROMPTS

1. How does Goodman introduce you to her thesis? (What is the context for this narrative essay?)

2. What does Goodman say about getting to Montana? (What is her thesis?)

3. How does she develop her argument? (What support does she use to expand on her thesis?)

4. The author uses sarcasm as she develops her argument. Do you find that sarcasm adds to or subtracts from the effectiveness of her argument? Why?

5. What experiences have you had on airplanes? Do you think Goodman exaggerates her experience, or is her story typical of air travel?

---

Did you notice a large difference in Greene's and Goodman's styles? One is not necessarily better than the other (although because of her very readable short sentences and paragraphs, Goodman is the more appealing at a glance)—just different.

As we stated in our definition, diction, or word choice, is an important element of style. As you saw in the Greene and Goodman essays, the *level of language* (*formal*, *informal*, or *nonstandard*), the use of *figurative language* (*similes* and *metaphors*), and *denotations* and *connotations* all influence an author's choice of vocabulary. Formal language is the language of all serious writing. Informal language is the language we use most of the time, the language of magazines, newspapers, and books for general audiences. Nonstandard language includes *slang* and *colloquialisms*. Similes and metaphors compare words to picture-making words. Similes use the words *like* or *as*: *She is as big as an elephant*. Metaphors just make the comparison without using a comparative word: *She's an elephant*. Denotation (the dictionary definition of a word) and connotation (the emotions or feelings a word triggers) also influence style by the way in which the words are used in a particular passage. The denotative definition of *elephant* is "either of two very large herbivorous mammals of south-central Asia or of Africa, having thick, almost hairless skin, a long flexible, prehensile trunk, upper incisors forming long, curved tusks, and, in the African species, large, fan-shaped ears" (*The American Heritage Dictionary*, 2nd College Edition, 1982). What you think of when you hear the word *elephant* to mean a large person is the connotative definition of the word.

In the following paragraph, taken from *Hard Times* by Charles Dickens, we have circled five words; think about the connotations you associate with each of these five words. Do they help Dickens create a negative picture of this factory town? Underline the similes and metaphors in this passage.

### Hard Times

It was a town of red brick, or of brick that would have been red if the smoke and ashes had allowed it; but as matters stood it was a town of unnatural red and black like the painted face of a (savage.) It was a town of machinery and tall chimneys out of which interminable (serpents) of smoke trailed themselves for ever and ever, and never got uncoiled. It had a (black) canal in it, and a river that ran purple with ill-smelling dye, and vast piles of buildings full of windows where there was a (rattling) and a trembling all day long, and where the piston of the steam-engine worked (monotonously)

up and down like the head of an elephant in a state of melancholy madness. It contained several large streets all very like one another, and many small streets still more like one another, inhabited by people equally like one another, who all went in and out at the same hours, with the same sound upon the pavements, to do the same work, and to whom every day was the same as yesterday and to-morrow, and every year the counterpart of the last and the next.

Charles Dickens, Hard Times

## Understanding Tone

A final contributing factor in the interpretive level of language is an author's tone, his attitude toward his work. Tone can be serious, even somber; humorous, even whimsical; or sarcastic, to name just several. To illustrate the possible differences in tone, we include two final essays: the first, "Don't Rewrite the Bible," is humorous; and the second, "I Want a Wife," is sarcastic. For a serious, somber tone, return to Bob Greene's essay, "It Took This Night to Make Us Know."

### DON'T REWRITE THE BIBLE

#### Michael Golden

1    In line with our national obsession with obliterating distinctions between men and women for fear of being labeled sexist, the National Council of Churches has recently released the "Inclusive Language Lectionary," a modernized translation of key Bible passages. The council, an organization of major Protestant denominations, apparently feels that masculine references to such eminent authority figures as Jesus Christ and even God offend the sensibilities of its distaff members. Thus the new volume of Bible readings, meant to be used in public worship services, refers to God as "Sovereign One" rather than "Lord"; "King" becomes "Monarch" and "Son of God" becomes "Child of God." Women's lib, it seems, has gone otherworldly; indeed, nothing is sacred in our manic quest for a perfectly egalitarian society.

2    Now, bra burning may be one thing, but before we start tinkering with the Bible we should seriously consider just what we're doing with this semantic sleight of hand. Before I'm called a chauvinist pig and worse, let me state that I'm all for the women's movement and its primary goals—equality of opportunity in the workplace, shared responsibilities in the home, political power, financial independence and so forth. I am fervently against discrimination of any kind to any group. But when the Bible is called sexist and is rewritten, I believe we're going just a bit overboard.

3    **Paternal:** There is, after all, something to be said for tradition, especially when one's fundamental beliefs are at stake. I suppose a case could be made for the sexual neutrality of God; after all, at the risk of sounding sacrilegious I submit that we can't really be sure what we're dealing with here. But for whatever historical, cultural, philosophical, psychological or theological reasons one wishes to choose, all the major religions have as their Almighty a paternal figure, whether it be God, Buddha, Allah, Muhammad or Confucius. And I suggest that this state of affairs in no way diminishes the status of women.

4    I cannot, for the life of me, understand why Jesus Christ must have his masculinity denied him for the sake of linguistic neutrality. What possibly can be accomplished by calling him (him?) the Child of God instead of Son of God? This may sound blasphemous, but what else is one to make of this bizarre form of heavenly hermaphroditism? Just how far do we go here? What becomes of all those magnificent Renaissance paintings depicting Jesus Christ with those sinewy muscles and dark beard?

5    What the National Council of Churches has done is not nonsexist; it is merely absurd.

6    By rewriting the Bible we are also opening up a Pandora's box for other traditions and disciplines. Perhaps there will be those who insist that history be rewritten. George Washington will no longer be referred to as the Father of Our Country; that appellation is blatantly sexist. How about Parent of Our Country? Not quite as catchy, but at least there is no paternal bias.

7    In the interest of fairness, of course, this gender genocide can work both ways. What will become of Mother Earth, Mother Nature, Mother Courage and Mother Goose? Certainly these maternal eminences must be neutered as well. Will we be reading to our children Parent Goose stories in the future? Will we arouse the wrath of Progenitor Nature?

8    There are instances where traditions can be changed in order to accommodate modern, nonsexist views, even when they are only token gestures. The National Weather Service avoided a storm of controversy several years ago when they began giving hurricanes and tropical tempests masculine as well as the traditional feminine names. Thus, we now have Tropical Storm Tommy as well as Hurricane Hilda, and meteorologists can no longer be accused of casting aspersions on the feminine temperament. But when we start looking skyward past those ominous clouds and gaze toward the heavens with an eye to eliminating sexual distinctions, then we're headed for trouble.

9    **Maternal:** In our egalitarian philosophy we are terribly afraid to admit that there are differences between sexes, or races, or nationalities or humans of any group at all. Somehow the possibility that physical or psychological differences of any sort exist strikes that fear that this will be equated with superiority or inferiority of certain groups. But the denial that differences exist, whether biological or otherwise, only leads to absurdities; indeed, it is a denial of our own humanity. We cannot respect differences among people unless we first admit to them. This is not sexism or racism; it is merely common sense.

What the council has done in its rewriting of the Bible is not progressive or nonsexist; it is merely absurd.

10    Instead of denying that differences occur between men and women, we should celebrate those differences. After all, Mother Earth—er, Ancestor Earth?—would be an awfully dull place if we couldn't distinguish between masculine and feminine characteristics. Different does not mean inferior. As one noted French—uh, Frenchperson—once said, *"Vive la difference!"*

11    And, for God's sake, let's leave the Bible alone!

## WRITING PROMPTS

1. Why does Golden think the Bible should not have to become politically correct?

2. What examples does he include other than those found in the Bible of both positive and negative changes regarding language?

3. Do you find Golden's humor effective, or does he exaggerate too much? Give examples from the essay to support your answer.

4. This essay was written at the peak of the feminist movement. Do you think people now accept the revised version of the Bible better than they did during the 1970s and early 1980s? Why or why not?

5. Can you think of any instances where political correctness has been carried to extremes? How can we make sure we treat people equitably without carrying political correctness too far?

---

## I WANT A WIFE

### Judy Brady

1    I belong to that classification of people known as wives. I am a Wife. And, not altogether incidentally, I am a mother.

2    Not too long ago a male friend of mine appeared on the scene fresh from a recent divorce. He had one child, who is, of course, with his ex-wife. He is obviously looking for another wife. As I thought about him while I was ironing one evening, it suddenly occurred to me that I, too, would like to have a wife. Why do I want a wife?

3    I would like to go back to school so that I can become economically independent, support myself, and, if need be, support those dependent upon me. I want a wife who will work and send me to school. And while I am going to school I want a wife to keep track of the children's doctor and dentist appointments. And to keep track of mine, too. I want a wife to make sure my children eat properly and are kept clean. I want a wife who will wash the children's clothes and keep them mended. I want a wife who is a good nurturant attendant

to my children, who arranges for their schooling, makes sure that they have an adequate social life with their peers, takes them to the park, the zoo, etc. I want a wife who takes care of the children when they are sick, a wife who arranges to be around when the children need special care, because, of course, I cannot miss classes at school. My wife must arrange to lose time at work and not lose the job. It may mean a small cut in my wife's income from time to time but I guess I can tolerate that. Needless to say, my wife will arrange and pay for the care of the children while my wife is working.

4    I want a wife who will take care of *my* physical needs. I want a wife who will keep my house clean. A wife who will pick up after me. I want a wife who will keep my clothes clean, ironed, mended, replaced when need be, and who will see to it that my personal things are kept in their proper place so that I can find what I need the minute I need it. I want a wife who cooks the meals, a wife who is a *good* cook. I want a wife who will plan the menus, do the necessary grocery shopping, prepare the meals, serve them pleasantly, and then do the cleaning up while I do my studying. I want a wife who will care for me when I am sick and sympathize with my pain and loss of time from school. I want a wife to go along when our family takes a vacation so that someone can continue to care for me and my children when I need a rest and change of scene.

5    I want a wife who will not bother me with rambling complaints about my wife's duties. But I want a wife who will listen to me when I feel the need to explain a rather difficult point I have come across in my course of studies. And I want a wife who will type my papers for me when I have written them.

6    I want a wife who will take care of the details of my social life. When my wife and I are invited out by my friends, I want a wife who will take care of the babysitting arrangements. When I meet people at school that I like and want to entertain, I want a wife who will have the house clean, will prepare a special meal, serve it to me and my friends, and not interrupt when I talk about the things that interest me and my friends. I want a wife who will have arranged that the children are fed and ready for bed before my guests arrive so that the children do not bother us. I want a wife who takes care of the needs of my guests so that they feel comfortable, who makes sure that they have an ashtray, that they are passed the hors d'oeuvres, that they are offered a second helping of the food, that their wine glasses are replenished when necessary, that their coffee is served to them as they like it.

7    And I want a wife who knows that sometimes I need a night out by myself.

8    I want a wife who is sensitive to my sexual needs, a wife who makes love passionately and eagerly when I feel like it, a wife who makes sure that I am satisfied. And, of course, I want a wife who will not demand sexual attention when I am not in the mood for it. I want a wife who assumes the complete responsibility for birth control, because I do not want more children. I want a wife who will remain sexually faithful to me so that I do not have to clutter up my intellectual life with jealousies. And I want a wife who understands that *my*

sexual needs may entail more than strict adherence to monogamy. I must, after all, be able to relate to people as fully as possible.

9    If, by chance, I find another person more suitable as a wife than the wife I already have, I want the liberty to replace my present wife with another one. Naturally I will expect a fresh, new life; my wife will take the children and be solely responsible for them so that I am left free.

10   When I am through with school and have a job, I want my wife to quit working and remain at home so that my wife can more fully and completely take care of a wife's duties.

11   My God, who *wouldn't* want a wife?

## WRITING PROMPTS

1. Brady writes in this argumentative essay that "wives" take care of a multitude of needs, and therefore, Brady wants her own "wife." What statement is she making about liberated women and the inequality between the lives of men and women?

2. What are the categories into which Brady lists routine activities that take time away from her more important endeavors and could be handled by a "wife"?

3. Describe Brady's tone and give examples from the essay that demonstrate this tone.

4. Do you think Brady perceives the roles of women and men accurately? Why or why not?

5. Would you like a servant (or wife) to take care of all of your everyday needs? How do you stay organized now without such a servant to share the responsibilities?

---

Michael Golden's purpose in "Don't Rewrite the Bible" is to persuade but also to entertain. His tone is light and playful, humorous. By using words and phrases such as "tinkering with the Bible" and "going just a bit overboard," he lets colloquial language provide humor as it is interspersed with informal and even formal diction. By employing *alliteration* (a writer's use of repeated beginning sounds of words), he continues with his humorous tone. "Semantic sleight of hand" in paragraph 2, "heavenly hermaphroditism" in paragraph 4, and "Hurricane Hilda" in paragraph 8 are three ways Golden uses alliteration.

Finally, Judy Brady's sarcasm and use of irony appear in "I Want a Wife" as she details her argument for wanting a wife. Her use of **parallel structure** (her beginning of many paragraphs with "I want a wife") and her continued use of **asides** (in paragraph 3, "And to keep track of mine, too" and

"It may mean a small cut in my wife's income from time to time, but I guess I can tolerate that"; in paragraph 4, "... a wife who is a *good* cook"), and her zinger of a last line, "My God, who *wouldn't* want a wife?" all develop her general tone.

## ANALYTICAL LEVEL

The **analytical level** includes the skills of recognizing an author's **rhetorical modes** (organization patterns), questioning content, marking text, annotating, outlining, mapping, and summarizing. These skills will be covered in greater detail as you learn about the writing process. They all reaffirm the connection between reading and writing.

## CRITICAL LEVEL

The **critical level** introduces the **Socratic method** (the use of questions). You also learn to separate fact and opinion by recognizing support (called *evidence* in argumentative writing).

## CREATIVE LEVEL

The **creative level** serves as a bridge between the first four levels of reading and the writing process. This level requires you to go beyond the words on a page, to take some kind of action. In an English class when you read at the creative level, you usually write a personal response to an essay you have read. You create a new work based on an existing text.

## CONCLUSION

To conclude this chapter, return to Danielle Vander Voort's assignment (pp. 6–12), which illustrates these five levels of reading. By examining her marked-up version of Nyhan's essay, we can get an idea of the reading she did at the first four levels. But the reading process is even more obvious when we examine her first and final drafts more closely. Her essay is the result of the reading she did at the creative level.

# CHAPTER 3

# Reading Improved and Reading Acquired

## READING IMPROVED

Now that you know reading is more than pronouncing words, how do you acquire the ability to read quickly and efficiently in order to wade through the thousands of words that a college degree will demand? Some of you may suffer from *dyslexia*, a condition in which the synchronization (combination) of vision and hearing does not occur easily. If you have been professionally diagnosed with dyslexia, for lengthy assignments you may want to resort to books on tape or computer software that lets you hear text as you read it. But even colleges exclusively for students with learning disabilities require their students to read because it is a skill so vital to success after graduation.

Others of you may find that after doing almost no reading in high school, it is almost impossible to look at print in a book for more than five minutes at a stretch without your attention wandering, your eyes watering, or your head pounding. In either of these cases, you may get discouraged and simply give up.

Regardless of the reason, if you did little or no reading during your secondary school career, you should increase your daily dose slowly. Start with five minutes at a stretch. Each day, increase the amount of time you spend at one sitting with reading assignments. By midsemester, you will be amazed at how you have lengthened your reading and attention span—but you have to want to make it happen. As we said before, the solution is to *practice*.

The forced practice you'll receive in college is, of course, a collection of assignments in textbooks and other course-related reading. You will not have a great deal of extra time for recreational reading, especially if you have dyslexia or are sorely out of practice. Pleasure reading can be a great stress reliever, however, so try to find some time for it, perhaps in the following instances: between classes when assignments are up to date; before going to sleep; while waiting in line for public transportation; or while waiting for a professor during office hours. Keep an appealing paperback ready for these slack times. Vacations, of course, can provide you with ample time to further your recreational reading habit (and to keep your eye muscles toned so reading assignments are easier the following semester).

Your speed will continue to increase the more you read, and you will be able to complete more books in a given time span than before you arrived at college. Once you develop the reading habit with easily readable material, try expanding your horizons by reading several books by the same author. Then attempt more challenging material, perhaps written by authors whose views you do not share, or sample some classics. With each new piece of fiction or nonfiction, you'll be building your background knowledge, thereby making your future reading easier, including assignments for your courses, because you have acquired a framework.

# READING ACQUIRED

A famous person who set an example for us regarding the development of reading ability is Malcolm X, one of the leaders of the civil rights movement. Although he completed only the eighth grade, he acquired a phenomenal amount of knowledge through self-education while he was serving time in prison. His leadership on the streets had been based on his speaking ability; however, once imprisoned, he needed to communicate with his followers in writing because he could not be with them daily. Malcolm X discovered that he did not possess the literacy skills necessary for satisfactory communication. In the following excerpt, "Learning to Read" from his work *The Autobiography of Malcolm X*, he explains how he taught himself to read. Notice, too, as you read his words, how important the reading/writing connection was in his education.

### LEARNING TO READ

#### Malcom X

1    It was because of my letters that I happened to stumble upon starting to acquire some kind of a homemade education.

2    I became increasingly frustrated at not being able to express what I wanted to convey in letters that I wrote, especially to Mr. Elijah Muhammad. In the street, I had been the most articulate hustler out there—I had commanded attention when I said something. But now, trying to write simple English, I not only wasn't articulate, I wasn't even functional. How would I sound writing in slang, the way I would *say* it, something such as, "Look, daddy, let me pull your coat about a cat, Elijah Muhammad—"

3    Many who today hear me somewhere in person, or on television, or those who read something I've said, will think I went to school far beyond the eighth grade. This impression is due entirely to my prison studies.

4    It had really begun back in the Charlestown Prison, when Bimbi first made me feel envy of his stock of knowledge. Bimbi had always taken charge of any conversations he was in, and I had tried to emulate him. But every book I picked up had few sentences which didn't contain anywhere from one to nearly all of the words that might as well have been in Chinese. When I just skipped those words, of course, I really ended up with little idea of what the book said. So I had come to the Norfolk Prison Colony still going through only book-reading motions. Pretty soon, I would have quit even these motions, unless I had received the motivation that I did.

5    I saw that the best thing I could do was get hold of a dictionary—to study, to learn some words. I was lucky enough to reason also that I should try to improve my penmanship. It was sad. I couldn't even write in a straight line. It was both ideas together that moved me to request a dictionary along with some tablets and pencils from the Norfolk Prison Colony school.

6    I spent two days just riffling uncertainly through the dictionary's pages. I'd never realized so many words existed! I didn't know *which* words I needed to learn. Finally, just to start some kind of action, I began copying.

7    In my slow, painstaking, ragged handwriting, I copied into my tablet everything printed on that first page, down to the punctuation marks.

8    I believe it took me a day. Then, aloud, I read back, to myself, everything I'd written on the tablet. Over and over, aloud, to myself, I read my own handwriting.

9    I woke up the next morning, thinking about those words—immensely proud to realize that not only had I written so much at one time, but I'd written words that I never knew were in the world. Moreover, with a little effort, I also could remember what many of these words meant. I reviewed the words whose meanings I didn't remember. Funny thing, from the dictionary first page right now, that "aardvark" springs to my mind. The dictionary had a picture of it, a long-tailed, long-eared, burrowing African mammal, which lives off termites caught by sticking out its tongue as an anteater does for ants.

10    I was so fascinated that I went on—I copied the dictionary's next page. And the same experience came when I studied that. With every succeeding page, I also learned of people and places and events from history. Actually the dictionary is like a miniature encyclopedia. Finally the dictionary's A section had filled a whole tablet—and I went on into the B's. That was the way I started copying what eventually became the entire dictionary. It went a lot faster after so much practice helped me to pick up handwriting speed. Between what I wrote in my tablet, and writing letters, during the rest of my time in prison I would guess I wrote a million words.

11    I suppose it was inevitable that as my word-base broadened, I could for the first time pick up a book and read and now begin to understand what the book was saying. Anyone who has read a great deal can imagine the new world that opened. Let me tell you something: from then until I left that prison, in every free moment I had, if I was not reading in the library, I was reading on my bunk. You couldn't have gotten me out of books with a wedge. Between

Mr. Muhammad's teachings, my correspondence, my visitors, . . . and my reading of books, months passed without my even thinking about being imprisoned. In fact, up to then, I never had been so truly free in my life.

## Writing Prompts

1. Why did Malcolm X need to learn to read and write?
2. How did he go about this process?
3. Why does he claim that he had never before in his life been "so truly free" as after he became literate?
4. How does Malcolm X's technique of learning to read and write compare with the way you learned these skills?
5. How valuable are these skills to you?
6. Do you consider yourself "truly free"? Why or why not?

---

We don't suggest you use Malcolm X's methods, but we do suggest you practice. To begin this practice, read the following essay written by the president of Drew University, Thomas H. Kean, entitled "The Crisis Coming to Campus," which appeared in the *Washington Post* (May 1, 1995). Before we give you any suggestions, read it as you normally would read anything.

## The Crisis Coming to Campus
### Thomas H. Kean

1    Our nation is lurching toward what is arguably the gravest crisis in higher education in a generation. It is a crisis of access: The high cost of college is limiting quality higher education opportunities for all but the wealthiest families. This crisis threatens more damage to campus diversity than all the high-profile battles in academia over race, gender and ethnicity.

2    That the United States sends more high school graduates to college than any other industrialized nation should not lull us to complacency. The continued willingness of students and families to incur an ever-growing mountain of debt partly masks the full impact of higher education's sky-rocketing costs. But cracks in the façade are beginning to appear.

3    After decades of working to expand access to all students, our nation's commitment now seems to be more in word than in deed. Today, educational opportunities are increasingly sorted according to the type of school a student can afford. For low and moderate-income students, particularly minorities, the likely prospect of massive indebtedness often means reconsidering four-year

college altogether. Nor are students the only ones reconsidering. Distressingly, some colleges, strapped for cash, have begun making admissions decisions based on a student's ability to pay rather than the ability to benefit.

4    Students also know that college loans cannot pay all the bills, so they work part-time jobs. More than half of all full-time students work—an average of 25 hours a week—and there is growing evidence that it harms academic performance. Income, not merit, is increasingly determining the type of school students attend.

5    And this is only the beginning. T. Rowe Price recently estimated that a parent of a newborn today will have to invest more than $450 a month in high-yield stocks for the next 18 years to send a child to a private college.

6    As a university president, I see the impact every day. Students continually visit my office to tell me they no longer can afford to stay in school. Many are minorities, and an alarming number are middle-class. One described how her parents lost their home so they could keep paying the college bills. College presidents nationwide tell similar stories.

7    Ever since the G.I. Bill half a century ago, higher education has served as the great leveler in our country. But more and more it is becoming the great stratifier. Political and business leaders tell young people that education is the key to their—and our—futures. But the message to the students who visit my office is that the future is available only to those who can afford it.

8    This is not just an academic issue. At no other time in history has the possession of knowledge been so strong an indicator of economic wealth. It used to be that colleges and universities graduated people to manage capital. Now, we look to them to create capital. The health and vitality of colleges and universities cannot be separated from the health and vitality of our economy and society.

9    There is no magic wand to reverse this trend, but we must act soon. Unfortunately, the level of dialogue in Washington suggests that our political leadership has not yet come to grips with this crisis.

10    In the name of deficit-cutting, some proposals in Congress would burden already stretched students by increasing the cost of borrowing for school and eliminating some matching federal scholarship programs.

11    But even if Washington awakens to the problem, solving it will require more than tinkering with policy. Attitudes must also change. In recent years, higher education has mistakenly come to be viewed less as an investment and more as an expense. States with excellent public institutions, such as California and Virginia, focus more on downsizing and cutting state universities rather than improving them. The increasing reliance on student loans instead of grants suggests we are shifting the cost of education to future generations because we are not willing to pay the price today.

12    We must also ask hard questions of colleges and universities. Should our nation's investment in higher education undergo something similar to the restructuring corporate America has experienced the last 15 years? Do we

lavish too much time and money on the top 10 percent of our institutions and not enough on improving the schools the majority of students attend? How can we use the new technologies to lower costs?

13    Debating these issues will be healthy, but it must be done in the context of enhancing—not diminishing—educational opportunity for all Americans. If we are to avoid becoming a nation of education haves and havenots, we must address the looming access crisis now.

---

Do you remember our definition of reading? We stated that the act of reading is not just about sounding out words but about recognizing words instantly, attaching meaning to those words, and being able to predict what comes next. When he began reading while in prison, Malcolm X realized he was "going through only book reading motions." He knew he needed to develop his **sight vocabulary**, so he copied every word in the dictionary. With his first word, *aardvark*, he made a connection to his background: He was of African heritage, and the aardvark is an African mammal. Near the end of his essay, Malcolm X states that once he developed a word base, he could understand an author's message. Adding to this idea, once we comprehend a passage, we can begin to predict where an author is going next.

In Thomas Kean's essay, you may have had a difficult time with the first two paragraphs if you did not attach meaning to such words as *lurching*, *access*, *academia*, *ethnicity*, *complacency*, *incur*, and *façade*. If you have learned good word attack skills, you might have been able to pronounce these words. But it is only with knowledge of the definitions of these words that you can comprehend Kean's opening and be able to predict where his essay is going to take you.

As a second step in reading practice, we provide you with a thinking exercise—a background questionnaire (page 51). Take some time to complete it now. The time you spend answering these questions may be the most valuable step you take in improving your reading and writing.

Now create a reading/writing connection. Read over your questionnaire and then reread "The Crisis Coming to Campus." Did Kean's essay seem easier when your eyes traveled over the lines for a second time? Did you instantly recognize some of the words this time that you stumbled over the first time? Did the passage take on any additional meanings when you connected to it personally? Which background statements from your questionnaire did you connect to the Kean essay during your second reading?

In addition to connecting background to words on a page, efficient reading requires following a strategy, a game plan. This process demands continually asking questions that help you analyze the text you are reading. As you can see by the following questions, we need to be active participants, not just passive bystanders, when we read.

# Background Questionnaire

## You/Your Family/Your Home

Full name? _____

Nickname? _____

Date of birth? _____

Family members in your home? _____

_____

_____

Extended family members? _____

_____

_____

Favorite relative? Why? _____

_____

_____

Home address? _____

_____

## Your Academic History

Schools attended? _____

_____

Approximate number of students
  in your secondary school? _____

Approximate high school
  grade point average? _____

Favorite subjects? _____

_____

_____

Least favorite subjects? _____

_____

_____

Favorite teacher? _____

Extracurricular activities? _____

_____

_____

Awards/scholarships? _____

_____

_____

## Other

Interests/hobbies? _____

_____

_____

Jobs held? _____

_____

_____

Places traveled? _____

_____

_____

Books read during high school? _____

_____

_____

Magazines/newspapers regularly read? _____

_____

_____

Tastes in music? _____

_____

Memorable events in your life? _____

_____

_____

Special accomplishments? _____

_____

_____

## Your College Experience

Reason for choosing this college? _____

_____

Method of financing your education? _____

_____

Initial reactions? _____

_____

Campus residence? _____

Major? _____

Feelings about this course? _____

_____

Dorothy Seyler, a reading textbook author, offers the Active Reader Checklist, strategies to assist you in your reading:

## Active Reader Checklist

| | |
|---|---|
| **When you *preview* a text, ask:** | **You will *discover*:** |
| What is the text about? | The topic |
| What is the author's most important idea about the topic? | The key idea |
| Why am I reading this? | Your own purpose and reading strategies |
| What do I already know about the topic | Associations or connections with your previous knowledge |
| What do I predict the author will say? | Insights into the topic |
| **When you *skim* a text, ask:** | **You will *discover*:** |
| What is the text about? | The topic and subtopics |
| What is the author's most important idea about the topic? | The key idea |
| What techniques or strategies did the author use to write this? | The structure and patterns of organization |
| **When you *study* a text, ask:** | **You will *discover*:** |
| What is this text about? | The topic and subtopics |
| What is the author's most important idea about the topic? | The key idea |
| Who? What? How? Why? Where? When? Which? Or What kind? | Supporting ideas and supporting details |
| **When you want to read a text *critically,* ask:** | **You will *assess*:** |
| Why did the author write this? | The author's purpose |
| What are the author's credentials and possible biases? | The author's credibility |
| What kind of evidence does the author offer? | The reliability of the author's author's evidence |
| How does the author interpret the evidence? | The author's reasoning |

Now that you have skimmed Seyler's questions, consider Thomas Kean's essay one last time. Apply some of Seyler's questions to the passage for maximum reading efficiency.

## EXERCISE

Consider the following questions for analytical reading:

1. What is Kean's text (essay) about?
2. What is Kean's most important idea about his topic?
3. What do I already know about Kean's topic?
4. What techniques or strategies does Kean use to develop his main point? What kinds of evidence does Kean use for support?
5. What do you think prompted Kean to write this essay?

After three readings of the same passage, some hard soul searching, and a "Q and A" treatment, you will obtain much more meaning than you did on your first attempt. You have achieved good comprehension of the passage—your major goal. You also read at the analytical level as you worked through Seyler's Active Reader Checklist and the questions from her outline.

# CHAPTER 4

# Responding to Reading

This chapter addresses the skills necessary to read at the critical level, the Socratic method of questioning, the requirements of arguments, and the separation of fact and opinion.

## THE SOCRATIC METHOD

Socrates was an ancient Greek philosopher who taught by questioning his students and drawing out information from them rather than just lecturing or giving them information. Thus, when we employ questioning as a way of learning, we refer to that way of teaching as the *Socratic method*. At the critical level of reading, you are continually asking yourself questions as you read, evaluating both content and your interpretation of the author's words.

Chapter 3 described the kinds of analytical questions you should be asking as you read and prepare to write about the reading. The Analytical and Critical Reading Practice exercise below follows the Socratic method by asking a series of questions to help you read.

## EXERCISE

*Analytical and Critical Reading Practice Exercise* Mark up your text, indicating the thesis and major supporting details. Remember to circle any unfamiliar words to define later and to make marginal notes to personalize the essay. Then answer the following ten questions:

1. What is the title?
2. What is the author's full name?
3. What do you know about the author's life?
4. What is the date of the original publication?
5. What was the original source?
6. What is the author's thesis?

7. What is the major type of support used (the major organization pattern)?

8. What are some of the minor types of support used? (Include examples.)

9. What is the author's tone? (Give one example from the essay that clues you in to the tone.)

10. What conclusions can you draw about the future of the situation the author is discussing?

# FACTS, LOGIC, AND EMOTION

Three words from the Greek—**ethos, logos,** and **pathos**—refer to three major characteristics of formal arguments—facts, logic, and emotion. And it is these three terms that differentiate persuasive and argumentative writing. Authors of persuasive writing try to convince their readers to believe their values or to take some type of action. This writing contains emotional language and tugs at the reader's heartstrings, but it is not necessarily logical. Argumentative writing also tries to persuade but with facts and logic. In fact, these essays should consist of a balance among facts, logic, and emotion.

## Facts (Ethos)

Facts, or ethos, refers to the credibility of an author; what do you know about the writer? When you answer this question, you are addressing his credibility, the ethos of his argument. Determining ethos comes from an examination of an author's credentials (his background) and his research. Ask yourself the following questions as part of the critical reading process:

- What do I know about this author?
- Does this writer really know his subject thoroughly?
- How much research experience does she have in her field?
- With what organizations and/or institutions is this person affiliated?
- Are the organizations/institutions with which she is associated prestigious?
- Should I believe this person?

In order to gain credibility, an author often includes facts about his own background and relates personal experience. But in addition to what he already knows, a writer often conducts research on a topic and then includes this new knowledge and its sources. To aid you in evaluating factual content gained from research, consider the following questions:

- Are what an author presents as facts really facts? (For anything to be considered a fact, it must be provable.)

- Are the facts sufficient? Are there enough facts for you to understand an author's point and for her to be convincing? (One generalization is not enough.)
- Are the facts recent? As we mentioned earlier, the date of a source is always important, but so are the dates of specific facts within the writing. (Remember, facts change: Before Columbus, the earth was perceived as flat!)
- Does the author cite other researchers who are legitimate authorities on the subject? (A world-renowned cardiac surgeon might be an authority on the quadruple bypass but not on holes in one on the golf links.)
- Does the author name all studies to which he refers? ("Recent studies indicate . . . " does not score credibility points unless the source from which he got his information is cited.)

If you can answer all of these questions affirmatively, the author under scrutiny has filled the requirement of ethos.

## Logic (Logos)

The second requirement of argumentative writing is logic, or logos, which translates neatly into logic. We do not have space here to discuss the various structures of reasoning—or the many flaws in logic caused by hasty, or simply poor, judgment. Simply put, two major structures provide logic in argument—induction and deduction. *Inductive reasoning* involves a list of examples followed by a conclusion based on the preceding evidence. *Deductive reasoning* proceeds from a general assumption to a specific conclusion. If all the statements in an argument are true, then the conclusion must be true.

To make the distinction between these two types of reasoning clear, let's get specific with a simple subject—green apples. Suppose you go to a fruit stand and sample a green apple, and you discover it is sour. Then you take a

bite of another green apple and learn this second apple is also sour. You decide to try one more, so you bite into one last green apple. Unsurprisingly, this apple is also sour. You reach the conclusion that all green apples are sour. You reached this conclusion by inductive reasoning.

For deduction, let's begin with your previously reached conclusion that all green apples are sour. Suppose you go to a different market on another day and find a bin of green apples. You remember your previous apple tasting and the conclusion you drew. This conclusion is your major premise on this new market day. You select a green apple from the bin and examining it you think, "This is a green apple." You have just stated your minor premise. Your new conclusion, which will have to be true if both the major and minor premises are true, is this one: "Therefore, this apple will be sour." You don't need to sample it. You've used deductive reasoning to reach your conclusion.

## Emotion (Pathos)

The third and final requirement of good argumentative writing is pathos, the level of emotion an author arouses. A successful argument contains a balance of facts and emotion; it doesn't present itself as a sob story or an account of terror. In the section on ethos, you learned how to evaluate facts. Now you will learn how to differentiate between facts and opinions.

# SEPARATING FACT AND OPINION

Let's begin by defining the words *fact* and *opinion*. A **fact**, as you just learned, can be proven, and it fits one of the minor detail categories of statistics, examples, reasons, or testimony. An **opinion** is what someone believes and is the result of that individual's biases. It is not something that can ever be proven. To be credible, if an author states an opinion, he or she needs to back it up with facts. We have marked the following *Newsweek* essay, "Can America Assimilate?" by Robert J. Samuelson, to help you understand the difference between fact and opinion.

### CAN AMERICA ASSIMILATE?
#### Robert J. Samuelson

1    *O*
The latest census seems to have been a consciousness-raising exercise—at
*F*
least for the press. It has inspired a series of stories recognizing that large-
*O*
scale immigration is transforming America. "Diversity" is, of course, the
reigning cliché, but even while the press overuses the term, there's been a
*O*
subtle and useful shift in tone and message. Stories increasingly abandon the

uncritical celebration of "diversity" for a more realistic assessment that immigration also brings new social problems and tensions.

F
2   Here's a sample of recent front-page articles:

3   • Troubling label for Hispanics: "Girls Most Likely to Drop Out" (the *New York Times,* March 25): "According to government data, 26 percent of Hispanic girls leave school without a diploma, compared with 13 percent of black girls and 6.9 percent of white girls. The only group that has a higher dropout rate among all students is Hispanic boys [31 percent] . . ."

F
4   • Hispanic Growth Reveals Isolation—Trend Might Take Decades to Reverse (*USA Today,* March 26): "The millions of Hispanic immigrants to the U.S.A. in the 1990s are spreading throughout the country, but they are living in increasingly segregated neighborhoods . . . The average Hispanic lives in a neighborhood that is 44 percent Hispanic."

F
5   • A Magnet for Illegal Immigrants—Surge in Undocumented Population Swamps Area Service Providers (the *Washington Post,* March 27): "Those who teach, counsel and heal low-income immigrants say they are struggling to help a group that has swelled beyond official estimates."

O
6   We may be glimpsing a new attitude toward immigration. What has long been ignored is America's capacity to assimilate immigrants—how many we can easily absorb. The bland assumption has been that a society as wealthy and tolerant as ours doesn't have to worry. Immigrants will enrich our culture, energize the economy and reconfirm our humanitarian heritage. Anyone who voiced doubts (who wondered, for example, whether our wealth or virtues might have limits) risked being labeled a racist or reactionary.

O
7   Well, the Census demolishes the case for complacency. The Census Bureau had estimated the nation's population would increase from 249 million in 1990 to 275 million in 2000, with about 35 percent of the gain coming from immigration. In fact, the Census counted 281 million—6 million more than estimated. Where did the extra people come from? No one knows, but the easiest explanation is illegal immigration. There are other possibilities: the Census simply

may have counted some people missing in 1990. Either way, immigration— *[O]*
mostly legal—has had a huge impact. Already, a fifth of school-age children *[F]*
come from immigrant families. (Most are citizens, having been born here.)

8    As a society, America's central interest lies in assimilating these families. *[O]*
This means more than having them join the economic mainstream. It also
means that they think of themselves primarily as Americans. If the United *[O]* *[O]*
States simply becomes a collection of self-designated "minorities," then the
country will have changed for the worse.

9    We first need to admit that assimilation is desirable. The term has fallen *[O]* *[O]*
into disrepute because it's viewed "by its antagonists as a means of imposing *[F]*
cultural conformity on America's minority groups," as Peter Salins recently
wrote in his book "Assimilation, American Style." To those who worship *[O]*
"multiculturalism" and "diversity," assimilation is dated and detestable.

10    American assimilation never demanded this sort of rigid cultural con- *[F]*
formity, said Salins, now provost of the State University of New York. People *[F]*
could retain ethnic traditions and affections. Italian-Americans could still love
Italy. But assimilation did require three things, he argued. First, immigrant *[F]* *[F]*
families had to adopt English as the national language. Second, they had "to *[F]*
take pride in their American identity" and the country's democratic principles. *[F]*
And, finally, they had to embrace the so-called Protestant ethic—"to be self-
reliant, hardworking, and morally upright."

11    Assimilation is mostly a spontaneous process, driven by the economy, *[O]*
popular culture and the belief in individual opportunity. People are caught in *[O]*
an updraft of activity, new ideas and temptations. A *Washington Post* survey *[F]*
last year asked Latinos the language of their TV programs. Among the first
generation, 31 percent watched mainly Spanish programs and 42 percent
watched "equally" in Spanish and English; by the third generation, 88 percent
watched English programs. On many issues, the attitudes of third-generation *[F]*
Latinos mirrored those of other Americans. But assimilation has never been *[O]*
easy for immigrants or Americans already here.

O

12    That's true now. Progress for many low-skilled immigrants has been
F
grudging. About 30 percent of immigrant children are in poverty, says a report
from the Urban Institute; in 1999, wages for immigrant Hispanic men were
O
only 68 percent those of U.S.-born workers. Meanwhile, there's always a
danger of an anti-immigrant backlash, particularly if there's a recession.
O                                                  F
Americans exhibit spasms of prejudice and insecurity. Benjamin Franklin once
complained about German immigrants, "who will shortly be so numerous as
F
to Germanize us instead of our Anglifying them." There are many stains on
the national record: anti-Irish sentiment in the 1840s; the Chinese Exclusion
Act of 1882, barring Chinese immigrants; the Immigration Act of 1924, whose
quotas tried to limit Italian and Jewish immigration.

O  13    We may face a paradox. To benefit from immigration, we may need a little
less of it. People need time to adjust. American institutions (schools, hospi-
tals) and sensibilities can be overwhelmed by too many newcomers—a reality
ignored in the recent economic boom, when the demand for workers seemed
insatiable. We may also need to favor skilled over unskilled immigrants, further improving the odds for assimilation. Of course, all these controversial
propositions pose difficult philosophical and practical problems. But we aren't
debating them. This is neglect—and not benign.

---

Now it's your turn to recognize the difference between facts and opinions. Read the following essay by Barbara Ehrenreich, "In Defense of Splitting Up," and label each statement fact or opinion.

## In Defense of Splitting Up
### Barbara Ehrenreich

1    No one seems much concerned about children when the subject is welfare
or Medicaid cuts, but mention divorce, and tears flow for their tender psyches.
Legislators in half a dozen states are planning to restrict divorce on the

grounds that it may cause teen suicide, an inability to "form lasting attach-ments" and possibly also the piercing of nipples and noses.

2    But if divorce itself hasn't reduced America's youth to emotional cripples, then the efforts to restrict it undoubtedly will. First, there's the effect all this antidivorce rhetoric is bound to have on the children of people already divorced—and we're not talking about some offbeat minority. At least 37% of American children live with divorced parents, and these children already face enough tricky interpersonal situations without having to cope with the public perception that they're damaged goods.

3    Fortunately for the future of the republic, the alleged psyche-scarring effects of divorce have been grossly exaggerated. The most frequently cited study, by California therapist Judith Wallerstein, found that 41% of the chil-dren of divorced couples are "doing poorly, worried, underachieving, depre-cating and often angry" years after their parents' divorce. But this study has been faulted for including only 60 couples, two-thirds of whom were deemed to lack "adequate psychological functioning" even before they split, and all of whom were self-selected seekers of family therapy. Furthermore, there was no control group of, say, miserable couples who stayed together.

4    As for some of the wilder claims, such as "teen suicide has tripled as divorces have tripled": well, roller-blading has probably tripled in the same time period too, and that's hardly a reason to ban in-line skates.

5    In fact, the current antidivorce rhetoric slanders millions of perfectly won-derful, high-functioning young people, my own children and most of their friends included. Studies that attempt to distinguish between the effects of divorce and those of the income decline so often experienced by divorced mothers have found no lasting psychological damage attributable to divorce per se. Check out a typical college dorm, and you'll find people enthusiastically achieving and forming attachments until late into the night. Ask about family, and you'll hear about Mom and Dad . . . and Stepmom and Stepdad.

6    The real problems for kids will begin when the antidivorce movement starts getting its way. For one thing, the more militant among its members want to "re-stigmatize" divorce with the cultural equivalent of a scarlet *D*. Sadly though, divorce is already stigmatized in ways that are harmful to children. Studies show that teachers consistently interpret children's behavior more negatively when they are told that the children are from "broken" homes—and, as we know, teachers' expectations have an effect on children's performance. If the idea is to help the children of divorce, then the goal should be to *de*-stigmatize divorce among all who interact with them—teachers, neighbors, playmates.

7    Then there are the likely effects on children of the proposed restrictions themselves. Antidivorce legislators want to repeal no-fault divorce laws and return to the system in which one parent has to prove the other guilty of adultery, addiction or worse. True, the divorce rate rose after the introduction of no-fault divorce in the late '60s and '70s. But the divorce rate was already rising at a healthy clip *before* that, so there's no guarantee that the repeal of no-fault laws will reduce the divorce rate now. In fact, one certain effect will be to generate more divorces of the rancorous, potentially childharming variety. If you think "Mommy and Daddy aren't getting along" sounds a little too blithe, would you rather "Daddy (or Mommy) has been sleeping around"?

8    Not that divorce is an enviable experience for any of the parties involved. But just as there are bad marriages, there are, as sociologist Constance Ahrons argues, "good divorces," in which both parents maintain their financial and emotional responsibility for the kids. Maybe the reformers should concentrate on improving the *quality* of divorces—by, for example, requiring prenuptial agreements specifying how the children will be cared for in the event of a split.

9    The antidivorce movement's interest in the emotional status of children would be more convincing if it were linked to some concern for their physical survival. The most destructive feature of divorce, many experts argue, is the

poverty that typically ensues when the children are left with a low-earning mother, and the way out of this would be to toughen child-support collection and strengthen the safety net of supportive services for low-income families— including childcare, Medicaid and welfare.

10     Too difficult? Too costly? Too ideologically distasteful compared with denouncing divorce and, by implication, the divorced and their children? Perhaps. But sometimes grownups have to do difficult and costly things, whether they feel like doing them or not. For the sake of the children, that is.

---

You've learned the levels of reading; you've learned how to improve your reading; you've learned about ethos (facts), logos (logic), and pathos (emotion) in arguments; and you've learned how to recognize and separate fact and opinion. Now it's time to take the information you've learned about reading and connect it to the writing process.

# PART III
# The Act of Writing

# CHAPTER 5

# Writing Defined

Writing is hard work! I'm afraid to write letters to my mother because she totally misunderstands what I'm saying. If I suggest that the weather has been gray for the past few days, she interprets my words to mean I'm depressed. Sometimes when I write, however, I look back over my words and think, "I didn't realize I thought that!" Then writing is fun! The difficulty or ease of writing depends primarily on the person(s) to whom you are writing and your purpose for writing. If you are writing for yourself, for whatever reason, writing is fun and easy. But the minute another person enters the dialogue, the act of writing becomes challenging because now you have to consider your purpose and your audience. What is your reason for writing? What does your reader know? What are the reader's biases? What is the level of vocabulary? So many factors enter into the dialogue.

*The American Heritage Dictionary* tells us that *to write* means "to form (letters, for example) on a surface with a tool such as a pen or pencil. To form (a word, for example) by inscribing letters or symbols on a surface." And often, when someone asks me what I teach, and I respond, "writing," that person stares at me blankly and responds, "You teach penmanship?"

The next meanings of *write* in the dictionary are "to compose and set down, esp. in literary or music form . . . to express . . . to communicate . . . to produce written material, such as articles or books" (1393). For the purposes of this text, writing means *to express one's thoughts on paper*. We hope to help you write expository essays that your readers will find "capable of being read easily" and "pleasurable or interesting to read" (1030).

What, you may ask, are expository essays? Turning again to the dictionary, we find that *essay*—from the French *essayer*, "to try," means "A short literary composition on a single subject, usually presenting the personal view of the author" (465). And *expository*, from the Latin *ex*—out and *ponere*—to put or place, "means exposing, or setting forth meaning or intent. . . . A precise statement intended to give information about or an explanation of difficult material." The following, an expository essay written by a college freshman, exemplifies the definitions set forth in this paragraph:

## ALCOHOL ABUSE

1   Alcohol abuse has been a problem for thousands of years, but we are only just beginning to understand the causes of alcoholism. Scientists have long suspected that a tendency to drink too much is in some part hereditary. I believe that the tendency to abuse alcohol may be a trait passed down through the generations just like blue eyes or red hair.

2   One reason I believe that alcoholism is hereditary is that I used to work with alcoholics as a volunteer. Several people enrolled in the program fit the pattern of hereditary alcoholism. For instance, George is a recovering alcoholic who drank heavily for forty years. George has four children, and all four children are alcoholics. Alice is an alcoholic whose mother and father both are alcoholics. Catherine is an alcoholic and her son and her mother are alcoholics. Harry is a 75-year-old alcoholic man whose son and grandson are recovering alcoholics.

3   Another reason that I believe that alcoholism is hereditary is from my research. According to an article in *Newsweek* magazine entitled "The Gene and the Bottle," children of alcoholics are not only more likely to become problem drinkers, but studies have shown that they share distinctive brain-wave patterns. A study conducted at the University of California in Los Angeles shows that an estimated 24 percent of the U.S. population has a genetic structure that limits the brain's ability to register and respond to the effects of certain external stimulants.

4   As a result, "they are prone to using excessive amounts of alcohol in quest of stimulation," says Ernest P. Noble, M.D., and Ph.D., professor of alcohol studies at the University of California School of Medicine in Los Angeles. Among the 70 subjects of the study, every carrier of the abnormal gene had a 77 percent chance of being an alcoholic; each noncarrier had a 72 percent chance of not being alcoholic.

5   My experience of working with alcoholics involved only a few of the nation's estimated 18 million alcoholics and an abnormal gene is but one piece of a larger puzzle. However, I believe that my experience and my research suggest that alcoholism may be hereditary.

---

This student's instructor made the following comment: "This essay exhibits a few weak ties to the student's thesis, but otherwise, it is a well-focused, good job. The essay needs a few more paragraphs in both personal experience and research for proper development." But notice that the student has a definite thesis supported with clear and specific supporting evidence.

# THE SPEAKING/WRITING CONNECTION

We discussed the reading/writing connection earlier. Let's take a look now at the speaking/writing connection to understand the vast differences between the two. Talking is natural behavior whereas writing is learned behavior. We listen first, even in the womb, and we begin to speak as we parrot the sounds of our parents. We begin to write when we go to school and are first taught how to form the letters of the alphabet, and then, after learning to read, how to form words by combining letters. Talking, therefore, is a natural process whereas writing is an artificial process. Like the wheel, writing is a primary technological device, but talking is natural and almost always performed earlier than writing.

Most talking is faster than most writing. Granted, the computer allows us to write with increased speed, but our minds generally work more quickly than our fingers. Thus we often see words left out of our initial drafts as we try to keep up with the thoughts pouring from our brains.

When we read, we have only the words on the page from which to decipher meaning, and often we read incorrectly "between the lines" (remember my mother's response to my letters). As writers we have only one chance to say what we have to say. But when we talk, others can hear tone, see nonverbal signals, and question confusing comments. When we write, we cannot just jump in; we must introduce the reader to the topic, provide some background, and then let the reader think about what we're saying.

Along the same lines, when talking, the listener is usually present; when writing, the audience is usually absent. Writing usually results in a visible product, whereas talking does not; therefore, perhaps because a product is involved, writing tends to be a more responsible and committed act than talking. We have the opportunity to think before we write, to consider our purpose, our audience, our tone, and to choose our words carefully. We often speak without thinking, "off the tops of our heads," and we speak carelessly. Finally, writing is more readily a form and source of learning than talking (Emig, *Writing as a Mode of Learning*). We don't know what we think until we see it in writing; the warm woolies that swirl around in our brains don't become substantial until we see them in print. We take notes in lecture classes, but some of us have to rewrite our notes in preparation for tests, for it is in the physical act of rewriting that we retain knowledge.

Thus speaking and writing are two very different activities, and for academic purposes, we can no longer put our speaking voice on paper. In fact, English is broken into **standard** and **nonstandard usage**. Nonstandard English includes words common to dialect (*ain't* instead of *am* or *are not*, *don't* instead of *doesn't*, *hisself* instead of *himself*). We may speak nonstandard English, and we might use it if we're writing dialogue in a narrative essay or writing in our journals or writing a letter to a friend. **Colloquial language** (the language you use with friends) and **slang** (trendy words that appear and disappear from everyday usage) are other examples of nonstandard English. Standard English is that English taught in schools.

As we mentioned before, within the broad scope of standard English lie two varieties, *informal* and *formal* English. **Informal English** is the language used by your professors in classes. Most of us use informal English most of the time. It is the language of general population magazines (as opposed to technical journals), newspapers, novels, and talks intended for general audiences. But it is *not* generally the language we use for academic writing. **Formal English** is the language of textbooks, speeches, and all serious academic writing. It rarely includes slang or contractions; it may use complex sentence structures and vocabulary not normally found in spoken language.

We generally have four levels of vocabulary knowledge: speaking, writing, reading, and listening. We use our spoken vocabulary in conversation; we use written vocabulary when we write. Depending on my audience to whom I am either speaking or writing, I may raise my level of vocabulary from conversational to more formal. My vocabulary responds to the expectations of my audience. When I speak with my fellow faculty members, I am more apt to use the "vocabulary of academia" (educational jargon) than I am with my students or my family. And in the workplace, we speak differently when speaking with our employer than with our customers or clients or fellow employees.

Our reading/listening vocabulary is largest. When we read we are able to grasp the meaning of many words from their context, but we are not apt to use those words when speaking until we are truly comfortable with their denotations and connotations.

Once you understand and accept that speaking and writing really are two different languages and that even within writing there are different levels of usage, you will have an easier time meeting the writing expectations of your professors. Going back to our definition of writing, we now see that to write essays that are capable of being read easily and are pleasurable or interesting to read, we must, together (student and professor), review or learn those processes and rules that underlie all writing.

## PRIVATE VERSUS PUBLIC WRITING

Generally we can separate writing into two parts: writing for "our eyes only" and writing for publication. When we use the word *publication*, we mean writing for the public or, more simply, writing for someone other than ourselves. Private writing means writing to discover, to express, and to learn and includes such activities as prewriting, journals, and writing to learn. Public writing means writing to inform, to entertain, and to persuade and includes any form of the written word with which we come in contact.

## Private Writing: Writing to Discover, Express, and Learn

How many times have you written a letter, a paper for one of your teachers, or a diary entry and, in reading over what you have written, thought, "I didn't realize I thought that!" Think about how you start to write a paper. If you have not done so in high school, you certainly will be taught now how to prewrite. In the process of prewriting, you will discover ideas to help you write on a particular topic.

Writing to express includes informal letters to friends, first drafts of emotional outpourings, like letters to the editor or a "Dear John" letter to an about-to-be ex-girl/boyfriend, or a parent who has denied you something you desperately need or want, and entries in your journal or diary.

Journals can also spark ideas for writing. I often find germs of ideas, feelings, descriptions, or characters in my daily jottings. I also work out problems in my journal.

I ask students to keep journals, and their responses have been enlightening. One student, after complaining bitterly for the first month, commented at the end of the semester that he could not go to bed at night without first "unloading" in his journal. An alumna wrote, five years after she graduated, that in cleaning out a closet, she came upon her freshman year notebooks, including her journal. She wept and howled at the record of her first semester at college. Journals are a wonderful way of record keeping for memories.

We ask you to keep a journal or diary during this course. Don't simply record your days, but reflect on the daily events as they occur. How did you feel about getting to your psych class unprepared and being asked to summarize the reading assigned for the weekend? How did you feel when the best-looking sophomore on your floor said, "Hi, how're you doing?" as you were on your way to your room from the shower, wrapped in a towel? Or how did you feel when you arrived half an hour late for a test because you had to pick up your sick child from school? I think you have the idea. Try keeping a journal for the semester. We find that journal writing, aside from the pleasure it may give you, greases your wheels, loosens your tongue, and strengthens your writing muscles.

## EXERCISE

Go to your bookstore or a local discount store and buy a spiral notebook or a bound journal. For the rest of this semester, write every day (including weekends!) for at least ten minutes. Please do *not* write

> I got up late this morning, grabbed a box of Captain Crunch to take to class and arrived ten minutes late for my 8 o'clock history lecture. Went to math class and fell asleep. Had lunch and went to the library to research

some material for my computer course. Took a nap. Had dinner with my roommate at Kentucky Fried Chicken and went back to the library to check out the chicks/guys. Nothing much. Went back to the dorm to watch *West Wing* and hang out. On my way to bed at 12:30.

Rather, think about your actions for the day. How did you feel when you awoke at 7:30 and had to be in class at 8? What was the response of the teacher and students to your falling asleep in math class? With whom did you have lunch? Did you have lunch? Meet any interesting people? Or same old, same old? How's the college library? Do you have trouble finding material? Are you comfortable using the microfiche, copy machines, computers? How's the library staff?

Writing to learn includes taking notes both in class and from textbooks, in-class writing that professors will ask you to do as a check on your understanding of material in a particular course, and preliminary writing as a way to prepare for class and exams.

These examples of writing are all personal; they are not "for publication," they are not graded, they are not for anyone else except you. Of course you may choose to have someone else share your personal writing, but the intended audience is you and you alone.

## Public Writing: Writing to Inform, Entertain, and Persuade

Unlike private writing, where you are the audience, public writing is intended to be read by an external audience. That audience may be anyone—your classmates, your professor, readers of a newspaper to which you write a letter, your parents, your significant other. And because this writing is public, your communication must be precise because you have only one chance to be understood. Unlike speaking, where you are able to repeat your idea until your listener completely understands your message, writing gives you only one chance to say what you mean. That concept is a bit formidable, but it only means you must consider carefully what you are writing. And consideration involves two primary concerns—purpose and audience.

**Purpose** has two meanings. First, what is your reason for writing? Is it to inform? Is it to entertain? Or is it to persuade? Second, what is your message? In other words, what main idea do you wish to get across to your reader? We call that main idea the *thesis*. You've already read about finding a thesis or main idea when you read, and you will learn much more about thesis when we talk about the writing process.

The second concern, *audience*, refers to your reader(s). Writing to one person narrows your responsibility considerably. If you are writing to your professor or to your father, your sister, your best friend or spouse, you generally know what is expected from your writing. Your papers for your professor will be written in fairly formal, standard English; your letters to your father, your sister, or your spouse will probably be fairly informal, filled with colloquialisms and clichés. You know what you can get away with in each of these instances.

But now broaden that audience, say to readers of your college newspaper or local town newspaper, or readers of the *New York Times*. Your tone, your style, and your voice will be different for each of these audiences.

Notice the differences in writing between the following two letters. The first is a letter from a college student to his father; the other is from a college student to the editor of the student newspaper:

> Hi Dad; Just a note to tell you about my first impressions of this place. The *most* important thing I've noticed is that the parking sucks. I'm almost sorry I brought the car 'cause I can't find anywhere to put it, and the campus cops spend their entire lives waiting to catch us poor innocent freshmen who haven't yet memorized the stupid parking symbols, and they slap us with $50 fines every time one of us parks where we're not supposed to. I'm gonna go broke just paying the dumb fines!

> To the Editor: This school has an excellent academic reputation, and I realize how fortunate I am to be a student here. The faculty is knowledgeable and caring, and I am impressed with the core curriculum and the course offerings; however, I'm sorry to say that I do not have the same kind words or feelings about the campus police. I have brought my car to school because I need it to get to and from my part-time job in town (the money I make at that job allows me to eat and pay for my books and my expenses). I understand that parking is tight here on campus, but I do not understand why we are fined $50 every time we make a mistake. I have been here three weeks and I have already been fined $150 for parking in the wrong place at the wrong time. Until we uninformed freshmen become familiar with the complicated parking symbols, I would hope the campus police would be a bit more understanding of our plight.

Do you sense the difference in audience for these two letters? In both instances, the message is clear, but certainly the tone, the style and the voice are quite different.

## EXERCISE

How is the college environment (library, cafeteria, faculty, staff, parking, etc.)? Try writing the following letters:

- Your spouse or best friend at home
- The dean of students
- The college newspaper

First, determine your purpose in writing. Are you writing to entertain, inform, or argue or persuade? Then, determine your audience and that audience's knowledge and level of understanding of you and your message.

You've learned what writing is and how writing varies depending on audience and purpose. We hope you will have the opportunity to do lots of private writing while you're in college. The rest of this text discusses public writing and how to write to be understood and, incidentally, appreciated as a writer.

# CHAPTER 6

# The Writing Process

For a long time the teaching of writing involved assigning in-class and out-of-class essays, usually one or two a week. The student wrote; the instructor read, bled all over with red ink, and returned the essay to the student. The student immediately balled up the essay and threw it into the wastebasket, never to be considered again.

Those times have changed. Today the teaching of writing involves helping students understand the **process** that writers undergo to produce a piece of writing. For example, today as I work on this chapter, I am surrounded by notes, texts, a dictionary, and my thoughts (which have been rattling around in my brain for the past month waiting to take shape on this page). When I have finished my writing for the day, I'll print the results, read them over tonight, and give them to a friend tomorrow to read and evaluate. Once she returns the draft to me with her suggestions, I'll revise and rewrite the draft. When I have completed that process for the entire chapter, I'll probably outline the chapter as I have written it, check it for organization and coherence, rewrite it once again, and then—before I give it to the members of the faculty to review—I'll proofread the chapter for errors of punctuation, grammar, and mechanics. And that, in a nutshell, is the process of writing you will experience during this course.

The writing process involves three elemental steps: planning or *prewriting*, drafting or *writing*, and revision or *rewriting*. But these steps are not linear; they do not happen one after another from beginning to end. In fact, these steps are recursive; writing is a process consisting of continually drafting and revising *toward* the finished product. In other words, prewriting, writing, and rewriting occur *throughout* the writing of the

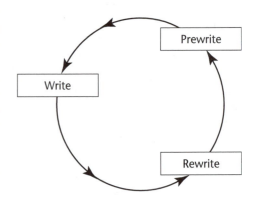

essay. They are ongoing steps that repeat and repeat as you work through the piece of writing.

# PREWRITING

The first stage of this process is **prewriting** or *planning*, the mental and physical activities that prepare you to put pen to paper. These activities may include peer collaboration to discuss topics and to consider purpose and audience. You might freewrite, map, or cluster your thoughts. Or, as you become more comfortable with this process, you may "prethink" (some of us keep self-stick notes beside our beds in case we have a stroke of brilliance in the middle of night!)

# WRITING

The second stage of the process, *writing* or *drafting*, involves many steps. At this point you are ready to put ideas to paper. (Like a dog who circles its sleeping place many times before finally settling down, I prepare to settle in by getting my coffee, my notes, and my dictionary, checking my voice mail, preparing my music for the siege, and generally "psyching myself" for the activity.) This first attempt at writing, the first draft, should be simply a regurgitation draft—an emptying of your brain of all ideas connected to the topic. This is *not* the time to worry about organization, audience, tone, style, or spelling; it is the time to simply get ideas on paper.

Once that is accomplished, thinking about intended **audience**, purpose, thesis, and focus become appropriate concerns. A second draft, paying attention to those elements, deserves an outside reading—peer review, a conference with your instructor, a meeting with your tutor.

# REWRITING

The final stage is **rewriting** or *revision*. Consider the word *revision*, from the Latin *revisere*, to visit or look at again, which means to prepare a new version of a text, to change, to modify. At this point in the process, give careful thought to organization, coherence, point of view, audience, tone, diction, and your intended purpose. To rewrite does *not* mean simply to proofread or to edit. Proofreading or editing is the final step in writing, accomplished just before you submit the document. Once you have made those revisions, you are ready to type, proofread, correct, and hand in your piece of writing.

Prewriting, writing, and rewriting present the three steps that writers follow again and again. Once you learn and understand this concept, you will truly appreciate each step and what it can do for you in any writing situation.

# CHAPTER 7

# Prewriting

Prewriting involves the planning you do every time you are called on to put pen to paper or fingers to computer keyboard. It occurs regardless of the writing situation. Prewriting can be as simple and uncomplicated as, "Hmmm, what do I want to tell my diary tonight?" and as complicated as the preplanning that has gone and continues to go into the writing of this book. Prewriting includes the considerations of purpose and audience, and it includes the techniques we use to develop and organize our thoughts.

## CONSIDERATIONS

### Purpose

As we mentioned in Chapter 2, the term *purpose* has two meanings: one is the message the author wishes to get across to an audience; the other is the form the writing will take—informative, argumentative or persuasive, or entertaining. Consider Ellen Goodman's essay "Flying into Air Rage" in Chapter 2. What is her message, and what form does it take? Her main idea (or thesis) is serious and important; she is discussing air rage or lack of civility on U.S. airlines. But what form does that message take? Goodman has chosen to couch this serious issue in humor; thus her primary purpose is to entertain even though she does inform and persuade. Notice the amount of reading that Goodman did in order to write this humorous essay. She not only narrates a humorous experience; she also cites statistics, the Consumer's Bill of Rights, and testimony of flight attendants before Congress. Clearly Goodman engaged in prewriting activities before she finished her column.

### Audience

Audience is the second consideration as you plan your writing task. For whom is the writing intended? Once you have answered that question, many other considerations come into play. How much does that audience already know about your subject? And how does that audience feel about your subject? What is the educational level of your reader(s)? What is their vocabulary level? How important are education, religion, work, family to this audience? Is the audience liberal or conservative in its political leanings? Will the topic make the audience angry or defensive? How can you carefully present unpopular ideas? Why should your audience read what you have written? What authority have you for writing your piece? How can you attract the attention of your readers? What tone should you use to best engage your readers?

A final word about audience. In a world that becomes more diverse daily, we ask you to write in language that can be universally understood. How many of you have tried to translate a computer manual, or an insurance policy, or *anything* written by the U.S. government? We live in a world of pretentious language, language meant to exclude us from a particular sector of our society. You will find perfect examples of exclusionary language in any journals in your library, be they in the fields of English, psychology, history, or computers. When you write, write for a universal audience. In other words, use vocabulary that everyone can understand, use simple sentence structures, and use your own voice.

# TECHNIQUES

## Analytical Reading

Much of the writing you do in college involves responding, in one way or another, to material you have read. Essay questions on tests and exams, research papers, class projects, and responding to articles and essays occur in all disciplines. Even the writing in this course will require that you read to gather information to add to your own knowledge or experience. Thus we start the prewriting techniques with the first step in the process of writing—reading. And the reading you will do here falls under the analytical level we first mentioned in Chapter 2.

When we read actively, we read with pen in hand. If you are reading your own books, you can mark them up as much as you wish. (Many of you appreciate buying secondhand books when a previous student has done your work for you—sometimes! Be careful because that student may not have been an efficient reader!) If you are doing research in the library, photocopy the articles or pages you want to study so you can mark those pages as you wish.

When you mark text, you are conversing with the author, examining and sometimes questioning the author's ideas. The following poem, "Catch" by Robert Francis, draws a wonderful analogy between reading and playing catch.

**Catch**

Two boys uncoached are tossing a poem together,

Overhand, underhand, backhand, sleight of hand, every hand,

Teasing with attitudes, latitudes, interludes, altitudes,

High, make him fly off the ground for it, low, make him stoop,

Make him scoop it up, make him as-almost-as-possible miss it,

Fast, let him sting from it, now fool him slowly,

Anything, everything tricky, risky, nonchalant,

Anything under the sun to outwit the prosy,

Over the tree and the long sweet cadence down,

Over his head, make him scramble to pick up the meaning,

And now, like a posy a pretty one plump in his hand.

Robert Francis

When you mark text, you are also noting the important information you want to remember and possibly use in your own work. And making marginal notes means you will not have to reread the article completely when you are ready to use the material.

Text marking includes underlining, numbering, circling, bracketing, starring, and annotating (making notes in the margins). Underline the author's thesis (main idea) and perhaps number the pieces of supporting evidence. Circle any unfamiliar words, look them up in a dictionary, and write their meanings in the margins. Bracket significant sentences or key passages you might want to quote or paraphrase. You might star or asterisk important phrases or sentences.

And finally, annotate, make notes in the margin about anything that will help you remember the piece. Take a look at the following essay, "Role Models, Bogus and Real," by Brent Staples, and see how one reader chose to mark the text.

2 kinds of
role models

## ROLE MODELS, BOGUS AND REAL
### Brent Staples

suburban kids—
shipped off to
malls

America deludes itself about why its children behave as they do. In the suburbs we herd them into malls and let them grow up bereft of community, under the impression that what you can buy is who you are. In the cities we

City kids—
parentless;
drugs & guns

raise them in devastated, parentless settings, where drug addiction and random gunfire rule the day.

After all that, <u>when children behave badly we inexplicably lay the blame at the tarnished feet of America's sports gods.</u> We blame <u>Michael Jordan</u> for gambling. We blame <u>Charles Barkley</u> for <u>spitting on a fan.</u> This week we're blaming <u>O.J. Simpson</u> for <u>battering his wife and for being accused of her murder.</u>

The <u>blame</u> of which I speak is indirectly assigned, a <u>consequence of that seemingly innocuous phrase "role model."</u> The term entered the language 30 years ago. <u>Initially a "role model" was someone whose successes other people—and especially children—might emulate. As the television age wore on, there came a subtle shift in meaning. A "role model" became someone who, by virtue of fame and money, was appointed surrogate parent to America's young.</u>

<u>These are peculiar "parents" indeed: They live behind television screens, never meet their "children" and are expected to inspire them by force of fame alone.</u> Any failing on their part is regarded as a betrayal of the nation, and a tragedy for all those doe-eyed kids in television land. These days, the term "role model" is almost exclusively heard when some modern-day Icarus[1] loses his wings and comes crashing back to earth proved mortal in the end.

In the days <u>since O.J. Simpson's arrest</u> for murder, there have probably been <u>hundreds of stories lamenting the loss of a vital "role model" for America's young.</u> This despite the fact that Mr. Simpson's glory years as a player ended 20 years ago. In popular culture, 20 years is an eternity. It's a safe bet that until Mr. Simpson's arrest, most kids had barely even heard of him.

<u>Why</u> then the constant <u>"role model" morality play?</u> Partly it's the <u>archaic notion that athletes need to be paragons of virtue and temperance, exempt from mortal flaw.</u> Beyond that, I think, lies a <u>deeper and more unfortunate presumption</u>: that <u>only stars can affect children's lives for the better, that the mere mortals among us are powerless to guide, shape or enlighten.</u> The sadness here is that the <u>reverse is true.</u> The <u>only legitimate "role model" is the person whom children can see, feel and interact with in their daily lives.</u>

**Notes (margin):** When essay was written · We blame sports heroes when kids misbehave (we should blame the parents) · orig. def. of role model—someone who is successful & should be copied · later—role model became someone who was a "surrogate parent" to kids · Gr. myth. ref. · Today we show someone as a bad role model when he fails. Ex. – O.J. Simpson · Why? We expect athletes to be perfect people. Worse—we think the only role models our kids can have are athletic stars seen on T.V. · TS *ex. of a real role model Joseph Marshall – saves kids.*

*Staples cites Marshall who says athletes can't help kids who have been abandoned by everyone.*

*Marshall runs a radio show to try to counteract inner city violence.*

*Real def. of a role model – What we should use as the def.*

*\*restatement of TS*

Enter <u>Joseph Marshall, Jr.,</u> the recipient of a 1994 "genius" award from the MacArthur Foundation and cofounder of San Francisco's Omega <u>Boys Club</u>, a place where young people between the ages of 11 and 25 find friendship, surrogate parents, academic training—and college scholarships. <u>Mr. Marshall</u> <u>says</u> that <u>inner-city kids are confused and violent because they've been</u> <u>"orphaned"—by family, community, government and the media. No athletes,</u> grinning or otherwise, <u>can reach them. His role</u> is <u>to recreate families for these</u> <u>children.</u>

<u>Mr. Marshall is also the host of "Street Soldiers,"</u> an extraordinary <u>violence-</u> <u>intervention project.</u> At a time when many <u>radio talk shows</u> have become little more than noise, Mr. Marshall's is the <u>equivalent of a radio "parent,"</u> broadcast weekly on San Francisco's KMEL. He reaches an <u>audience of 40,000 to</u> <u>50,000 young people,</u> many of whom he advises on such pressing matters as how not to shoot people and how to avoid being shot.

The <u>results speak for themselves.</u> <u>"Street Soldiers" has a proven record of</u> <u>averting the reprisal shootings that often follow initial episodes of violence.</u> And <u>since the Omega Boys Club opened in 1987, more than 100 young people</u> who might well have gone to jail, or to graveyards, <u>have gone to college</u> instead.

That's <u>what a role model is: someone who loves and works and encourages</u> <u>and lays on hands.</u> All the rest is noise and empty air.

A role model needs to be a real person in a community who works directly with children. Because a true role model actually must interact with the young people he influences, to make a difference. The old definition of role model (one who is successful and, therefore, should be copied) no longer applies.

[1]Character in Greek mythology who wore wax wings invented by his father but flew too close to the sun and fell to his death when the wax melted.

## WRITING PROMPTS

1. According to Staples, what changes have occurred over the years in the definition of the term *role model?*
2. Why does Staples think sports heroes cannot be role models?

3. What kinds of supporting examples does he include to show both unsuccessful and successful role models?

4. Do you think good role models can prevent violence and drug abuse among adolescents? Why or why not?

5. Do you agree with Staples that a role model must be someone living in the community rather than someone in professional sports? Why or why not?

6. Who have some of your heroes been, and why do you think they were role models?

## EXERCISE

Read the following essay, "A Civility Lesson for Students" by Ilene Grinna. Using the techniques we offered, mark the text of this essay. Share your text marking with your classmates to see if you came up with the same responses.

## A CIVILITY LESSON FOR STUDENTS
### Ilene Grinna

I have had enough! I am tired of the way students misbehave in my classroom. Every day students wander into class late, leave whenever they feel like it, eat a meal while class is conducted, and display downright rude behavior. Many students seem unaware that they need to be considerate of others and conscious of how their behavior is perceived. I have to ask myself, do I do students any favor by allowing them to act in such a crude manner? I believe it is time for college professors everywhere to set standards for student behavior in class.

I know I am not alone feeling this way. Fellow teachers at other colleges and universities nationwide complain about what they see in their classes. When a chemistry professor at Virginia Tech asked his class how to solve an equation, a student in the back of the room shouted, "Who gives a shit?" When a professor at Utah State University refused to change a grade, a student screamed at her, "Well, you damn bitch, I'm going to the department head, and he'll straighten you out!" Some professors have been stalked by angry students, and a few have been physically attacked.

Even at my small college, students have lost any semblance of civility. Last semester, I had a student confront me in front of the whole class when she received a B on a paper instead of the A she thought she deserved. My students are unprepared for class. Many don't bother to do any assigned work. Others may read the material quickly, but they don't read it carefully and aren't ready to discuss ideas. Even worse are the students who, when asked a question, blurt out an answer without giving the question any thought. Then there are those students who feel free to walk into class ten minutes late or get up whenever they need to get a drink or use the restroom. In many instances, students see class as a social occasion where they converse with their friends instead of participating or listening. I can't tell you the number of times I've seen students pass around photos of a weekend party when they were supposed to be working on a group case study. I get particularly upset when students regard class as a time to have breakfast or lunch. They eat food that smells up the whole classroom, and they leave wrappers and bottles lying around on the desks and floor when they leave. Putting their messes in the garbage wouldn't occur to them. Frankly, I'm just tired of seeing students reclining with their feet up on the desks in front of them, wearing their baseball caps, belching and making inappropriate comments. They act like slobs instead of serious students.

I think many of the problems would disappear if students understood simple civility. We should set up rules of conduct and punish students who don't follow them. Here are the rules all students should follow:

- All students will address faculty as "Professor _____."
- Classroom doors will be closed at the official class time, and no student may enter after the door has been closed.
- Students are not allowed to leave during class, except in an emergency.
- Students will sit at their desks without slouching or putting their feet up on the furniture.

- Students will not wear caps of any sort during class.
- Students may not eat or drink during class, and should not be chewing gum loudly.
- If students wish to talk in class, they will raise their hands.
- Students will not chat with each other.
- Students will turn off all cell phones.
- Students will not use obscene language in the classroom.

I believe that students who violate these rules should be kicked out of class for that day and marked absent. If they continue with their uncivil behavior, the professor should be allowed to withdraw them from the class. Professors should not have to tolerate such rude behavior, behavior that ruins the learning that is supposed to take place.

Just imagine what the classrooms would be like if students followed these rules. They would be cleaner and smell better. Class would start on time with no interruptions from students walking in or out. The classroom "atmosphere" would be quiet and decorous, and learning could take place undisturbed by rude outbursts. I think all students would benefit because they would learn the most valuable lesson: that they must be civil if they want to succeed in the "real" world.

## WRITING PROMPTS

1. What does Grinna think of student behavior in the classroom? What examples does she give to support her points?
2. Have you seen uncivil behavior in classes at your college? How did the instructor handle the situation? Have you witnessed uncivil behavior outside the classroom?
3. What kind of behavior do you think is appropriate in college classrooms? Do you think Grinna's rules are good ones or would you suggest others?
4. If you come from another country, what kind of behavior is considered appropriate in a college classroom in your home country? Do students behave differently than American students?

## Brainstorming

**Brainstorming** is the easiest of the prewriting techniques in that it requires nothing more than emptying your brain! When you brainstorm, you take the topic about which you wish to write, and you simply list, in the order in which the words flow from your pen, all the ideas that come to mind relative to that topic.

Here is a list of rules for brainstorming:

1. Don't criticize or evaluate ideas during the session. Simply write down every idea that emerges. Save the criticism and evaluation until later.
2. Use your imagination for "free wheeling." The wilder the idea the better because it might lead to some valuable insights later.
3. Strive for quantity; more ideas increase chances for a winner to emerge.
4. Combine and improve ideas as you proceed. (Osborne, *Applied Imagination* 84)

In graduate school when I took a course from one of the country's leading process writing advocates, I was told to write at least 100 words or phrases, each on a separate note card, about a place I loved. (The list never materialized into an essay, but it did, eventually, become a poem.)

## EXERCISE

Try brainstorming now. Take a topic you know well—a person, place, or thing (a family member, your home, your pet) and make a list of all the words and phrases that come to mind about that topic. Write down everything, no matter how silly it may seem at the time. You might be surprised at the ideas you generate for a vivid picture of something or someone that you care about. Stretch. Write *at least* 25 words or phrases.

Brainstorming also works well for groupthink. When I taught public speaking classes, students broke into groups to present a panel discussion about a topic of their choosing. We spent a class period as a group brainstorming possible topics for those discussions, narrowing down the choices until groups of five could agree on a topic listed on the blackboard for their project. This process worked well because the students had some ownership of the topic and were much more creative than I would have been in coming up with possible interesting subject matter.

## Freewriting

**Freewriting,** a technique much like brainstorming, allows you again to write anything that comes to mind about a particular topic. Peter Elbow explains freewriting this way:

**Freewriting**

The idea is simply to write for ten minutes (later on, perhaps fifteen or twenty). Don't stop for anything. Go quickly without rushing. Never stop to look back, to cross something out, to wonder how to spell something, to wonder what word or thought to use, or to think about what you are doing. If you can't think of a word or a spelling, just use a squiggle or else write, "I can't think of it." Just put down something. The easiest thing is just to put down whatever is in your mind. If you get stuck it's fine to write "I can't think what to say, I can't think what to say" as many times as you want: or repeat the last word you wrote over and over again: or anything else. The only requirement is that you *never* stop.

*Writing Without Teachers*, 3

The major difference between brainstorming and freewriting is the manner in which you write. With brainstorming you are listing words and phrases related to your topic; with freewriting you are writing continuously.

## EXERCISE

School! You've been at college long enough now to have formed some initial impressions. On a piece of paper write for at least ten minutes about your time at college thus far. This exercise can be shared with your classmates before, during, or after class. You'll probably have many similarities and many differences about your first impressions.

## EXERCISE

Return to Ellen Goodman's "Flying into Air Rage" and freewrite your response to her essay. Don't worry about form (spelling, complete sentences, etc.), and put *everything* that pops into your head regarding this essay on paper—ideas, facts, feelings. Write for at least ten minutes without stopping.

## Mapping or Clustering

**Mapping** or **clustering** can be used both when reading and writing or at any point in the writing process. You map as a prewriting device or during the writing process to spark ideas for sections of the essay as you draft or revise. This technique involves visually arranging ideas so you can see where ideas belong, how they relate to each other, and whether or not you need to write more. Begin clustering by writing your topic in the middle of a sheet of paper. Circle the word and then surround it with words and phrases that identify the major points you intend to discuss. Circle these words and phrases and connect them to the topic in the center. Then construct other

**Figure 7.1**
Clustering/Mapping

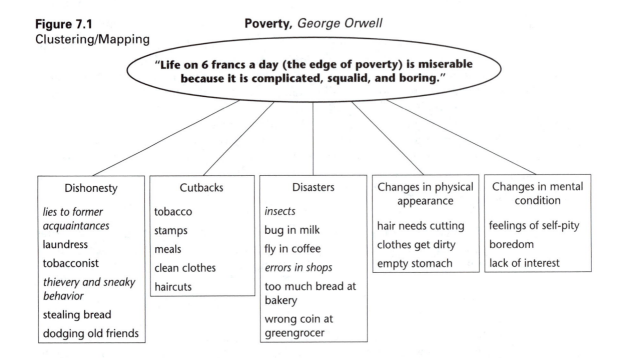

**Poverty,** *George Orwell*

clusters of ideas relating to each major point and draw lines connecting them to the appropriate point. By dividing and subdividing your points, you get more specific as you move outward from the center of the page. In the process you can identify facts, details, examples, and opinions that illustrate and expand your main points. Clustering or mapping works particularly well for those of us who need to visualize our ideas on paper.

Figure 7.1 (above) shows how clustering can be used when you read, and Figure 7.2 (at the top of the next page) gives you an example of the clustering I did for writing this chapter.

## EXERCISE

Remember the list you made of campus impressions? Try taking one of those topics (parking, finances, dorms, parties, faculty, facilities) and mapping it. Remember, put the word in the middle of your paper and go from there.

## Outlining

Outlining is another reading and writing technique you can use as you plan your essay. Recall Danielle's outline in Chapter 1 for the Nyhan essay. When you're writing, if you know your topic well, a preliminary outline

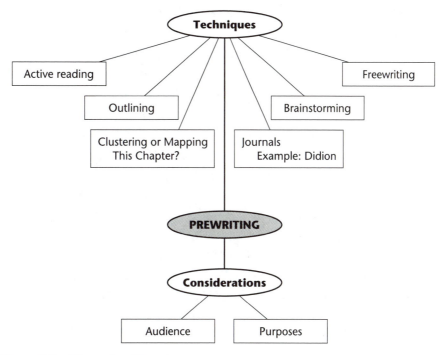

**Figure 7.2**   Clustering/Mapping

helps you focus your ideas, and you can freewrite or brainstorm from the initial outline. But outlines are probably most useful after you have done your initial prewriting or written the first draft. At this point it is often useful to put your ideas into outline form to see how the parts of your ideas fit together, how they relate, and what you might need to add. Formal outlines follow a pattern of numbers and letters in parallel form with at least two parts to each section. A typical outline for an argument essay could look like this:

I. Introduction

   A. Context

   B. Thesis Statement

   C. Definition of terms

   D. Direction

II. Body

   A. First main idea

      1. First supporting idea

         (a) First supporting detail

         (b) Second supporting detail

2. Second supporting idea

    (a) First supporting detail

    (b) Second supporting detail

B. Second main idea

    1. First supporting idea

        (a) First supporting detail

        (b) Second supporting detail

    2. Second supporting idea

        (a) First supporting detail

        (b) Second supporting detail

III. Conclusion

    A. Restatement of thesis

    B. How body supported thesis

    C. Call for action

Keep your outline flexible and remember it is only a guide. The best use of an outline is usually after the first draft when you can use it to check on the organization of your writing.

## Journals

We mentioned the journal in Chapter 5 as an example of private writing, and we spoke about using the journal as a reflective diary of events. Now, let's look at the journal as a prewriting technique. In your journal you can practice freewriting, respond to reading assignments, jot down questions you might have for class discussion, work on assignments, keep track of particular problems with grammar, mechanics, or personal spelling demons, and keep ideas for possible writing tasks.

## EXERCISE

In your notebook, add one more section—a writing journal. This journal will include in-class writing, jottings about potential topics for writing, responses to readings, prewriting exercises, rough drafts, anything that has to do with writing you are doing this year (in any course!).

A few other ideas to help you at the prewriting stage include defining a term, comparing and contrasting topics, considering cause and effect, and checking out what others have said about your topic. *The Oxford English Dictionary* (if you've never seen it, go find it in a library; it's worth the trip)

---

### Using a Computer in the Prewriting Process

- You don't have to look as you write/type. Just pour your heart out without worrying about the mechanics.
- Check out some of the software programs that prompt writers. *Idea Generator Plus* and *Writer's Helper* are both popular programs.
- Type notes to yourself in parentheses or put asterisks in places that may need more work.
- If you start wandering, just start a new page for those thoughts.
- Keep your journal on your computer. You might have the seeds for an assignment somewhere within those jottings.
- Once you've finished your generating exercises, rearrange them, by cutting and pasting, into some semblance of order.
- Save *everything* on your hard drive or floppy. You never know when something you wrote might come in handy.
- Date all work. Otherwise, at some point in the writing process, you might become confused by all the drafts you have saved.

---

not only defines terms; it also traces the etymology (history) of the word, showing how meanings of words can change in time. This dictionary also explores the roots of words, explaining where words came from (for example, *education* comes from the Latin word *duco, ducare,* meaning "to lead." The prefix *e* means "out of" or "away from". Understanding these root words helped me understand Socrates' philosophy of education: Teachers should bring out or elicit information from students rather than spoon-feeding it in like sausage into a casing). Comparing and contrasting your topic with other topics will also help you generate ideas. (How is writing similar to or different from playing catch?) Vacations! (Who or what determined that we need them and what results stem from taking them?) And finally, depending on how much you already know about your topic, you might want to read or interview to find what others have said or have to say about your topic.

## EXERCISE

If your instructor does not give you a topic, take a topic of your choice and using the methods just described, generate ideas about that topic. Not every method works for every writer for every topic, but by experimenting with these methods, you may find a way or ways to loosen ideas that are lodged somewhere in the back of your mind.

Prewriting exercises will help you develop ideas and details that will strengthen your writing in all aspects. And prewriting happens not only at the start of a writing assignment; it can and should occur at any time during the writing process when you see a need to develop an idea or detail further.

# CHAPTER 8

# Writing Paragraphs

The *American Heritage Dictionary* (2nd ed.) defines a paragraph as "A distinct division of a written work or composition that expresses a thought or point relevant to the whole but is complete in itself." Alexander Bain, in his book *English Composition and Rhetoric* (1866), first defined a paragraph as a topic sentence that announces the main idea of a paragraph and is followed by subsidiary sentences that develop or illustrate the main idea.

In Part II, we defined a **topic sentence** as the sentence in the paragraph that specifies the major idea of the entire paragraph and functions as the heading for the rest of the sentences in that paragraph. English teachers have given and will continue to give rules relating to the development of those paragraphs.

Bain offers seven laws for effective paragraphing that range from unity to parallel structure to order of sentences. You will hear that every paragraph must have a topic sentence, that a paragraph must have at least three or five or seven sentences (depending on the idiosyncrasy of the particular teacher), and, for beginning essay writers, that the topic sentence should be the first sentence in the paragraph. All of these statements may have validity, but the reality is that we do not write by formula.

A **paragraph** is simply a new idea. It may be another illustration of support, it may at times signal a transition, or it may present a counterargument. A paragraph should be developed according to a definite plan that is logical and unified. You should discuss the idea you are presenting thoroughly enough for your reader to clearly understand your message.

Chapter 2 includes various examples of paragraphs with topic sentences scattered throughout the paragraphs. As you saw, you may read paragraphs with no specific topic sentence; the topic will be implied. If you do a lot of reading of newspapers, you'll find one-sentence paragraphs throughout the articles you read.

So, although we teach you rules, those rules can be broken once you clearly understand the purpose of the paragraph. And understanding the paragraph is important because in many ways a paragraph is a mini essay. It deals with one topic, which it introduces, develops fully, and then ends.

# EXERCISE

Read again "The Three New Yorks" by E. B. White.

### The Three New Yorks

There are roughly three New Yorks. There is, first, the New York of the man or woman who was born here, who takes the city for granted and accepts its size and its turbulence as natural and inevitable. Second, there is the New York of the commuter—the city that is devoured by locusts each day and spat out each night. Third, there is the New York of the person who was born somewhere else and came to New York in quest of something. Of these three trembling cities the greatest is the last—the city of final destination, the city that is a goal. It is this third city that accounts for New York's high-strung disposition, its poetical deportment, its dedication to the arts, and its incomparable achievements. Commuters give the city its tidal restlessness, natives give it solidarity and continuity, but the settlers give it passion. And whether it is a farmer arriving from Italy to set up a small grocery store in a slum, or a young girl arriving from a small town in Mississippi to escape the indignity of being observed by her neighbors, or a boy arriving from the Corn Belt with a manuscript in his suitcase and a pain in his heart, it makes no difference: each embraces New York with the intense excitement of first love, each absorbs New York with the fresh eyes of an adventurer, each generates heat and light to dwarf the Consolidated Edison Company.

1. Assume the first sentence in the paragraph is the topic sentence. Copy the sentence at the left margin of a piece of paper and number it 1.

2. Examine the second sentence. Does it continue the idea of the first sentence, or does it comment on the idea? If it continues the idea, it is parallel with the first sentence. Thus write it directly beneath the first sentence, and number it 1. If, as is usually the case, it comments on, refers to, or clarifies the idea of the first sentence, then it is subordinate to the first sentence. In that case, number it 2, and indent it one-half inch when you write it down under the first sentence.

3. Look at the third sentence. Does it continue or comment on the first sentence? How does it relate to the second sentence? If it continues the structure or ideas of the second sentence, it is like the second sentence. Number it 2, and write it directly under the second sentence. If, however, it comments on, refers to, or clarifies the structure or ideas of the second sentence, it is subordinate to that sentence, so write it and indent it a full inch from the left-hand margin and number it 3.

4. Continue your analysis with the rest of the sentences in the paragraph. The essential test will always be the question of whether the next sentence continues or comments on the sentences above it. Make sure you keep checking each new sentence against the sentences that precede it.

## EXERCISE

Try writing a paragraph of your own. Your topic sentence should include a word such as *reasons, causes,* or *uses.* Write a topic sentence. Add a sentence that supports it. Add a second supporting sentence. Add a third supporting sentence. Conclude with a final supporting sentence.

Your sequence should look like this:

1.
  2.
  2.
  2.
  2.

Next, write the topic sentence. Qualify that sentence. (Write a sentence that comments on the first sentence.) Add a specific detail. Add another detail. Qualify that detail. Conclude with the final supporting sentence.

Your sequence should look like this:

1.
  2.
    3.
    3.
      4.
  2.

Share your paragraphs with a classmate to see if he or she can determine the patterns you have used (Frank D'Angelo, "The Topic Sentence Revisited," *College English* 37 (1986): 431–441).

# INTRODUCTORY PARAGRAPHS

In Chapter 7, Prewriting, we gave you a possible outline for an essay. The introduction included *context, thesis statement, definition of terms,* and *direction.* Let's look at those four points in terms of the introductory paragraph. **Context** as used here means the connection between you and the audience. Many writers call that a "hook." It is usually an attention grabber that hooks the audience and makes them want to continue to read. A variety of methods can serve as context:

- *Statistics*   Remember David Nyhan's essay on TV? "Four hours a day is what the average kid watches. That twenty-eight hours per week, over the year, is more time than he spends in school (less than one-fourth of the day for less than 180 days)." Almanacs and encyclopedias provide good sources of statistics.

- *Direct quotes*   Taking the words of another person, especially one who is well known, adds interest and credibility to your writing. If you are able, in a quote, to capture the essence of your idea, you show your readers you have researched others' ideas about your subject.

- *Narration*   Relating an anecdote, a joke, a personal experience, or a dramatic event is sure to hook your reader's attention and add spice to your essay. Consider David Nyhan's opening sentence for his essay "The Prison Population Is Rising—Politicians Must be Very Proud," which you will read later in its entirety. "If I told you that my prescription for making America a bit safer from crime was to lock up every blessed soul living in Maine and New Hampshire, you'd think I was nutty."

- *Description*   Describing a scene appeals to the senses and will often elicit an emotional response. Description can also enhance curiosity if the person or place being described is not discovered until the end. Picture Mike Rosen's description: "It is not committed with guns and knives, but with great, relentless bulldozers and thundering dump trucks, with giant shovels like mythological creatures, their girded necks lifting massive steel mouths high above the tallest trees." Rosen is beginning an argument essay about strip mining.

The **thesis statement** makes a promise to your audience. You make a statement, you give your opinion about that statement, and you then proceed to support that opinion. The thesis statement represents the essay-length equivalent of a topic sentence of a paragraph and is probably the most difficult part of the essay to write. If you can make a statement and follow that statement with a *because* clause, you have organized your essay.

Consider the following: The topic assigned is water and its effect on you. As a writer you have tremendous leeway in terms of where to go with that very general topic. Because I am sitting at my computer looking out the window at the Atlantic Ocean pounding at the cliffs below me, I choose to write about the effect of the ocean on my well-being. My sister lives on a lake, and we are constantly arguing over which is "better," so I am going to argue that the ocean is more soothing to the soul than a lake. Now where do I go? First of all, notice that my statement is not a fact; it is my opinion. I now need to think about how or why I believe that statement to be true. See what happens when I add the word *because* to that statement. The ocean is more soothing to the soul than a lake because . . . Now I am forced to consider the reasons, and, once I have done that and am able to articulate those reasons, I have a working thesis that will organize my entire piece.

So why do I believe that statement is true? Because the ocean appeals to my senses and that appeal soothes my soul. Aha! I have a working thesis statement. The ocean is more soothing to the soul than a lake because the ocean appeals to all the senses. Now you, the reader, and I, the writer, know where I am going with this essay. The senses include sight, sound, smell, touch, taste, and feel. I may or may not include that particular thesis in my beginning paragraph, but I certainly have given myself direction.

The next two parts of an introductory paragraph, according to the outline we presented earlier, would be **definition of terms** and **direction.** If any words in the thesis statement might cause confusion to the reader, now would be the time to define those terms in the way that you, the author, wish them to be understood for the purposes of this essay. Do I need to define appeal? Soul? Senses? I think not, so I can skip that part. Do I need to provide direction for the paper? No! I have a clear thesis that allows both me and the audience to follow along with no difficulty. I would probably use description or narration as the context for this essay. So I would open the paragraph with two or three sentences of context, then state my thesis, and then be ready to argue or persuade you, my audience, that the ocean is far superior to a lake for its effect on one's peace of mind.

## EXERCISE

Your topic is water and its effect on you. Design an opening paragraph that includes context, a thesis statement, and, if necessary, definition of terms and direction. Don't be influenced by my response to this topic. Water has many more connotations than simply oceans and lakes. Use your imagination and have fun!

## DEVELOPING BODY PARAGRAPHS: RHETORICAL MODES

You've written your introductory paragraph, and now you're ready to write the body of the essay. It's time to examine the patterns into which writing falls. You've already seen two of these patterns, also called *rhetorical modes*, in our discussion of introductory paragraphs. Narration and description are two of the most common ways of structuring ideas. These patterns will help you mold your ideas into coherent form in your writing; they will also improve your reading comprehension if you are able to recognize these patterns in your reading. Thus, once again, you can see the close tie between writing and reading. If you want to be easily understood as a writer, you will follow conventions that will make your writing easy to be read and understood.

Listed next are the nine major organization patterns and the signal words that accompany them. These words can guide your writing of the paragraph and will help your audience identify the pattern as they read your work. We discuss these patterns in greater detail in the following chapters.

- *Narration:* first, second, third, etc.; next; then; after; finally; last
- *Description:* above, before, behind, beside, below, beyond, in front of, on the left, on the right, next
- *Exemplification (illustration):* for example, to illustrate, such as
- *Process:* the same time-order words used in narration, steps to follow
- *Comparison/Contrast:* two kinds of_____, similar to, different from, compares to, contrasts with
- *Classification/Division:* three (or more) kinds of_____, is divided into
- *Cause/Effect:* causes, reasons why, results, consequences, therefore, thus, hence
- *Definition:* is, are, means, is defined as
- *Argument and persuasion:* believe, think, opinion

## CONCLUDING PARAGRAPHS

Your conclusion should leave the reader with the feeling that you have satisfactorily ended your piece of work and are ready to wrap it up. A concluding paragraph should summarize or reemphasize your major points. We suggested earlier in the prewriting techniques that an expository outline should, in the conclusion, restate the thesis, show how the body supports the thesis, and call for action (if appropriate). Many argue that steps A and B in the conclusion are dreary. They are! And as you become more comfortable with your writing, you will enjoy breaking away from this model. A noted writer from Yale University, William Zinsser, suggests that a good ending should be "a joy in itself." He suggests, "when you are ready to stop, stop. If you have presented all the facts and made the point that you want to make, look for the nearest exit." I agree. I also find that, along with composing the first sentence of a piece of writing, composing an appropriate ending is laborious and painstaking—but extremely gratifying when it is well done.

# CHAPTER 9

# Narration, Description, and Exemplification

Now let's take a look at the patterns used to develop your ideas in more detail:

## NARRATION

Simply put, *narration* means relating events in chronological or temporal (time) order or storytelling. The writer of a narrative usually includes events in the order in which they occur. A narrative can be factual or fictional, and it can be personal or objective. As you have already discovered, you can use narration for your opening hook or you can use personal experience to support your thesis.

In her autobiography, *I Know Why the Caged Bird Sings*, Maya Angelou writes about her grandmother's two commandments, "Thou shall not be dirty" and "Thou shall not be impudent" and in a paragraph of narration supports her statement, "Everyone I knew respected these customary laws, except for the powhitetrash children."

### I Know Why the Caged Bird Sings

Some families of powhitetrash lived on Momma's farm land behind the school. Sometimes a gaggle of them came to the Store, filling the whole room, chasing out the air and even changing the well-known scents. The children crawled over the shelves and into the potato and onion bins, twanging all the time in their sharp voices like cigar-box guitars. They took liberties in my Store that I would never dare. Since Momma told us that the less you say to white-folks (or even powhitetrash) the better, Bailey and I would stand, solemn, quiet, in the displaced air. But if one of the playful apparitions got close to us, I pinched it. Partly out of angry frustration and partly because I didn't believe in its flesh reality.

Maya Angelou, *I Know Why the Caged Bird Sings*

Narration occurs in two other formats in addition to the subjective personal narrative you just read. The first of these is *factual narration*, the kind you read in news stories. Unlike personal narratives, these accounts, which are more objective, are written in third person. Read Martin Gansburg's "Thirty-Eight Who Saw Murder Didn't Call the Police," which originally appeared in the *New York Times* shortly after the brutal murder it chronicles.

## THIRTY-EIGHT WHO SAW MURDER DIDN'T CALL THE POLICE

### Martin Gansburg

1    For more than half an hour 38 respectable, law-abiding citizens in Queens watched a killer stalk and stab a woman in three separate attacks in Kew Gardens.

2    Twice their chatter and the sudden glow of their bedroom lights interrupted him and frightened him off. Each time he returned, sought her out, and stabbed her again. Not one person telephoned the police during the assault; one witness called after the woman was dead.

3    That was two weeks ago today.

4    Still shocked is Assistant Chief Inspector Frederick M. Lussen, in charge of the borough's detectives and a veteran of 25 years of homicide investigations. He can give a matter-of-fact recitation on many murders. But the Kew Gardens slaying baffles him—not because it is a murder, but because the "good people" failed to call the police.

5    "As we have reconstructed the crime," he said, "the assailant had three chances to kill this woman during a 35-minute period. He returned twice to complete the job. If we had been called when he first attacked, the woman might not be dead now."

6    This is what the police say happened beginning at 3:20 A.M. in the staid, middle-class, tree-lined Austin Street area:

7    Twenty-eight-year-old Catherine Genovese, who was called Kitty by almost everyone in the neighborhood, was returning home from her job as manager of a bar in Hollis. She parked her red Fiat in a lot adjacent to the Kew Gardens Long Island Rail Road Station, facing Mowbray Place. Like many residents of the neighborhood, she had parked there day after day since her arrival from Connecticut a year ago, although the railroad frowns on the practice.

8    She turned off the lights of her car, locked the door, and started to walk the 100 feet to the entrance of her apartment at 82-70 Austin Street, which is in a Tudor building, with stores in the first floor and apartments on the second.

9    The entrance to the apartment is in the rear of the building because the front is rented to retail stores. At night the quiet neighborhood is shrouded in the slumbering darkness that marks most residential areas.

10    Miss Genovese noticed a man at the far end of the lot, near a seven-story apartment house at 82-40 Austin Street. She halted. Then, nervously, she headed up Austin Street toward Lefferts Boulevard, where there is a call box to the 102nd Police Precinct in nearby Richmond Hill.

11    She got as far as a street light in front of a bookstore before the man grabbed her. She screamed. Lights went on in the 10-story apartment house at 82-67 Austin Street, which faces the bookstore. Windows slid open and voices punctuated the early-morning stillness.

12    Miss Genovese screamed: "Oh, my God, he stabbed me! Please help me! Please help me!"

13    From one of the upper windows in the apartment house, a man called down: "Let that girl alone!"

14    The assailant looked up at him, shrugged, and walked down Austin Street toward a white sedan parked a short distance away. Miss Genovese struggled to her feet.

15    Lights went out. The killer returned to Miss Genovese, now trying to make her way around the side of the building by the parking lot to get to her apartment. The assailant stabbed her again.

16    "I'm dying!" she shrieked. "I'm dying!"

17    Windows were opened again, and lights went on in many apartments. The assailant got into his car and drove away. Miss Genovese staggered to her feet. A city bus, Q-10, the Lefferts Boulevard line to Kennedy International Airport, passed. It was 3:35 A.M.

18    The assailant returned. By then, Miss Genovese had crawled to the back of the building, where the freshly painted brown doors apartment house held out hope for safety. The killer tried the first door; she wasn't there. At the second door, 82-62 Austin Street, he saw her slumped on the floor at the foot of the stairs. He stabbed her a third time—fatally.

19    It was 3:50 A.M. by the time the police received their first call, from a man who was a neighbor of Miss Genovese. In two minutes they were at the scene. The neighbor, a 70-year-old woman, and another woman were the only persons on the street. Nobody else came forward.

20    The man explained that he had called the police after much deliberation. He had phoned a friend in Nassau County for advice and then he had crossed the roof of the building to the apartment of the elderly woman to get her to make the call.

21    "I didn't want to get involved," he sheepishly told police.

22    Six days later, the police arrested Winston Moseley, a 29-year-old business machine operator, and charged him with homicide. Moseley had no previous record. He is married, has two children and owns a home at 133-19 Sutter Avenue, South Ozone Park, Queens. On Wednesday, a court committed him to Kings County Hospital for psychiatric observation.

23    When questioned by the police, Moseley also said that he had slain Mrs. Annie May Johnson, 24, of 146-12 133rd Avenue, Jamaica, on February 29 and

Barbara Kralik, 15, of 174-17 140th Avenue, Springfield Gardens, last July. In the Kralik case, the police are holding Alvin L. Mitchell, who is said to have confessed to that slaying.

24    The police stressed how simple it would have been to have gotten in touch with them. "A phone call," said one of the detectives, "would have done it." The police may be reached by dialing "0" for operator or SPring 7-3100.

25    Today witnesses from the neighborhood, which is made up of one-family homes in the $35,000 to $60,000 range with the exception of the two apartment houses near the railroad station, find it difficult to explain why they didn't call the police.

26    A housewife, knowingly if quite casually, said, "We thought it was a lovers' quarrel." A husband and wife both said, "Frankly, we were afraid." They seemed aware of the fact that events might have been different. A distraught woman, wiping her hands in her apron, said, "I didn't want my husband to get involved."

27    One couple, now willing to talk about that night, said they heard the first screams. The husband looked thoughtfully at the bookstore where the killer first grabbed Miss Genovese.

28    "We went to the window to see what was happening," he said, "but the light from our bedroom made it difficult to see the street." The wife, still apprehensive, added: "I put out the light and we were able to see better."

29    Asked why they hadn't called the police, she shrugged and replied: "I don't know."

30    A man peeked out from a slight opening in the doorway to his apartment and rattled off an account of the killer's second attack. Why hadn't he called the police at the time? "I was tired," he said without emotion. "I went back to bed."

31    It was 4:25 A.M. when the ambulance arrived to take the body of Miss Genovese. It drove off. "Then," a solemn police detective said, "the people came out."

## WRITING PROMPTS

1. What was the shocking event that prompted Gansburg to write this piece of factual narration for the *New York Times?*

2. In addition to his chronology of events, what support does Gansburg include to increase the impact of this incident?

3. Do you think the journalistic style (very short paragraphs) enhances or detracts from the message? Why?

4. If you had been a neighbor of Kitty Genovese on the night of her murder, would you have called the police or in some other way tried to help?

5. Have you ever witnessed a person or group of people harming another without anyone getting involved to prevent this harm?

Leigh Montville, in his essay "Requiem for a Super Featherweight" written for *Sports Illustrated* immediately after the death of Jimmy Garcia, uses the narrative form effectively in this moving account of the time following Garcia's last fight. Notice that the paragraphs in this essay do not follow the typical expository formula of the topic sentence being the initial sentence; in fact, they often do not have topic sentences at all. Notice also the short paragraphs.

## REQUIEM FOR A SUPER FEATHERWEIGHT
### Leigh Montville

1    The father tried to make the son move just the slightest bit. There had been all those years, all those nights in the gym in the faraway port town of Barranquilla, Colombia, where he had tried to teach the son the most complicated movements, asked for the jabs and feints, the dips and weaves, the lethal choreography of the prizefight ring, but now he would settle for much, much less. Any movement would do.

2    *"Mueve la mano,"* Manuel Garcia said in Spanish. Move your hand.

3    The son lay on a hospital bed in a blue-green gown, his arms and legs exposed, the tubes and wires of modern science attached to his body. The tubes that had been inserted into his nose were part of his life-support system. A bandage, wrapped like a turban around his head, covered the spot where doctors had operated for more than two hours to remove a blood clot and relieve pressure on his brain. The right side of his face was absurdly swollen. He was still unresponsive.

4    *"Mueve la mano,"* the father said again and again.

5    He was rewarded sometimes with a spasm, a slight reflex from the son's left hand. He could detect hardly any movement from the right. Less than twenty-four hours earlier—it was May 7 now, five o'clock, visiting hours at the University Medical Center in Las Vegas—the son, Jimmy Garcia, twenty-three years old, challenger for the WBC super featherweight title, had slid to the canvas in the hectic moments after his futile, one-sided fight against Gabriel Ruelas had been stopped in the eleventh round at Caesars Palace.

6    Garcia was still conscious as he was removed from the ring on a stretcher. Indeed, public-address announcer Michael Buffer asked the crowd to give Garcia a hand, which it did. The fight card then proceeded to the top-billed bouts, including Oscar De La Hoya's second-round knockout of Ruelas's younger brother, Rafael. Garcia was unconscious by the time he reached the ambulance. He was in surgery within forty minutes.

7    His mother, Carmen Perez, had worried about something like this. She had refused to travel to Las Vegas for the fight, refused even to listen to the broadcast in Colombia. She had gone to church, instead, to pray for Jimmy's safety. The son had shared none of her concern. Danger? He could not worry about danger. He described himself as a prince. He said he was "born to box."

8 "I'm not going to live long," he used to say. "Maybe thirty or thirty-five years. The lives of princes are short like that. And I am a prince of sport. There's no doubt about it, so there's no reason to fear death."

9 He had a 35-4 record before he fought Ruelas. He had never been knocked out and had been knocked down only once. He had two daughters and a common-law wife. His friends said he had a photographic memory. He read Gabriel Garcia Marquez. He read Edgar Allan Poe. He had plans to go to college after he won a world championship. All that seemed long ago. He had lost 30 pounds to make the 130-pound weight limit to fight Ruelas. He had been hammered for all eleven rounds.

10 *"Mueve la mano,"* Manuel Garcia said.

11 The room was quiet. There was a moment when the father put a finger inside the son's left hand and the son seemed to squeeze lightly. There were moments when nothing happened. Nothing ever seemed to happen on the right side. The father walked around the bed, touching parts of the son's body, naming them in Spanish.

12 *"Los ojos."* The eyes.

13 *"La boca."* The mouth.

14 *"Los pies."* The feet.

15 Any movement seemed to be a historic victory. No movement was a terrible defeat. At the end of his circuit the father held one of his son's feet and rubbed it softly, repeating three times the words *"Eres bravo."* You are brave. By the middle of last week the son's condition had worsened. There was no movement. The mother had arrived from Colombia. The doctors feared that his death was imminent.

16 His condition brought easy calls for the abolition of boxing. It is a familiar debate, which will ultimately go nowhere. Boxing will stay. Boxing will be the same. Instead of engaging in that debate, everyone connected with the sport should have to go inside a room like this. Everyone should see. The boxers should see, and the fans who watch on pay-per-view should see, and the promoters should see, and the sportswriters and the broadcasters and the headline writers and the cool, blithe heads everywhere should see.

17 No one is invincible. The princes of sport can be as vulnerable as anyone else who shares the human condition. The price of this cruel game can be very, very high. The people who are involved, in even the slightest way, should know.

18 Jimmy Garcia died last Friday.

## WRITING PROMPTS

1. Montville uses this sad narrative to state an opinion about boxing. What is Montville's belief?

2. What does the author tell readers about Jimmy Garcia, both before and after the accident? Why is it necessary to show this contrast?

3. Is the author optimistic that this incident will change the sport of boxing? Why or why not?

4. Do you know of any young athletes who have died or been permanently harmed from injuries received while participating in their chosen sport? Could anything have been done to prevent those injuries?

5. Can you think of any sports in which personal injury is common? What suggestions can you make for changes in safety standards?

# DESCRIPTION

Just as narrative writing follows a time order, *description* follows a spatial order; its details are arranged in space. With this type of writing, the focus is on sensory images, how something looks, sounds, smells, feels, or tastes. The aim of its writer is to create a dominant impression from these sensory images. Also typical of description is concrete language, so an author can make a subject crystal clear. Description can be of people, places, or things. The important elements of descriptive paragraphs include (1) an abundance of specific concrete and sensory details, and (2) the use of figurative language (metaphors and similes).

In the following selection, you will read a description of both a location and a character. Notice how H. G. Wells places his character, chubby Miss Polly, into a setting, the Potwell Inn. Wells bombards his reader with sensory images, and he demonstrates two other characteristics of good writing in the process. First, his description shows a logical arrangement of details in space as he moves us toward the Inn and then inside. Once inside, he focuses on an extremely relaxed woman. Second, his final three words in the second paragraph are an effective conclusion to show the ultimate in relaxation and to complement the topic sentence in his first paragraph. The inclusion of a very short sentence after long ones is also a good means of grabbing a reader's attention—or to signal a conclusion to the work.

## THE POTWELL INN

### H. G. Wells

1    The nearer he came to the place the more he liked it. The windows on the ground floor were long and low and they had pleasing red blinds. The green tables outside were agreeably ringed with memories of former drinks, and an extensive grape vine spread level branches across the whole front of the place. Against the wall was a broken oar, two boat-hooks and the stained and faded red cushions of a pleasure boat. One went up three steps to the glass-panelled door and peeped into a broad, low room with a bar and beer engine, behind which were many bright and helpful looking bottles against mirrors, and great

and little pewter measures, and bottles fastened in brass wire upside down with their corks replaced by taps, and a white china cask labelled "Shrub," and cigar boxes and boxes of cigarettes, and a couple of Toby jugs and a beautifully coloured hunting scene framed and glazed, showing the most elegant and beautiful people taking Piter's Cherry Brandy, and cards such as the law required about the dilution of spirits and the illegality of bringing children into bars, and satirical verses about swearing and asking for credit, and three very bright red-cheeked wax apples and a round-shaped clock.

2    But these were the mere background to the really pleasant thing in the spectacle, which was quite the plumpest woman Mr. Polly had ever seen seated in an armchair in the midst of all these bottles and glasses and glittering things, peacefully and tranquilly, and without the slightest loss of dignity, asleep. Many people would have called her a fat woman, but Mr. Polly's innate sense of epithet told him from the outset that plump was the word. She had shapely brows and a straight, well-shaped nose, kind lines and contentment about her mouth and beneath it the jolly chins clustered like chubby little cherubim about the feet of an Assumptioning-Madonna. Her plumpness was firm and pink and wholesome, and her hands, dimpled at every joint, were clasped in front of her; she seemed as it were to embrace herself with infinite confidence and kindliness as one who knew herself good in substance, good in essence, and would show her gratitude to God by that ready acceptance of all that he had given her. Her head was a little on one side, not much, but just enough to speak of trustfulness, and rob her of the stiff effect of self-reliance. And she slept.

For essays that describe a person or place, read Toshio Mori's "The Woman Who Makes Swell Doughnuts," Nelson George's "Rare Jordan," and William Least Heat Moon's "Arizona 87." As you read these essays, notice the sensory images and dominant impressions they establish.

## THE WOMAN WHO MAKES SWELL DOUGHNUTS
### Toshio Mori

1    There is nothing I like to do better than to go to her house and knock on the door and when she opens the door, to go in. It is one of the experiences I will long remember—perhaps the only immortality that I will ever be lucky to meet in my short life—and when I say experience I do not mean the actual movement, the motor of our lives. I mean by experience the dancing of emotions before our eyes and inside of us, the dance that is still but is the roar and the force capable of stirring the earth and the people.

2    Of course, she, the woman I visit, is old and of her youthful beauty there is little left. Her face of today is coarse with hard water and there is no question that she has lived her life: given birth to six children, worked side by side with her man for forty years, working in the fields, working in the house, caring for the grandchildren, facing the summers and winters and also the springs and autumns, running the household that is completely her little world. And when I came on the scene, when I discovered her in her little house on Seventh Street, all of her life was behind, all of her task in this world was tabbed, looked into, thoroughly attended, and all that is before her in life and the world, all that could be before her now was to sit and be served; duty done, work done, time clock punched; old-age pension or old-age security; easy chair; soft serene hours till death take her. But this was not of her, not the least bit of her.

3    When I visit her she takes me to the coziest chair in the living room, where are her magazines and books in Japanese and English. "Sit down," she says, "Make yourself comfortable. I will come back with some hot doughnuts just out of oil."

4    And before I can turn a page of a magazine she is back with a plateful of hot doughnuts. There is nothing I can do to describe her doughnut; it is in a class by itself, without words, without demonstration. It is a doughnut, just a plain doughnut just out of oil but it is different, unique. Perhaps when I am eating her doughnuts I am really eating her; I have this foolish notion in my head many times and whenever I catch myself doing so I say, that is not so, that is not true. Her doughnuts really taste swell, she is the best cook I have ever known, Oriental dishes or American dishes.

5    I bow humbly that such a room, such a house exists in my neighborhood so I may dash in and out when my spirit wanes, when hell is loose. I sing gratefully that such a simple and common experience becomes an event, an event

of necessity and growth. It is an event that is part of me, an addition to the elements of the earth, water, fire, and air, and I seek the day when it will become a part of everyone.

6   All her friends, old and young, call her Mama. Everybody calls her Mama. That is not new, it is logical. I suppose there is in every block of every city in America a woman who can be called Mama by her friends and the strangers meeting her. This is commonplace, it is not new and the old sentimentality may be the undoing of the moniker. But what of a woman who isn't a mama but is, and instead of priding in the expansion of her little world, takes her little circle, living out her days in the little circle, perhaps never to be exploited in a biography or on everybody's tongue, but enclosed, shut, excluded from world news and newsreels; just sitting, just moving, just alive, planting the plants in the fields, caring for the children and the grandchildren and baking the tastiest doughnuts this side of the next world.

7   When I sit with her I do not need to ask deep questions, I do not need to know Plato or The Sacred Books of the East or dancing. I do not need to be on guard. But I am on guard and foot-loose because the room is alive.

8   "Where are the grandchildren?" I say. "Where are Mickey, Tadao, and Yaeko?"

9   "They are out in the yard," she says. "I say to them, play, play hard, go out there and play hard. You will be glad later for everything you have done with all your might."

10   Sometimes we sit many minutes in silence. Silence does not bother her. She says silence is the most beautiful symphony, she says the air breathed in silence is sweeter and sadder. That is about all we talk of. Sometimes I sit and gaze out the window and watch the Southern Pacific trains rumble by and the vehicles whizz with speed. And sometimes she catches me doing this and she nods her head and I know she understands that I think the silence in the room is great, and also the roar and the dust of the outside is great, and when she is nodding I understand that she is saying that this, her little room, her little circle, is a depot, a pause, for the weary traveler, but outside, outside of her little world there is dissonance, hugeness of another kind, and the travel to do. So she has her little house, she bakes the grandest doughnuts, and inside of her she houses a little depot.

11   Most stories would end with her death, would wait till she is peacefully dead and peacefully at rest but I cannot wait that long. I think she will grow, and her hot doughnuts just out of the oil will grow with softness and touch. And I think it would be a shame to talk of her doughnuts after she is dead, after she is formless.

12   Instead I take today to talk of her and her wonderful doughnuts when the earth is something to her, when the people from all parts of the earth may drop in and taste the flavor, her flavor, which is everyone's and all flavor; talk to her, sit with her, and also taste the silence of her room and the silence that is herself; and finally go away to hope and keep alive what is alive in her, on earth and in men, expressly myself.

## WRITING PROMPTS

1. Why does Mori feel compelled to visit the old woman who lives in the little house on Seventh Street and makes doughnuts?

2. How does he contrast the woman's early life with her life now?

3. What feelings does the author claim he experiences when he visits this woman?

4. Do you agree with Mori that we all need a place where we can go to rest and to relieve stress?

5. What active elderly people do you admire? Why do you admire them?

---

# RARE JORDAN

### Nelson George

1    A few seasons ago, in the now-defunct Chicago Stadium, Michael Jordan was being guarded by the eager but over-matched John Starks. I sat fifteen rows behind them, wearing my Knicks cap amid a sea of Bulls red and black. I'd flown in the day before and scalped tickets, determined to see Starks and the rest of my beloved New York team finally dethrone the Bulls.

2    What a joke.

3    Sometime during the second half, Jordan rises, the No. 23 on his chest suspended in air as Starks elevates. The Knick, who earlier in the series jammed in Jordan's face, has hopes, but no one is Jordan. Starks begins his journey back to earth, but Jordan continues to hang, defying gravity. He releases the ball and, like a bird of prey, the potential three-pointer soars toward the hoop. The shot is good. The crowd explodes. I cringe and of course the Knicks lose. Of the fifty-four points Jordan scores that night, it is this single shot that lingers in my mind.

4    This is my Jordan moment. You probably have your own. Built one by one, they have lifted him to the enviable, extraordinary and undoubtedly taxing position of African-American hero—with equal emphasis placed on the African and the American. His achievement comes in an era when unqualified Black male heroism is rare and thus particularly precious. While White-chosen heroes (Christopher Darden, Clarence Thomas), flawed icons (Tupac Shakur, Mike Tyson) and polarizing forces (Marion Barry, Louis Farrakhan) proliferate, Jordan has universal respect from women and men, Blacks and Whites and children of all ages.

5    That's not to say the ride has always been smooth. There have been failures, eccentric choices and profound tragedies in his otherwise charmed life. These trials, along with the triumphs, have shaped him into something of a living, breathing Rorschach test. When this country looks at Jordan, it sees its dreams, obsessions—even its fears.

6    After all, there are many Michael Jordans. There is Jordan the star. Jordan the athlete. Jordan the family man. Jordan the sex symbol. Jordan the Commodity. Jordan the role model. And Jordan the personification of Black masculinity. By that I mean that Michael embodies some of the deepest fantasies Black men have of themselves. Like those of Jack Johnson, Joe Louis, "Sugar" Ray Robinson, Jackie Robinson, Willie Mays, Muhammad Ali, Julius Erving and a handful of others, Michael Jordan's movements, boldness and skill allow African-American men to see the best of themselves projected in the symbolic war of sports.

7    In every culture the warrior plays the role of elemental icon of a community's spirit. In America our history of enslavement sometimes makes us nervous about how much emotion we should invest in these athletes. Are they not just well-paid studs? Do they not entertain at the whim of wealthy White men? No doubt both observations have some merit.

8    But to negate the individual will of these men, to ignore the power and glory of their prowess, is to deny ourselves access to the purity and strength they display. There is a thrill, a kinetic quality of life that a Louis, a Mays, a Jordan taps into that we need. Now African-Americans need other things too. (An emphasis on literacy would be a great start.) Yet Michael's brand of Black masculinity—explosive, graceful, yet grounded in work and morality—is quite simply beautiful and essential.

9    Jordan, of course, consistently transcends his role as mere player. Through a series of megabuck endorsement deals, he hovers above the game as a commercial staple, a Black face with the mass appeal to sell goods (and himself), rivaled only by prime time's favorite sepia pitchman, Bill Cosby. Plying the media with his cool southern charm, while playing the game spectacularly, Jordan defies the stereotypes of the street-hardened, inner-city athlete. He grew up in the Sunbelt state of North Carolina in a solid nuclear family.

10    Religious, well-spoken and with none of the wariness of Whites that hampers many African-American men, Michael Jordan represents the flip side of the crack dealers who populate the local news broadcasts of big cities. With the exception of Julius Erving, no previous African-American basketball hero has had the same balance of tremendous talent, public poise and personal charisma. But it's the late tennis great Arthur Ashe whom because of his southern background, charm and crossover appeal, Jordan calls to mind. While Ashe was the real-life Sidney Poitier amid the country-club set, Jordan, with his clean-cut, starched shirt on Sunday morning, epitomizes Black masculinity—without the rough edges of so many Generation X players.

11    More than any other contemporary African-American athlete, he thrives in the pressure cooker of corporate commitments—appearances at charitable events, golf tournaments and commercial shoots—while never making any embarrassing "I'm not Black, I'm universal" comments and without selling his soul. He works in the system while retaining his Black identity, and he has arrived without a nose job or a White wife.

12    Just as he succeeded Erving on the court, Jordan followed the elegant Dr. J as the preeminent Black athletic sex symbol. And Jordan's smooth, chocolate handsomeness has made it easier for brothers to get dates when the Bulls come to town. His wagging tongue, baggy (now standard issue) shorts and 800-watt smile reflect a stylish, idiosyncratic and confident man. By coolly accepting his baldness, he made his glistening Black dome the defining African-American hairstyle of the era, chasing out the seemingly entrenched high-top fad. At the same time Jordan's public-speaking style grew increasingly polished, a welcome alternative to the you-know what-I'm-sayin' syndrome that too many other brothers display.

13    When I ask women what they like about Jordan, the answer is often, "He married the mother of his children," which they felt spoke to his morality and class. Unlike many other Black sports superstars of this era, Michael never let himself be perceived as a dog. He married Juanita Vanoy in September 1989, within a year of the birth of their first child, Jeffrey Michael. Two more children, Marcus and Jasmine, followed. Though Jordan wisely guards his home life with his wife and children, it's clear that his professional accomplishments are made possible by the solid foundation he and Juanita have created at home.

14    The credit for Jordan's character goes back to the steadying influence of his parents. During his childhood, they set the kind of hardworking example so many Black men lack. His late father, James, a smallish, relaxed southern man,

worked his way up from forklift operator to a supervisor at Wilmington's General Electric plant. His mother, Deloris, who recently authored a book on child rearing and was the stern disciplinarian, worked as a clerical supervisor at United Carolina Bank. On occasions when Michael had misbehaved, she wasn't averse to taking him along to sit beside her and do his homework.

15    But Jordan's loving childhood and his astute decision making haven't immunized him against the violence that rocks our community. Which brings me to my next Jordan moment, one that is sure to linger in my mind long after he retires. In fact, for anyone who saw it, it helped redefine the man. The moment came right after the Bulls knocked out the Seattle Supersonics in game six last June, when Jordan snatched the game ball and fell to the floor, clutching it as teammates and fans began celebrating around him.

16    Then, seeking privacy, he sprinted to the locker room, where despite all the frivolity, he sought a moment of solitude. Of course he didn't get it. Cameras, a constant in his life, dogged his steps, and with them came the eyes of the whole world. We watched as he lay on the floor, crying for the man who could not be there. It was Father's Day, and the basketball great grieved anew for his father, who had been murdered three years before.

17    Unlike so many contemporary public figures, Michael never used his tragedy to gain sympathy for himself. No cheap sentimentality. No playing the victim. No sobbing on Oprah. He has handled the entire matter with a dignity as heroic as any jump shot. And yet, in a moment of profound public triumph, he gave in to private pain. The journey Jordan has taken in recent years—retirement, baseball career, the difficult comeback—arguably had as its catalyst his father's death. So it was only fitting that James Jordan's presence loomed large in that championship locker room.

18    Over time, the lesson of Michael's career may be to illustrate how even the great can be humbled. Steeled by fire, he returned to basketball with heightened appreciation for the game and his role within it. Moreover he has made peace with aging. These days, his atmospheric forays to the hoop are far less frequent. Instead he attacks with a pump fake, turning a defender's legs into jelly and then burying a jump shot. No more a sprinter, he, like a canny distance runner, paces himself until the crucial third and fourth quarters.

19    Ultimately, history will not judge Jordan's greatness by his vicious slam dunks or clever ad campaigns. Rather it will judge him as a father and a son, and as a man, a Black man—one of the best we've ever had.

## WRITING PROMPTS

1. For what reasons does George claim Michael Jordan should be admired?

2. Why does the author say Jordan has universal appeal?

3. Why does George believe this star athlete "epitomizes Black masculinity"?

4. What examples does George include of Jordan's humility despite all the stardom?

5. Do you agree that Jordan is a person who will go down in history as a great person? Why or why not?

6. Can you think of any other outstanding professional athletes who also have universal appeal and are of exemplary character?

---

## ARIZONA 87

### William Least Heat Moon

1   I don't suppose that saguaros mean to give comic relief to the otherwise solemn face of the desert, but they do. Standing on the friable slopes they are quite persnickety about, saguaros mimic men as they salute, bow, dance, raise arms to wave, and grin with faces carved in by woodpeckers. Older plants, having survived odds against their reaching maturity of sixty million to one, have every right to smile.

2   The saguaro is ninety percent water, and a big, two-hundred-year-old cactus may hold a ton of it—a two-year supply. With this weight a plant that begins to lean is soon on the ground: one theory now says that the arms, which begin sprouting only after forty or fifty years when the cactus has some height, are counterweights to keep the plant erect.

3   The Monday I drove northeast out of Phoenix, saguaros were in bloom—comparatively small, greenish-white blossoms perched on top of the trunks like undersized Easter bonnets; at night, long-nosed bats came to pollinate them. But by day, cactus wrens, birds of daring aerial skill, put on the show as they made kamikaze dives between toothpick-size thorns into nest cavities, where they were safe from everything except the incredible ascents over the spines by black racers in search of eggs the snakes would swallow whole.

4   It was hot. The only shade along Arizona 87 lay under the bottomsides of rocks; the desert gives space then closes it up with heat. To the east, in profile, rose the Superstition Mountains, an evil place, Pima and Maricopa Indians say, which brings on diabolic possession to those who enter. Somewhere among the granite and greasewood was the Lost Dutchman gold mine, important not for whatever cache it might hide as for providing a white dream.

5   North of the Sycamore River, saguaro, ocotillo, paloverde, and cholla surrendered the hills to pads of prickly pear the size of a man's head. The road climbed and the temperature dropped. At Payson, a mile high on the northern slope of the Mazatzal Mountain, I had to pull on a jacket.

6   Settlers once ran into Payson for protection from marauding Apaches; after the Apache let things calm down, citizens tried to liven them up again by holding rodeos in the main street. Now, streets paved, Payson lay quiet but for the whine of sawmills releasing the sweet scent of cut timber.

7   I stopped at an old log hotel to quench a desert thirst. A sign on the door: NO LIVE ANIMALS ALLOWED. I guess you could bring in all the dead ones you wanted. A

woman shouted, "Ain't servin' now." Her unmoving eyes, heavy as if cast from lead, watched suspiciously for a live badger under my jacket or a weasel up my pantleg.

8    "This is a fine old hotel," I said. She ignored me. "Do you mind if I look at your big map?" She shrugged and moved away, safe from any live animal attack. I was hunting a place to go next. Someone had marked the Hopi Reservation to the north in red. Why not? As I left, I asked where I could water my lizard. She ignored that too.

9    Highway 260, winding through the pine forests of central Arizona, let the mountains be boss as it followed whatever avenues they left open, crossing ridges only when necessary, slipping unobtrusively on narrow spans over streams of rounded boulders. But when 260 reached the massive escarpment called the Mogollon Rim, it had to challenge geography and climb the face.

10   I shifted to low, and Ghost Dancing pulled hard. A man with a dusty, leathery face creased like an old boot strained on a bicycle—the old style with fat tires. I called a hello, he said nothing. At the summit, I waited to see whether he would make the ascent. Far below lay two cars, crumpled wads. Through the clear air I could count nine ranges of mountains, each successively grayer in a way reminiscent of old Chinese woodblock prints. The Mogollon was a spectacular place; the more so because I had not been anesthetized to it by endless Kodachromes. When the cyclist passed, I called out, "Bravo!" but he acknowledged nothing. I would have liked to talk to a man who, while his contemporaries were consolidating their little empires, rides up the Mogollon Rim on a child's toy. Surely he knew something about desperate men.

11   The top of the great scarp, elevation sixty-five hundred feet, lay flat and covered with big ponderosas standing between dirty snowdrifts and black pools of snowmelt. I began anticipating Heber, the next town. One of the best moments of any day on the road was, toward sunset, looking forward to the last stop. At Heber I hoped for an old hotel with a little bar off to the side where they would serve A-1 on draft under a stuffed moosehead; or maybe I'd find a grill dishing up steak and eggs on blue-rimmed platters. I hoped for people who had good stories, people who sometimes took you home to see their collection of carved peach pits.

12   That was the hope. But Heber was box houses and a dingy sawmill, a couple of motels and filling stations, a glass-and-Formica cafe. Heber had no center, no focus for the eye and soul: neither a courthouse, nor high church steeple, nor hotel. Nothing has done more to take a sense of civic identity, a feeling of community, from small-town America than the loss of old hotels to the motel business. The hotel was once where things coalesced, where you could meet both townspeople and travelers. Not so in a motel. No matter how you build it, the motel remains a haunt of the quick and dirty, where the only locals are Chamber of Commerce boys every fourth Thursday. Who ever heard the returning traveler exclaim over one of the great motels of the world he stayed in? Motels can be big, but never grand.

## WRITING PROMPTS

1. What is the dominant impression that Heat Moon gives of the Arizona desert?

2. What visual images does he include as he describes his trip through the desert?

3. Although this essay, which is a chapter from his book *Blue Highways*, is primarily one of description, Heat Moon offers several contrasts. What are some of these contrasts?

4. Have you ever traveled through a desert? If so, do you think the author's description is accurate? Add any differences that you remember from your desert trip.

5. If you were Heat Moon and traveling across America, would you have needed human companionship as he seemed to need? Would you have tried harder than he did to converse with the man on the bicycle and the woman in the hotel? Why or why not?

---

# EXERCISE

Read the following essay, "The Subway Station" by Gilbert Highet. As you read, underline all the examples of sensory images (those "pictures" that appeal to your six senses). When you have finished, write a paragraph in which you describe either a place or a person using as much sensory description as you can. Present that place or person so vividly that your audience members can picture it in their minds. Remember that you want to present a dominant impression of what you are describing. Your audience is a person who has been blind from birth.

## THE SUBWAY STATION
### Gilbert Highet

1      Standing in a subway station, I began to appreciate the place—almost to enjoy it. First of all, I looked at the lighting: a row of meager electric bulbs, unscreened, yellow, and coated with filth, stretched toward the black mouth of the tunnel, as though it were a bolt hole in an abandoned coal mine. Then I lingered, with zest, on the walls and ceiling: lavatory tiles which had been white about fifty years ago, and were now encrusted with soot, coated with the remains of a dirty liquid which might be either atmospheric humidity mingled

with smog or the result of a perfunctory attempt to clean them with cold water; and, above them, gloomy vaulting from which dingy paint was peeling off like scabs from an old wound, sick black paint leaving a leprous white undersurface. Beneath my feet, the floor was a nauseating dark brown with black stains upon it which might be stale oil or dry chewing gum or some worse defilement; it looked like the hallway of a condemned slum building. Then my eye traveled to the tracks, where two lines of glittering steel—the only positively clean objects in the whole place—ran out of darkness into darkness above an unspeakable mass of congealed oil, puddles of dubious liquid, and a mishmash of old cigarette packets, mutilated and filthy newspapers, and the debris that filtered down from the street above through a barred grating in the roof. As I looked up toward the sunlight I could see more debris sifting slowly downward, and making an abominable pattern in the slanting beam of dirt-laden sunlight. I was going on to relish more features of this unique scene: such as the advertisement posters on the walls—here a text from the Bible, there a half-naked girl, here a woman wearing a hat consisting of a hen sitting on a nest full of eggs, and there a pair of girl's legs walking up the keys of a cash register—all scribbled over with unknown names and well-known obscenities in black crayon and red lipstick; but then my train came in at last, I boarded it, and began to read. The experience was over for the time.

---

# EXEMPLIFICATION

The pattern of *exemplification*, generalization followed by one or more illustrations, appears almost everywhere in prose. Your textbooks are filled with paragraphs of examples, and for essays of thesis and support (those which you will most commonly write in college) using examples is probably the easiest way to prove your point. See how Hal Espen, in his paragraph "The Woodstock Wars," supports his topic sentence with examples:

### The Woodstock Wars

In most respects, after all, Woodstock was a disaster. To begin with, it rained and rained for weeks before the festival, and then, of course, it rained during the festival. The promoters lost weeks of preparation time when the site had to be switched twice. They rented Yasgur's field less than a month before the concert. The stage wasn't finished, and the sound system was stitched together perilously close to the start of the show. As soon as the festival opened, the water- and food-delivery arrangements broke down, the gates and fences disintegrated, and tens of thousands of new bodies kept pouring in. (One powerful lure was the rumor that the revered Bob Dylan was going to perform; he wasn't.) In response to an emergency appeal for volunteers, fifty doctors were flown in. The Air Force brought in food on Huey helicopters, and the Women's Community Center in Monticello sent thirty thousand sandwiches. One kid was killed as he was run over by a tractor, one died of appendicitis, and another died of a drug overdose.

Hal Espen, "The Woodstock Wars"

For additional pieces of writing demonstrating exemplification, read "What the Nose Knows" by James Gorman, Ellen Goodman's "In the New Wave of Chick Flicks, a New Kind of Man," and "Custom Made" by Tara Parker-Pope.

## WHAT THE NOSE KNOWS

### James Gorman

1    Society is losing its odor integrity. Some enterprising souls are actually marketing aerosol cans filled with the aromas of pizza, new cars, anything that might entice people to buy something they would otherwise not. From the inexhaustible engine of commerce have come Aroma Discs, which when warmed in a special container (only $22.50) emit such scents as Passion, Fireplace and After Dinner Mints. And, in what may be the odor crime of the century, a company in Ohio is selling a cherry-scented garden hose.

2    I may seem like a weird curmudgeon looking for something new to complain about, but it's only the fake smells I don't like, the ones that are meant to fool you. This is a dangerous business because the human nose is emotional and not very bright. Inside the brain, smell seems snuggled right up to the centers for cooking, sex and memory.

3    I recently discovered a substance whose odor stimulates my memory of childhood like nothing else: Crayola crayons.

4    I don't expect you to experience the effect of this odor memory just by thinking about crayons, since most people can't recall smells the way they can recall pictures or sounds. But once you get a good whiff of waxy crayon odor, the bells of childhood will ring. Go out and buy a box. Get your nose right down on the crayons and inhale deeply. Pull that crayon smell right up into the old reptile brain. You'll be flooded with a new-crayon, untouched-coloring-book feeling—you're young, the world is new, the next thing you know your parents may bring home a puppy.

5    The smell is part of our culture, in the same class as the Howdy Doody song. Long after my daughters have stopped drawing with crayons, they will have in their brains, as I do now, the subconscious knowledge that if you smell stearic acid—the major component in the smell of Crayola crayons—you're about to have a good time.

6    Crayons have odor integrity. The Crayola people didn't stick stearic acid into their product to make you buy it. Nobody in his right mind would buy something because it smelled like a fatty acid. If there were a national odor museum, I would give crayons pride of place in it. And I would surround them with other objects emitting the honest aromas that make up American odor culture.

7    I have a few ideas of what these other objects should be. I got them from William Cain of Yale University and the John B. Pierce Foundation Laboratory in New Haven, Conn. Cain studies what he calls the smell game. He had people sniff 80 everyday things, and then he ranked the substances by how recognizable their odors were. His list is the place for the aroma preservationist to begin.

8    On it are Juicy Fruit gum and Vicks VapoRub (remember getting it rubbed on your chest?), Ivory soap, Johnson's baby powder and Lysol. Cain also tested Band-Aids, nail-polish remover, shoe polish (which reminds me of church) and bleach.

9    Crayons are on the list, ranked eighteenth in recognizability. Coffee was first, peanut butter second. Not on the list, but favorites of mine, are rubber cement (which I remember from my newspaper days) and Cutter insect Repellent.

10    I know there will be judgment calls. Some people will want to preserve Brut after shave and Herbal Essence shampoo, numbers 35 and 53 on Cain's list, while I will not. Others won't want fresh cow manure in the museum. I think it's a must.

11    Whatever the choices, it's time to start paying attention to our odor culture. We're responsible for what posterity will smell, and like to smell. If we're not careful, we may end up with a country in which everyone thinks garden hoses are supposed to smell like cherries.

## Writing Prompts

1. Why is Gorman concerned that "society is losing its odor integrity"?

2. What are some of the smells that reflect American culture that Gorman would place in an odor museum?

3. What are some of his examples of odors being added to products to encourage purchases of these products?

4. In addition to Crayola crayons, can you remember any smells from the past that cause you to remember specific incidents?

5. Do you think manufacturers are being dishonest by adding pleasant smells to products so customers will be more apt to buy, or do you think these manufacturers lack "odor integrity"?

---

## IN THE NEW WAVE OF CHICK FLICKS, A NEW KIND OF MAN
### Ellen Goodman

1    I have spent this spring watching smart women make smart choices, or at least avoid foolish ones. Not just in life, but in love. Not just in the real world, but in the reel world.

2    I have, you see, been to the chick flicks. This is the rather dismissive term generally used by Hollywood producers and 14-year-old boys to describe movies in which more tears than blood are shed.

3    Only in these flicks the heroines are most decidedly not chicks.

4    The female leads who have been drawing me and my gender into the cineplex are an independent lot. These are not women who follow "The Rules" but make them.

5    Yet far from being disqualified from true love on account of her uppity-ness—an Old Hollywood staple—these women are managing a romantic runoff. They seem to be parading male contenders across the screen for the current cultural title of Mr. Right.

6    Let us begin with Kate Winslet—Who else?—on her "Titanic" voyage to American marital prison. She's rebellious in a circa-1912 sort of way, in everything from her taste in art to men.

7    Next is Jennifer Aniston, the social worker in "The Object of My Affection" who tells her teenage charges: "Keeping your boyfriend happy is not your full-time job. You call the shots."

8    Finally in this box-office-blitzing trio is Meg Ryan, the cardiovascular surgeon in "City of Angels" who keeps hearts throbbing on and off the operating table.

9    In the old days, heroines were swept off their feet and gone with the wind by heroes like Clark Gable. A true woman was supposed to swoon with gratitude whenever John Wayne uttered another monosyllable.

10    But today they are looking for something and someone else. Say, for example, Leonardo DiCaprio.

11    Now, I realize that American mothers have heard all they can bear of Leo. He has teenage girls everywhere embezzling the baby-sitters club funds to see their ninth drowning. But maybe there's more to this pick than a safe fantasy figure.

12    After all, in this movie, Kate makes a choice between the fiancé who wants to dominate her and the steroidfree artist who enables her liberation. Even the love scenes have a gentle and misty mutuality. When Kate takes off her

clothes, Leo draws her instead of assaulting her. She does the initiating in her own time. Is Leo adored by the young female audience because he is a harbor for their sexual awakening?

13    Of course, in a thoroughly modern Manhattan, Jennifer Aniston has a boyfriend in "Object of My Affection" she refers to as "a bulldozer," and a male roommate who knows how to listen. In this movie, the boyfriend is straight, the roommate is gay, the emotional plot is complicated. But the woman's real search is for a man who can be both friend and lover.

14    And what of Nicholas Cage? I found his angelic puss a touch creepy, but his character fits the man-of-the-year model. Before Cage makes his move, Meg Ryan is contemplating the proposal of another surgeon who says, "I'm not very good at matters of the heart . . . please be my wife." Instead she chooses the angel who gives up heaven in order to get in touch, literally, with his feelings.

15    There you are. The chick-flick pantheon. The box office hits. Women choosing men who can feel, listen, free, and befriend them. Women who don't have to sacrifice their lives, their spirituality, their work for love.

16    These movies don't all have happily-ever-afters, but you get the point. Hollywood is romancing a new generation of women with a new collection of men. The men women want.

17    The only problem with this new male role modeling is that these romance films and figures attract mostly women. It's girls who are the repeat customers at "Titanic" and women who are looking for the object of their affection.

18    I wonder if men and women are getting different male messages. While teenage girls are looking for Leo, are teenage boys emulating Bruce Willis? While women want fallen angels, do men want Mercury Rising? Are girls and boys, women and men, still being offered opposite male role models in and out of Hollywood?

19    The male heroes for young boys are the men who hurl balls, crash cars, and wave Uzis at enemies. The male heroes for young girls are the lads who lift them on the prow of a ship.

20    What happens if boys grow up wanting to be different kinds of men than the men women want? Isn't this where we came in?

21    And while we are on the subject, when do these stop being flicks for only chicks?

## WRITING PROMPTS

1. How does Goodman define chick flicks, and what is her attitude toward those playing currently in theaters?

2. What examples does she include of today's leading men and women in films, and how does she compare them to such actors of the past?

3. How do current audiences view the change in traditional male and female roles in films?

4. What conflict does Goodman see based on the audiences of today's films?

5. Do you think the portrayal of actors and actresses in these new gender roles will have a positive impact on society (i.e., less violence and more nurturing)?

6. In addition to these new film images, what suggestions can you make to help break down stereotypical, old-fashioned gender roles?

---

## CUSTOM MADE

### Tara Parker-Pope

1    Pity the poor Domino's Pizza Inc. delivery man.

2    In Britain, customers don't like the idea of him knocking on their doors—they think it's rude. In Japan, houses aren't numbered sequentially—finding an address means searching among rows of houses numbered willy-nilly. And in Kuwait, pizza is more likely to be delivered to a waiting limousine than to someone's front door.

3    "We honestly believe we have the best pizza delivery system in the world," says Gary McCausland, managing director of Domino's international division. "But delivering pizza isn't the same all over the world."

4    And neither is making cars, selling soap, or packaging toilet paper. International marketers have found that just because a product plays in Peoria, that doesn't mean it will be a hit in Helsinki.

5    To satisfy local tastes, products ranging from Heinz ketchup to Cheetos chips are tweaked, reformulated, and reflavored. Fast-food companies such as McDonald's Corp., popular for the "sameness" they offer all over the world, have discovered that to succeed, they also need to offer some local appeal—like selling beer in Germany and adding British Cadbury chocolate sticks to their ice-cream cones in England.

6    The result is a delicate balancing act for international marketers: How does a company exploit the economies of scale that can be gained by global marketing while at the same time making its products appeal to local tastes?

7    The answer: Be flexible, even when it means changing a tried-and-true recipe, even when consumer preferences, like Haagen-Dazs green tea ice cream, sound awful to the Western palate.

8    "It's a dilemma we all live with every day," says Nick Harding, H. J. Heinz Co.'s managing director for Northern Europe. Heinz varies the recipe of its famous ketchup in different markets, selling a less-sweet version in Belgium and Holland, for instance, because consumers there use ketchup as a pasta sauce (and mayonnaise on french fries). "We're looking for the economies from globalizing our ideas, but we want to maintain the differences necessary for local markets," says Mr. Harding.

9    For those who don't heed such advice, the costs are high. U.S. auto makers, for instance, have done poorly in Japan, at least in part because they failed to adapt. Until recently, most didn't bother even to put steering wheels on the

right, as is the standard in Japan. While some American makers are beginning to conform, European companies such as Volkswagen AG, Daimler-Benz AG, and Bayerische Motoren Werke AG did it much sooner, and have done far better in the Japanese market as a result.

10      For Domino's, the balancing act has meant maintaining the same basic pizza delivery system world-wide—and then teaming up with local franchisers to tailor the system to each country's needs. In Japan, detailed wall maps, three times larger than those used in its stores elsewhere, help delivery people find the proper address despite the odd street numbering system.

11      In Iceland, where much of the population doesn't have phone service, Domino's has teamed with a Reykjavik drive-in movie theater to gain access to consumers. Customers craving a reindeer-sausage pizza (a popular flavor there) flash their turn signal, and a theater employee brings them a cellular phone to order a pizza, which is then delivered to the car.

12      Local Domino's managers have developed new pizza flavors, including *mayo jaga* (mayonnaise and potato) in Tokyo and pickled ginger in India. The company, which now has 1,160 stores in 46 countries, is currently trying to develop a nonbeef pepperoni topping for its stores in India.

13      When Pillsbury Co., a unit of Britain's Grand Metropolitan PLC, wanted to begin marketing its Green Giant brand vegetables outside the United States, it decided to start with canned sweet corn, a basic product unlikely to require any flavor changes across international markets. But to Pillsbury's surprise, the product still was subject to local influences. Instead of being eaten as a hot side dish, the French add it to salad and eat it cold. In Britain, corn is used as a sandwich and pizza topping. In Japan, school children gobble down canned corn as an after-school treat. And in Korea, the sweet corn is sprinkled over ice cream.

14      So Green Giant tailored its advertising to different markets. Spots show corn kernels falling off a cob into salads and pastas, or topping an ice-cream sundae.

15      "Initially we thought it would be used the same as in the United States," says Stephen Moss, vice president, strategy and development, for Green Giant. "But we've found there are very different uses for corn all over the world."

16      And Green Giant has faced some cultural hurdles in its race to foreign markets. Although vegetables are a significant part of the Asian diet, Green Giant discovered that Japanese mothers, in particular, take pride in the time they take to prepare a family meal and saw frozen vegetables as an unwelcome shortcut. "Along with the convenience comes a little bit of guilt," says Mr. Moss.

17      The solution? Convince moms that using frozen vegetables gives them the opportunity to prepare their families' favorite foods more often. To that end, Green Giant focused on a frozen mixture of julienned carrots and burdock root, a traditional favorite root vegetable that requires several hours of tedious preparation.

18      The company also has introduced individual seasoned vegetable servings for school lunch boxes, with such flavors as sesame-seasoned lotus root. Although fresh vegetables still dominate the market, Green Giant says its

strategy is starting to show results, and frozen varieties now account for half the vegetable company's sales in Japan.

19   The drive for localization has been taken to extremes in some cases: Cheetos, the bright orange and cheesy-tasting chip brand of PepsiCo Inc.'s Frito-Lay unit, are cheeseless in China. The reason? Chinese consumers generally don't like cheese, in part because many of them are lactose-intolerant. So Cheetos tested such flavors as Peking duck, fried egg, and even dog to tempt the palates of Chinese.

20   Ultimately, says Tom Kuthy, vice president of marketing for PepsiCo Foods International's Asia-Pacific operations, the company picked a butter flavor, called American cream, and an Asianized barbecue flavor called Japanese steak. Last year, Frito rolled out its third flavor, seafood.

21   In addition to changing the taste, the company also packaged Cheetos 15-gram size priced at one yuan, about 12 cents, so that even kids with little spending money can afford them.

22   The bottom line: These efforts to adapt to the local market have paid off. Mr. Kuthy estimates that close to 300 million packages of Cheetos have been sold since they were introduced two years ago in Guangzhou. Cheetos are now available in Shanghai and Beijing as well.

23   Frito isn't through trying to adapt. Now the company is introducing a 33-gram pack for two yuan. Mr. Kuthy also is considering more flavors, but dog won't be one of them. "Yes, we tested the concept, but it was never made into a product," he says. "Its performance was mediocre."

24   Other PepsiCo units have followed with their own flavor variations. In Thailand, Pizza Hut has a *tom-yan*-flavored pizza based on the spices of the traditional Thai soup. In Singapore, you can get a KFC Zinger chicken burger that is hot and spicy with Asia's ubiquitous chili. The Singaporean pizza at Pizza Hut comes with ground beef, green peppers and chili. Elsewhere in Asia, pizzas come in flavors such as Mongolian, with pork, chili, and garlic; salmon, with a creamy lobster sauce; and Satay, with grilled chicken and beef.

25   Coming up with the right flavor combinations for international consumers isn't easy. Part of the challenge is building relationships with customers in far-flung markets. For years, the founders of Ben & Jerry's Homemade Inc. had relied on friends, co-workers, and their own taste buds to concoct such unusual ice-cream flavors as Chunky Monkey and Cherry Garcia.

26   But introducing their ice cream abroad, by definition, meant losing that close connection with their customers that made them successful. "For Ben and me, since we've grown up in the United States, our customers were people like us, and the flavors we made appealed to us," says co-founder Jerry Greenfield, scooping ice cream at a media event in the Royal Albert Hall in London. "I don't think we have the same seat-of-the-pants feel for places like England. It's a different culture."

27   As a result, one of the company's most popular flavors in the United States, Chocolate Chip Cookie Dough, flopped in Britain. The nostalgia quotient of the ice cream, vanilla-flavored with chunks of raw cookie dough, was simply lost

on the Brits, who historically haven't eaten chocolate-chip cookies. "People didn't grow up in this country sneaking raw cookie-dough batter from Mom," says Mr. Greenfield.

28    The solution? Hold a contest to concoct a quintessential British ice cream. After reviewing hundreds of entries, including Choc Ness Monster and Cream Victoria, the company in July introduced Cool Britannia, a combination of vanilla ice cream, strawberries, and chocolate-covered Scottish shortbread. (The company plans to sell Cool Britannia in the United States eventually.)

29    And in a stab at building a quirky relationship with Brits, the duo opted for a publicity stunt when Britain's beef crisis meant farmers were left with herds of cattle that couldn't be sold at market. Ben & Jerry's creative solution: Use the cows to advertise. The company's logo was draped across the backs of grazing cattle, and the stunt made the front page of major London newspapers.

30    The company has just begun selling ice cream in France but isn't sure whether the company will try contests for a French flavor in that market. One reason: It's unclear whether Ben & Jerry's wry humor, amusing to the Brits, will be understood by the laconic French. "We're going to try to get more in touch, more comfortable with the feel of the French market first," says Mr. Greenfield.

31    But for every success story, there have been a slew of global marketing mistakes. In Japan, consumer-products marketer Procter & Gamble Co. made several stumbles when it first entered the market in the early 1970s.

32    The company thought its thicker, more-absorbent Pampers diapers in big packs like those favored in America would be big sellers in Japan. But Japanese women change their babies twice as often as Americans and prefer thin diapers. Moreover, they often have tiny apartments and no room to store huge diaper packs.

33    The company adapted by making thinner diapers packaged in smaller bags. Because the company shifted gears quickly, Procter & Gamble is now one of the largest and most successful consumer-goods companies in Japan, with more than $1 billion in annual sales and market leadership in several categories.

## WRITING PROMPTS

1. What does Parker-Pope say is important to consider in international marketing?

2. What kinds of support does she include?

3. Parker-Pope claims "the costs are high" for businesspeople who do not consider local preferences when opening American businesses abroad. What examples does she include to demonstrate both good and poor decision making regarding local tastes?

4. If you have traveled out of the United States, what American products did you see and use? Were they marketed the same in that country (those countries) as they are here?

5. Do you prefer exactly the same menu in all fast food locations, or do you think each restaurant should reflect local tastes and traditions?

## EXERCISE

What is your favorite kind of food? Your favorite kind of music? Your favorite kind of movie? Take one of these topics and write a topic sentence followed by a paragraph giving examples. You are writing this paragraph for your roommate.

# CHAPTER 10

# Process, Comparison/Contrast, and Classification/Division

## PROCESS

Similar to narrative writing, *process* writing carries the same signal words and follows chronological order. Here you are telling your audience how to do something or how something was completed. It is the one kind of college prose that allows the use of the second person ("you"). Recipes and directions are two examples of process writing. Carin C. Quinn's "The Jeaning of America—and the World" provides a wonderful example of process.

### THE JEANING OF AMERICA—AND THE WORLD
#### Carin C. Quinn

1    This is the story of a sturdy American symbol which has now spread throughout most of the world. The symbol is not the dollar. It is not even Coca-Cola. It is a simple pair of pants called blue jeans, and what the pants symbolize is what Alexis de Tocqueville called "a manly and legitimate passion for equality. . . ." Blue jeans are favored equally by bureaucrats and cowboys; bankers and deadbeats; fashion designers and beer drinkers. They draw no distinctions and recognize no classes; they are merely American. Yet they are sought after almost everywhere in the world—including Russia, where authorities recently broke up a teenaged gang that was selling them on the black market for two hundred dollars a pair. They have been around for a long time, and it seems likely that they will outlive even the necktie.

2    This ubiquitous American symbol was the invention of a Bavarian-born Jew. His name was Levi Strauss.

3    He was born in Bad Ocheim, Germany, in 1829, and during the European political turmoil of 1848 decided to take his chances in New York, to which his two brothers already had emigrated. Upon arrival, Levi soon found that his two brothers had exaggerated their tales of an easy life in the land of the main

chance. They were landowners, they had told him; instead, he found them pushing needles, thread, pots, pans, ribbons, yarn, scissors, and buttons to housewives. For two years he was a lowly peddler, hauling some 180 pounds of sundries door-to-door to eke out a marginal living. When a married sister in San Francisco offered to pay his way West in 1850, he jumped at the opportunity, taking with him bolts of canvas he hoped to sell for tenting.

4     It was the wrong kind of canvas for that purpose, but while talking with a miner down from the mother lode, he learned that pants—sturdy pants that would stand up to the rigors of the diggings—were almost impossible to find. Opportunity beckoned. On the spot, Strauss measured the man's girth and inseam with a piece of string and, for six dollars in gold dust, had [the canvas] tailored into a pair of stiff but rugged pants. The miner was delighted with the result, word got around about "those pants of Levi's," and Strauss was in business. The company has been in business ever since.

5     When Strauss ran out of canvas, he wrote his two brothers to send more. He received instead a rough, brown cotton cloth made in Nimes, France— called serge de Nimes and swiftly shortened to "denim" (the word "jeans" derives from *Gênes,* the French word for Genoa, where a similar cloth was produced). Almost from the first, Strauss had his cloth dyed the distinctive indigo that gave blue jeans their name, but it was not until the 1870s that he added the copper rivets which have long since become a company trademark. The rivets were the idea of a Virginia City, Nevada, tailor, Jacob W. Davis, who added them to pacify a mean-tempered miner called Alkali Ike. Alkali, the

story goes, complained that the pockets of his jeans always tore when he stuffed them with ore samples and demanded that Davis do something about it. As a kind of joke, Davis took the pants to a blacksmith and had the pockets riveted; once again, the idea worked so well that word got around; in 1873 Strauss appropriated and patented the gimmick—and hired Davis as a regional manager.

6     By this time, Strauss had taken both his brothers and two brothers-in-law into the company and was ready for his third San Francisco store. Over the ensuing years the company prospered locally and by the time of his death in 1902, Strauss had become a man of prominence from California. For three decades thereafter the business remained profitable though small, with sales largely confined to the working people of the West—cowboys, lumberjacks, railroad workers, and the like. Levi's jeans were first introduced to the East, apparently, during the dude-ranch craze of the 1930s, when vacationing Easterners returned and spread the word about the wonderful pants with rivets. Another boost came in World War II, when blue jeans were declared an essential commodity and were sold only to people engaged in defense work. From a company with fifteen salespeople, two plants, and almost no business east of the Mississippi in 1946, the organization grew in thirty years to include a sales force of more than twenty-two thousand, with fifty plants and offices in thirty-five countries. Each year, more than 250,000,000 items of Levi's clothing are sold—including more than 83,000,000 pairs of riveted blue jeans. They have become, through marketing, word of mouth, and demonstrable reliability, the common pants of America. They can be purchased pre-washed, pre-faded, and pre-shrunk for the suitably proletarian look. They adapt themselves to any sort of idiosyncratic use; women slit them at the inseams and convert them into long skirts, men chop them off above the knees and turn them into something to be worn while challenging the surf. Decorations and ornamentations abound.

7     The pants have become a tradition, and along the way have acquired a history of their own—so much so that the company has opened a museum in San Francisco. There was, for example, the turn-of-the-century trainman who replaced a faulty coupling with a pair of jeans; the Wyoming man who used his jeans as a tow-rope to haul his car out of a ditch; the Californian who found several pairs in an abandoned mine, wore them, then discovered they were sixty-three years old and still as good as new and turned them over to the Smithsonian as a tribute to their toughness. And then there is the particularly terrifying story of the careless construction worker who dangled fifty-two stories above the street until rescued, his sole support the Levi's belt loop through which his rope was hooked.

## WRITING PROMPTS

1. What does Quinn claim blue jeans symbolize?
2. What steps occurred for Levi Strauss to create his blue jeans empire?

3. What are some of the unique uses for blue jeans that Quinn describes?

4. Do you wear jeans for a symbolic reason or just because they are comfortable?

5. Can you think of any other products that are considered American by other nations? Are they as popular as blue jeans?

## EXERCISE

Here is one of our favorite assignments. Write a paragraph that tells your reader how to make a peanut butter and jelly sandwich. Ask your instructor to bring a loaf of bread, peanut butter and jelly, and a knife to class. Ask him or her to follow your directions! Your audience is your instructor and your classmates.

# COMPARISON/CONTRAST

With the fifth of the nine rhetorical modes, *comparison/contrast*, you focus on the similarities and/or differences between two people, places, or things. Comparison refers to similarities and contrast focuses on differences. The structure of comparison/contrast writing follows either of two forms—*subject by subject*, also called block form, or *point by point*, also referred to as alternating form. With subject by subject, you describe subject A fully and then shift attention to subject B. You explain how A and B are similar or dissimilar by selecting certain points for both. Here is a diagram of the block method:

Subject A

    Point 1

    Point 2

    Point 3

Subject B

    Point 1

    Point 2

    Point 3

With the point-by-point method, you state the points of comparison or contrast first and then fill in each of the two subjects under each point. This diagram demonstrates this alternating format:

Point 1

    Subject A

    Subject B

Point 2

    Subject A

    Subject B

Point 3

    Subject A

    Subject B

To understand these two diagrams in paragraph fashion, read the following two excerpts. The first, which demonstrates the block pattern, is about the different ways men and women converse and is taken from Merrill Markoe's "Men, Women, and Conversation." The second, taken from Arthur Schlesinger, Jr.'s, "What If RFK Had Survived?" presents an alternating form of comparison/contrast between Robert Kennedy and his older brother, John F. Kennedy.

### Men, Women, and Conversation

First, it is important to note that men and women regard conversation quite differently. For women it is a passion, a sport, an activity even more important to life than eating because it doesn't involve weight gain. The first sign of closeness among women is when they find themselves engaging in endless, secretless rounds of conversation with one another. And as soon as a woman begins to relax and feel comfortable in a relationship with a man, she tries to have that type of conversation with him as well. However, the first sign that a man is feeling close to a woman is when he admits that he'd rather she please quiet down so he can hear the TV. A man who feels truly intimate with a woman often reserves for her and her alone the precious gift of one-word answers. Everyone knows that the surest way to spot a successful long-term relationship is to look around a restaurant for the table where no one is talking. Ah . . . now *that's* real love.

Merrill Markoe, "Men, Women, and Conversation"

### What If RFK Had Survived?

Oddly, Robert Kennedy seems to strike more of a nerve today than his older brother does. Though two men could hardly have been closer, the eight-and-a-half year gap between them was in fact generational. JFK's character was fixed by the war. He was reserved, ironic, laconic, self-contained, self-determined, self-sufficient. A self-described "idealist without illusions," he hoped through reason to rally the latent idealism of the American people. Robert Kennedy was postwar, ever in flux, moved by the urgencies and perplexities of history. Where JFK was cool, RFK was hot. JFK was a man of reason; RFK a man of passion. JFK was graceful and urbane; RFK blunt and abrasive. The older brother was objective, the younger subjective. JFK would monitor his own performance as from a distance; RFK, as Tom Wicker said, "lost himself in the event."

Arthur Schlesinger, Jr., "What If RFK Had Survived?"

Can you see the two subjects and their points of comparison emerging? By assigning the letters and numbers to the subjects and points in each, you can recognize the parallel structure that the authors use. Read the student essay "Bob and Warren." Notice the student's use of *signal words*, which both identify the mode and provide smooth transitions for the reader as she goes back and forth between the two in a point-by-point or alternating style. Read also "They Shut My Grandmother's Room Door" by Andrew Lam. In this essay Lam contrasts dying in America and dying in Vietnam. In "The Middle-Class Black's Burden," Leanita McClain considers her difficult position of fitting neither in the black nor white worlds in which she finds herself.

## BOB AND WARREN
### Student Essay

1    Strolling in to work at 8:45 A.M., Bob makes it obvious that work is of little importance in his life. Warren, on the other hand, is at his desk promptly at 7:30 and lives for his work. Bob is frequently leaving early to be somewhere with his family, to pick up the kids, or pack for a weekend away. Warren stays long after closing time, takes work home at night, and often stops by the office on weekends.

2    Upon first impression, Bob seems to be the boss in the group. He is confident with himself, has answers to every question, and frequently hurls insults or barbs at Warren, all in fun, of course. Warren, in reality, is boss over Bob but is green on the job and unsure of himself. He times his "digs" very carefully and uses a dry sense of humor to give subtle messages.

3    Bob is as easy-going and open as Warren is cold and calculating. Bob is funny, witty, and always carefree. Warren is funny only when he's not trying to be; he is perfection in detail to its ultimate—and everything he does has a hidden purpose. Whereas Bob is always good for easing tension, breaking the ice, or calming nerves, Warren is the one who creates the tension, stiffens the quills on my spine, and creates the ulcers in our department.

4    Bob is an extremely intelligent man, highly educated and very knowledgeable. Bob recently received his second master's degree, has seven years of related work experience with this company, and has more common sense than anyone I know. Warren is currently working on his bachelor's degree and has only been with the company three years. He has no related experience to fall back on, and his common sense is definitely lacking. While Bob has spent numerous years learning all aspects of manufacturing, Warren has spent only

a little over a year in the Auditing Department, learning nothing but the technical side of auditing.

5   Bob and Warren are as opposite as night and day in everything from looks to personality to work traits. Where Bob is short, blond, and pleasantly plump, Warren is tall, dark, and lean. Bob walks with a serious limp caused by a knee injury on a previous job. Warren could sustain nothing more serious than a paper cut.

6   These two opposites do have a few things in common, however. Both men are dedicated enough to really put forth the extra effort when a project comes down to the wire. Even though Bob is carefree and easy-going, he can be as work-oriented as Warren when the situation demands it. The other way they are alike is in their absent-mindedness. Bob and Warren both have a bad habit of misplacing pens or memos, or forgetting messages and phone numbers. As proficient and educated and intelligent as these men are, they are only human, and we forgive them their forgetfulness.

## WRITING PROMPTS

1. On what statement does the author of this essay base her comparison and contrast of Bob and Warren?

2. What does she tell us about Bob? About Warren?

3. Which man would you rather work for? Why?

4. Which man would you rather have as a friend? Why?

---

## THEY SHUT MY GRANDMOTHER'S ROOM DOOR
### Andrew Lam

1   When someone dies in the convalescent home where my grandmother lives, the nurses rush to close all the patient's doors. Though as a policy death is not to be seen at the home, she can always tell when it visits. The series of doors being slammed shut remind her of the firecrackers during Tet.

2   The nurses' efforts to shield death are more comical to my grandmother than reassuring. Those old ladies die so often," she quips in Vietnamese, "everyday's like new year."

3   Still, it is lonely to die in such a place. I imagine some wasted old body under a white sheet being carted silently through the empty corridor on its way to the morgue. While in America a person may be born surrounded by loved ones, in old age one is often left to take the last leg of life's journey alone.

4   Perhaps that is why my grandmother talks now mainly of her hometown, Bac-Lieu: its river and green rich rice fields. Having lost everything during the

war, she can now offer me only her distant memories: Life was not disjointed back home; one lived in a gentle rhythm with the land; people died in their homes surrounded by neighbors and relatives. And no one shut your door.

5    So it goes. The once gentle, connected world of the past is but the language of dreams. In this fast-paced society of disjointed lives, we are swept along and have little time left for spiritual comfort. Instead of relying on neighbors and relatives, on the river and land, we deal with the language of materialism: overtime, escrow, stress, down payment, credit cards, tax shelter. Instead of going to the temple to pray for good health we pay life and health insurance religiously.

6    My grandmother's children and grandchildren share a certain pang of guilt. After a stroke which paralyzed her, we could no longer keep her at home. And although we visit her regularly, we are not living up to the filial piety standard expected of us in the old country. My father silently grieves and my mother suffers from headaches. (Does she see herself in such a home in a decade or two?)

7    Once, a long time ago, living in Vietnam we used to stare death in the face. The war in many ways had heightened our sensibilities toward living and dying. I can still hear the wails of widows and grieving mothers. Though the fear of death and dying is a universal one, the Vietnamese did not hide from it. Instead we dwelt in its tragedy. Death pervaded our poems, novels, fairy tales and songs.

8    But if agony and pain are part of Vietnamese culture, pleasure is at the center of America's culture. While Vietnamese holidays are based on death anniversaries, birthdays are celebrated here. American popular culture translates death with something like nauseating humor. People laugh and scream at blood and guts movies. The wealthy freeze their dead relatives in liquid nitrogen. Cemeteries are places of big business, complete with colorful brochures. I hear there are even drive-by funerals where you don't have to get out of your own car to pay your respects to the deceased.

9    That America relies upon the pleasure principle and happy endings in its entertainments does not, however, assist us in evading suffering. The reality of the suffering of old age is apparent in the convalescent home. There is an old man, once an accomplished concert pianist, now rendered helpless by arthritis. Every morning he sits staring at the piano. One feeble woman who outlived her children keeps repeating, "My son will take me home." Then there are those mindless, bedridden bodies kept alive through a series of tubes and pulsating machines.

10    But despair is not newsworthy. Death itself must be embellished or satirized or deep-frozen in order to catch the public's attention.

11    Last week on her 82nd birthday I went to see my grandmother. She smiled her sweet sad smile.

12    "Where will you end up in your old age?" she asked me, her mind as sharp as ever.

13　The memories of monsoon rain and tropical sun and relatives and friends came to mind. Not here, not here, I wanted to tell her. But the soft moaning of a patient next door and the smell of alcohol wafting from the sterile corridor brought me back to reality.

14　"Anywhere is fine," I told her instead, trying to keep up with her courageous spirit. "All I am asking for is that they don't shut my door."

## WRITING PROMPTS

1. What is Lam comparing and contrasting in this essay?
2. Of what significance is the shutting of the door?
3. What examples does Lam use to compare and contrast American and Vietnamese attitudes toward death?
4. Lam uses both point-by-point and block organization in this essay. Give examples of each from the essay.
5. Do you agree or disagree with Lam's evaluation of Americans' attitudes toward death? Why?

---

## THE MIDDLE-CLASS BLACK'S BURDEN

### Leanita McClain

1　I am a member of the black middle class who has had it with being patted on the head by white hands and slapped in the face by black hands for my success.

2　Here's a discovery that too many people still find startling: when given equal opportunities at white-collar pencil pushing, blacks want the same things from life that everyone else wants. These include the proverbial dream house, two cars, an above-average school, and a vacation for the kids at Disneyland. We may, in fact, want these things more than other Americans because most of us have been denied them so long.

3　Meanwhile, a considerable number of the folks we left behind in the "old country," commonly called the ghetto, and the militants we left behind in their antiquated ideology can't berate middle-class blacks enough for "forgetting where we came from" We have forsaken the revolution, we are told, we have sold out. We are Oreos, they say, black on the outside, white within.

4　The truth is, we have not forgotten; we would not dare. We are simply fighting on different fronts and are no less war weary, and possibly more heartbroken, for we know the black and white worlds can meld, that there can be a better world.

5　It is impossible for me to forget where I came from as long as I am prey to the jive hustler who does not hesitate to exploit my childhood friendship. I am reminded, too, when I go back to the old neighborhood in fear—and have my purse snatched—and when I sit down to a business lunch and have an old classmate wait on my table. I recall the girl I played dolls with who now rears five children on welfare, the boy from church who is in prison for murder, the pal found dead of a drug overdose in the alley where we once played tag.

6    My life abounds in incongruities. Fresh from a vacation in Paris, I may, a week later, be on the milk-run Trailways bus in Deep South back-country attending the funeral of an ancient uncle whose world stretched only 50 miles and who never learned to read. Sometimes when I wait at the bus stop with my attaché case, I meet my aunt getting off the bus with other cleaning ladies on their way to do my neighbors' floors.

7    But I am not ashamed. Black progress has surpassed our greatest expectations; we never even saw much hope for it, and the achievement has taken us by surprise.

8    In my heart, however, there is no safe distance from the wretched past of my ancestors or the purposeless present of some of my contemporaries; I fear such a fate can reclaim me. I am not comfortably middle class; I am uncomfortably middle class.

9    I have made it, but where? Racism still dogs my people. There are still communities in which crosses are burned on the lawns of black families who have the money and grit to move in.

10    What a hollow victory we have won when my sister, dressed in her designer everything, is driven to the rear door of the luxury high rise in which she lives because the cab driver, noting only her skin color, assumes she is the maid, or the nanny, or the cook, but certainly not the lady of any house at this address.

11    I have heard the immigrants' bootstrap tales, the simplistic reproach of "why can't you people be like us." I have fulfilled the entry requirements of the American middle class, yet I am left, at times, feeling unwelcome and stereotyped. I have overcome the problems of food, clothing and shelter, but I have not overcome my old nemesis, prejudice. Life is easier, being black is not.

12    I am burdened daily with showing whites that blacks are people. I am, in the old vernacular, a credit to my race. I am my brothers' keeper, and my sisters', though many of them have abandoned me because they think that I have abandoned them.

13    I run a gauntlet between two worlds, and I am cursed and blessed by both. I travel, observe, and take part in both; I can also be used by both. I am a rope in a tug of war. If I am a token in my downtown office, so am I at my cousin's church tea. I assuage white guilt. I disprove black inadequacy and prove to my parents' generation that their patience was indeed a virtue.

14    I have a foot in each world, but I cannot fool myself about either. I can see the transparent deceptions of some whites and the bitter hopelessness of some blacks. I know how tenuous my grip on one way of life is, and how strangling the grip of the other way of life can be.

15    Many whites have lulled themselves into thinking that race relations are just grand because they were the first on their block to discuss crab grass with the new black family. Yet too few blacks and whites in this country send their children to school together, entertain each other, or call each other friend. Blacks and whites dining out together draw stares. Many of my coworkers see no black faces from the time the train pulls out Friday evening until they meet me at the coffee machine Monday morning. I remain a novelty.

16    Some of my "liberal" white acquaintances pat me on the head, hinting that I am a freak, that my success is less a matter of talent than of luck and affirmative action. I may live among them, but it is difficult to live with them. How can they be sincere about respecting me, yet hold my fellows in contempt? And if I am silent when they attempt to sever me from my own, how can I live with myself?

17    Whites won't believe I remain culturally different; blacks won't believe I remain culturally the same.

18    I need only look in a mirror to know my true allegiance, and I am painfully aware that, even with my off-white trappings, I am prejudged by my color.

19    As for the envy of my own people, am I to give up my career, my standard of living, to pacify them and set my conscience at ease? No. I have worked for these amenities and deserve them, though I can never enjoy them without feeling guilty.

20    These comforts do not make me less black, nor oblivious to the woe in which many of my people are drowning. As long as we are denigrated as a group, no one of us has made it. Inasmuch as we all suffer for everyone left behind, we all gain for everyone who conquers the hurdle.

## WRITING PROMPTS

1. What is McClain comparing and contrasting in this essay?

2. What is her relationship to the middle class? Why?

3. What points of comparison does she develop?

4. Describe a situation in which you didn't feel comfortable because you didn't "fit in." What was your solution to the problem?

5. What can white Americans do to make people from other races and ethnic groups feel more comfortable?

## EXERCISE

Write a paragraph in which you compare and contrast high school with college. Use either point-by-point or the block method, and write a topic sentence that controls the points you make. This paragraph will be read to this year's graduating class at your high school.

# CLASSIFICATION/DIVISION

Like comparison/contrast, *classification/division* go together as a single mode even though they do not indicate the same behavior. To *classify* means to start with a pool of three or more related items and then to search for a common category, whereas to *divide* means to begin with a whole and then to break it into its parts. Look at the following paragraphs, each of which illustrates how to write a classification/division paragraph:

### How to Mark a Book

There are three kinds of book owners. The first has all the standard sets and best sellers—unread, untouched. (This deluded individual owns wood-pulp and ink, not books.) The second has a great many books—a few of them read through, most of them dipped into, but all of them as clean and shiny as the day they were bought. (This person would probably like to make books his own, but is restrained by a false respect for their physical appearance.) The third has a few books or many—every one of them dog-eared and dilapidated, shaken and loosened by continual use, marked and scribbled in from front to back. (This man owns books.)

From "How to Mark a Book" by Mortimer Adler

### From Cakewalks to Concert Halls

Ragtime's complex historical legacy was perhaps a major reason for its widespread appeal among both blacks and whites. First and foremost, it was a dance music which grew on both European and African traditions. Second, ragtime was a style grounded in an ongoing, cross-cultural, racial parody: the slaves' parody of their masters, blackface minstrels trope of the slaves' parody, black minstrels trope of the blackface parody, and so on. In addition, ragtime was a rural folk music transposed to an urban and industrial context, where its machine-like rhythms became an expression of the lost innocence of bygone days and ways. And finally, as a novel popular music created by the first generation of African Americans born after slavery, ragtime represented an affirmation of their newly experienced freedoms and an optimistic vision of the future.

From "From Cakewalks to Concert Halls" by Thomas L. Morgan and William Barlow

Judith Viorst's "Friends, Good Friends—and Such Good Friends" and Martin Luther King, Jr.'s "Three Types of Resistance to Oppression" exemplify the technique of classifying and dividing material in a paragraph or essay.

## FRIENDS, GOOD FRIENDS—AND SUCH GOOD FRIENDS
### Judith Viorst

1    Women are friends, I once would have said, when they totally love and support and trust each other, and bare to each other the secrets of their souls, and

run—no questions asked—to help each other and tell harsh truths to each other (no, you can't wear that dress unless you lose ten pounds first) when harsh truths must be told.

2     Women are friends, I once would have said, when they share the same affection for Ingmar Bergman, plus train rides, cats, warm rain, charades, Camus, and hate with equal ardor Newark and brussels sprouts and Lawrence Welk and camping.

3     In other words, I once would have said that a friend is a friend all the way, but now I believe that's a narrow point of view. For the friendships I have and the friendships I see are conducted at many levels of intensity, serve many different functions, meet different needs and range from those as all-the-way as the friendship of the soul sisters mentioned above to that of the most nonchalant and casual playmates.

4     Consider these varieties of friendship:

5     1. Convenience friends. These are the women with whom if our paths weren't crossing all the time, we'd have no particular reason to be friends: a next-door neighbor, a woman in our car pool, the mother of one of our children's closest friends or maybe some mommy with whom we serve juice and cookies each week at the Glenwood Co-op Nursery.

6     Convenience friends are convenient indeed. They'll lend us their cups and silverware for a party. They'll drive our kids to soccer when we're sick. They'll take us to pick up our car when we need a lift to the garage. They'll even take our cats when we go on vacation. As we will for them.

7    But we don't, with convenience friends, ever come too close or tell too much; we maintain our public face and emotional distance. "Which means," says Elaine, "that I'll talk about being overweight but not about being depressed. Which means I'll admit being mad but not blind with rage. Which means I might say that we're pinched this month but never that I'm worried sick over money."

8    But which doesn't mean that there isn't sufficient value to be found in these friendships of mutual aid, in convenience friends.

9    2. Special-interest friends. These friendships aren't intimate, and they needn't involve kids or silverware or cats. Their value lies in some interest jointly shared. And so we may have an office friend or a yoga friend or a tennis friend or a friend from the Women's Democratic Club.

10   "I've got one woman friend," says Joyce, "who likes, as I do, to take psychology courses. Which makes it nice for me—and nice for her. It's fun to go with someone you know and it's fun to discuss what you've learned, driving back from the classes." And for the most part, she says, that's all they discuss.

11   "I'd say that what we're *doing* is *doing* together, not being together," Suzanne says of her Tuesday-doubles friends. "It's mainly a tennis relationship, but we play together well. And I guess we all need to have a couple of playmates."

12   I agree.

13   *My* playmate is a shopping friend, a woman of marvelous taste, a woman who knows exactly *where* to buy *what,* and furthermore is a woman who always knows beyond a doubt what one ought to be buying. I don't have the time to keep up with what's new in eyeshadow, hemlines and shoes and whether the smock look is in or finished already. But since (oh shame!) I care a lot about eyeshadow, hemlines and shoes, and since I don't *want* to wear smocks if the smock look is finished, I'm very glad to have a shopping friend.

14   3. Historical friends. We all have a friend who knew us when . . . maybe way back in Miss Meltzer's second grade, when our family lived in that three-room flat in Brooklyn, when our dad was out of work for seven months, when our brother Allie got in that fight where they had to call the police, when our sister married the endodontist from Yonkers and when, the morning after we lost our virginity, she was the first, the only friend we told.

15   The years have gone by and we've gone separate ways and we've little in common now, but we're still an intimate part of each other's past. And so whenever we go to Detroit we always go to visit this friend of our girlhood. Who knows how we looked before our teeth were straightened. Who knows how we talked before our voice got unBrooklyned. Who knows what we ate before we learned about artichokes. And who, by her presence, puts us in touch with an earlier part of ourself, a part of ourself it's important never to lose.

16   "What this friend means to me and what I mean to her," says Grace, "is having a sister without sibling rivalry. We know the texture of each other's lives. She remembers my grandmother's cabbage soup. I remember the way

her uncle played the piano. There's simply no other friend who remembers those things."

17    4. Crossroads friends. Like historical friends, our crossroads friends are important for *what was—for* the friendship we shared at a crucial, now past, time of life. A time, perhaps, when we roomed in college together; or worked as eager young singles in the Big City together; or went together, as my friend Elizabeth and I did through pregnancy, birth and that scary first year of new motherhood.

18    Crossroads friends forge powerful links, links strong enough to endure with not much more contact than once-a-year letters at Christmas. And out of respect for those crossroads years, for those dramas and dreams we once shared, we will always be friends.

19    5. Cross-generational friends. Historical friends and crossroads friends seem to maintain a special kind of intimacy—dormant but always ready to be revived—and though we may rarely meet, whenever we do connect, it's personal and intense. Another kind of intimacy exists in the friendships that form across generations in what one woman calls her daughter-mother and her mother-daughter relationships.

20    Evelyn's friend is her mother's age—"but I share so much more than I ever could with my mother"—a woman she talks to of music, of books and of life. "What I get from her is the benefit of her experience. What she gets—and enjoys—from me is a youthful perspective. It's a pleasure for both of us."

21    I have in my own life a precious friend, a woman of 65 who has lived very hard, who is wise, who listens well; who has been where I am and can help me understand it; and who represents not only an ultimate ideal mother to me but also the person I'd like to be when I grow up.

22    In our daughter role we tend to do more than our share of self-revelation; in our mother role we tend to receive what's revealed. It's another kind of pleasure—playing wise mother to a questing younger person. It's another very lovely kind of friendship.

23    6. Part-of-a-couple friends. Some of the women we call our friends we never see alone—we see them as part of a couple at couples' parties. And though we share interests in many things and respect each other's views, we aren't moved to deepen the relationship. Whatever the reason, a lack of time or—and this is more likely—a lack of chemistry, our friendship remains in the context of a group. But the fact that our feeling on seeing each other is always, "I'm *so* glad she's here" and the fact that we spend half the evening talking together says that this too, in its own way, counts as a friendship.

24    (Other part-of-a-couple friends are the friends that came with the marriage, and some of these are friends we could live without. But sometimes, alas, she married our husband's best friend; and sometimes, alas, she *is* our husband's best friend. And so we find ourself dealing with her, somewhat against our will, in a spirit of what I'll call *reluctant* friendship.)

25    7. Men who are friends. I wanted to write just of women friends, but the women I've talked to won't let me—they say I must mention manwoman

friendships too. For these friendships can be just as close and as dear as those that we form with women. Listen to Lucy's description of one such friendship:

26  "We've found we have things to talk about that are different from what he talks about with my husband and different from what I talk about with his wife. So sometimes we call on the phone or meet for lunch. There are similar intellectual interests— we always pass on to each other the books that we love-but there's also something tender and caring too."

27  In a couple of crises, Lucy says, "he offered himself, for talking and for helping. And when someone died in his family he wanted me there. The sexual, flirty part of our friendship is very small, but *some*—just enough to make it fun and different." She thinks—and I agree—that the sexual part, though small is always *some,* is always there when a man and a woman are friends.

28  It's only in the past few years that I've made friends with men, in the sense of a friendship that's *mine,* not just part of two couples. And achieving with them the ease and the trust I've found with women friends has value indeed. Under the dryer at home last week, putting on mascara and rouge, I comfortably sat and talked with a fellow named Peter. Peter, I finally decided, could handle the shock of me minus mascara under the dryer. Because we care for each other. Because we're friends.

29  8. There are medium friends, and pretty good friends, and very good friends, indeed, and these friendships are defined by their level of intimacy. And what we'll reveal at each of these levels of intimacy is calibrated with care. We might tell a medium friend, for example, that yesterday we had a fight with our husband. And we might tell a pretty good friend that this fight with our husband made us so mad that we slept on the couch. And we might tell a very good friend that the reason we got so mad in that fight that we slept on the couch had something to do with that girl who works in his office. But it's only to our very best friends that we're willing to tell all, to tell what's going on with that girl in his office.

30  The best of friends, I still believe, totally love and support and trust each other, and bare to each other the secrets of their souls, and run—no questions asked—to help each other, and tell harsh truths to each other when they must be told.

31  But we needn't agree about everything (only 12-year-old girl friends agree about *everything*) to tolerate each other's point of view. To accept without judgment. To give and to take without ever keeping score. And to *be* there, as I am for them and as they are for me, to comfort our sorrows, to celebrate our joys.

## WRITING PROMPTS

1. What does Viorst say about friendship?
2. How does she classify her friends?
3. What kinds of support does she include?

4. Do you agree with her categories of friendship, including her levels of intensity? Why or why not?

5. Can you think of any additional categories into which some of your friends fall?

6. How do you select your friends?

---

## THREE TYPES OF RESISTANCE TO OPPRESSION

### Martin Luther King, Jr.

1    Oppressed people deal with their oppression in three characteristic ways. One way is acquiescence: the oppressed resign themselves to their doom. They tacitly adjust themselves to oppression, and thereby become conditioned to it. In every movement toward freedom some of the oppressed prefer to remain oppressed. Almost 2800 years ago Moses set out to lead the children of Israel from the slavery of Egypt to the freedom of the promised land. He soon discovered that slaves do not always welcome their deliverers. They become accustomed to being slaves. They would rather bear those ills they have, as Shakespeare pointed out, than flee to others that they know not of. They prefer the "fleshpots of Egypt" to the ordeals of emancipation.

2    There is such a thing as the freedom of exhaustion. Some people are so worn down by the yoke of oppression that they give up. A few years ago in the slum areas of Atlanta, a Negro guitarist used to sing almost daily, "Ben down so long that down don't bother me." This is the type of negative freedom and resignation that often engulfs the life of the oppressed.

3    But this is not the way out. To accept passively an unjust system is to cooperate with that system; thereby the oppressed become as evil as the oppressor. Noncooperation with evil is as much a moral obligation as is cooperation with good. The oppressed must never allow the conscience of the oppressor to slumber. Religion reminds every man that he is his brother's keeper. To accept injustice or segregation passively is to say to the oppressor that his actions are morally right. It is a way of allowing his conscience to fall asleep. At this moment the oppressed fails to be his brother's keeper. So acquiescence—while often the easier way—is not the moral way. It is the way of the coward. The Negro cannot win the respect of his oppressor by acquiescing; he merely increases the oppressor's arrogance and contempt. Acquiescence is interpreted as proof of the Negro's inferiority. The Negro cannot win the respect of the white people of the South or the peoples of the world if he is willing to sell the future of his children for his personal and immediate comfort and safety.

4    A second way that oppressed people sometimes deal with oppression is to resort to physical violence and corroding hatred. Violence often brings about momentary results. Nations have frequently won their independence in battle.

But in spite of temporary victories, violence never brings permanent peace. It solves no social problem; it merely creates new and more complicated ones.

5    Violence as a way of achieving racial justice is both impractical and immoral. It is impractical because it is a descending spiral ending in destruction for all. The old law of an eye for an eye leaves everybody blind. It is immoral because it seeks to humiliate the opponent rather than win his understanding; it seeks to annihilate rather than to convert. Violence is immoral because it thrives on hatred rather than love. It destroys community and makes brotherhood impossible. It leaves society in monologue rather than dialogue. Violence ends by defeating itself. It creates bitterness in the survivors and brutality in the destroyers. A voice echoes through time saying to every potential Peter, "Put up your sword." History is cluttered with the wreckage of nations that failed to follow this command.

6    If the American Negro and other victims of oppression succumb to the temptation of using violence in the struggle for freedom, future generations will be the recipients of a desolate night of bitterness, and our chief legacy to them will be an endless reign of meaningless chaos. Violence is not the way.

7    The third way open to oppressed people in their quest for freedom is the way of non-violent resistance. Like the synthesis in Hegelian philosophy, the principle of nonviolent resistance seeks to reconcile the truths of two opposites—acquiescence and violence—while avoiding the extremes and immoralities of both. The nonviolent resister agrees with the person who acquiesces that one should not be physically aggressive toward his opponent; but he balances the equation by agreeing with the person of violence that evil must be resisted. He avoids the nonresistance of the former and the violent resistance of the latter. With nonviolent resistance, no individual or group need submit to any wrong, nor need anyone resort to violence in order to right a wrong.

8    It seems to me that this is the method that must guide the actions of the Negro in the present crisis in race relations. Through nonviolent resistance the Negro will be able to rise to the noble height of opposing the unjust system while loving the perpetrators of the system. The Negro must work passionately and unrelentingly for full stature as a citizen, but he must not use inferior methods to gain it. He must never come to terms with falsehood, malice, hate, or destruction.

9    Nonviolent resistance makes it possible for the Negro to remain in the South and struggle for his rights. The Negro's problem will not be solved by running away. He cannot listen to the glib suggestion of those who would urge him to migrate en masse to other sections of the country. By grasping his great opportunity in the South he can make a lasting contribution to the moral strength of the nation and set a sublime example of courage for generations yet unborn.

10    By nonviolent resistance, the Negro can also enlist all men of good will in his struggle for equality. The problem is not a purely racial one, with Negroes set against whites. In the end, it is not a struggle between people at all, but a tension between justice and injustice. Nonviolent resistance is not aimed

against oppressors but against oppression. Under its banner consciences, not racial groups, are enlisted.

11    If the Negro is to achieve the goal of integration, he must organize himself into a militant and nonviolent mass movement. All three elements are indispensable. The movement for equality and justice can only be a success if it has both a mass and militant character; the barriers to be overcome require both. Nonviolence is an imperative in order to bring about ultimate community.

12    A mass movement of militant quality that is not at the same time committed to nonviolence tends to generate conflict, which in turn breeds anarchy. The support of the participants and the sympathy of the uncommitted are both inhibited by the threat that bloodshed will engulf the community. This reaction in turn encourages the opposition to threaten and resort to force. When, however, the mass movement repudiates violence while moving resolutely toward its goal, its opponents are revealed as the instigators and practitioners of violence if it occurs. Then public support is magnetically attracted to the advocates of nonviolence, while those who employ violence are literally disarmed by overwhelming sentiment against their stand.

## WRITING PROMPTS

1. In what ways does Martin Luther King say oppressed people may behave?
2. Which of these types of behavior does he advocate, and why?
3. Why does he claim the other types are unsuccessful?
4. What examples can you find in this essay of King's religious training and career as a minister?
5. What kinds of support does King include for his argument?
6. Based on what you know about the civil rights movement in America, do you think King's preferred method has been the answer? Why or why not?
7. Are there groups of people today who could benefit from King's advice from half a century ago? Who and why?

## EXERCISE

Write a paragraph in which you classify and divide different kinds of relationships in your life. Write a topic sentence that suggests the importance of those relationships in your life. Your audience is your parents or your significant other.

# CHAPTER 11

# Cause/Effect, Definition, Argument and Persuasion

## CAUSE/EFFECT

A seventh mode of development is called *cause/effect* or causal analysis. Some textbook authors add still another title to this category: problem/solution writing. It doesn't matter what you call these patterns; what's important is that you understand them as ways to organize your thoughts.

With the cause/effect pattern you might start with one cause or a series of causes and, using the process of induction, build up to a conclusion (the effect). Reversing this process, you could begin with an event and flash back to its cause(s). Usually there is an immediate cause that triggers an event, but in most cases multiple causes build up to a major noticeable occurrence.

Occasionally an author will reach out, starting with one event that has two possible consequences. He will then turn to each of those consequences as if they are already completed and branch from each to two or more other consequences.

In so doing, he makes the original effects become the causes of further events. To illustrate causal analysis, here is a paragraph written by civil rights leader Martin Luther King, Jr. As you read, see if you can identify statements that indicate causes and those that refer to results:

### Rosa Parks

On December 1, 1955, an attractive Negro seamstress, Mrs. Rosa Parks, boarded the Cleveland Avenue Bus in downtown Montgomery. She was returning home after her regular day's work in the Montgomery Fair—a leading department store. Tired from the long hours on her feet, Mrs. Parks sat down in the first seat behind the section reserved for whites. Not long after she took her seat, the bus operator ordered her, along with three other Negro passengers, to move back in order to accommodate boarding white passengers. By this time every seat in the bus was taken.

This meant that if Mrs. Parks followed the driver's command she would have to stand while a white male passenger, who had just boarded the bus, would sit. The other three Negro passengers immediately complied with the driver's request. But Mrs. Parks quietly refused. The result was her arrest.

Martin Luther King, Jr.

See if you can find the causes and effects in the following paragraph, "Why Eat Junk Food?" from *Eating Your Way Through Life* by Judith Wurtman:

### Why Eat Junk Food?

We crunch and chew our way through vast quantities of snacks and confectionaries and relieve our thirst with multicolored, flavored soft drinks, with and without calories, for two basic reasons. The first is simple: the food tastes good, and we enjoy the sensation of eating it. Second, we associate these foods, often without being aware of it, with the highly pleasurable experiences depicted in the advertisements used to promote their sale. Current television advertisements demonstrate this point: people turn from grumpiness to euphoria after crunching a corn chip. Others water ski into the sunset with their loved ones while drinking a popular soft drink. People entertain on the patio with friends, cook over camp-fires without mosquitoes, or go to carnivals with granddad munching away at the latest candy or snack food. The people portrayed in these scenarios are all healthy, vigorous, and good looking; one wonders how popular the food they convince us to eat would be if they would crunch or drink away while complaining about low back pain or clogged sinuses.

Judith Wurtman, "Why Eat Junk Food?"

The following essay, "The Prison Population Is Rising—Politicians Must be Very Proud" by David Nyhan, uses cause and effect to develop the author's ideas.

## THE PRISON POPULATION IS RISING—POLITICIANS MUST BE VERY PROUD
### David Nyhan

1    If I told you that my prescription for making America a bit safer from crime was to lock up every blessed soul living in Maine and New Hampshire, you'd think I was nutty.

2    But official government policy in this country has almost that many people behind bars this morning, more than 1.7 million. And if you throw in all the employees who report to prison or jail every day, the guards, cooks, nurses, and administrators, the total of Americans who spend their day inside prison walls is more than the combined populations of Maine and New Hampshire.

3    Now for more news: The prison and jail population will probably top 2 million in time for 2000. Sure, crime rates are falling, but prison and jail populations are rising. How so? Longer sentences. Since Ronald Reagan's tough talk on crime proved politically popular in the mid-'80s, your typical inmate has had five months tacked on to his time in the jug, from an average of 20 months to 25 months.

4    Just ask yourself: Have you ever seen a politician brag that he's for shorter sentences? Easier time? More parole and probation? Have you forgotten what George Bush's hatchetmen did to Michael Dukakis over Willie Horton in the presidential election 10 years ago? No politician has forgotten that lesson.

5    So sentences get longer, rhetoric gets harsher, and candidates outdo themselves in bragging how tough they'll be on miscreants. Remember Bill Weld riding into office promising to introduce his prisoners to "the joy of breaking rocks"? It's still a trend.

6    And that average sentence gets longer each month, with longer minimums, three-strikes-and-you're-out, stricter sentencing rules that prevent judges from weighing a defendant's youth, IQ, mitigating circumstance, or general stupidity in easing prison stays. We are also cracking down on parole violators.

Nearly one-third of all inmates are back where they are because they did something really stupid all over again.

7    You thought our hottest growth industry was something in the computer line? Try prison construction. All through the '90s, our prison population expanded by about 64,000 per year. That means every month, we need new cells for 5,350 men—they are overwhelmingly men. That's a roof, a bed, a barred door, a toilet, three squares and medical care, plus the custodial charges, for a net increase of 175 men per day.

8    You are paying for all this. You are hiring, as taxpayers, on average, every day of the year, weekends and holidays included, a fresh crew of 175 prisoners, whom you will now have to feed, clothe, medicate, guard, and entertain, plus another crew to watch over them and make sure they don't leave their new home before their 25-months-and-growing, on average, is up.

9    Make sense to you? Do you feel safer because going on 2 million of your fellow Americans are locked up? In many cases, yes, we know there are dangerous people who deserve to be locked away. The most violent and felonious, sure, no problem, keep them tucked away.

10    But why do we have so many more prisoners per capita than any other industrial nation, save Russia? That is the only country with more inmates per head than we have. Our rate of incarcerating 645 out of every 100,000 citizens is six to 10 times higher than the rest of the so-called civilized world.

11    Sound bites elect politicians, and three-strikes-and-you're-out sounds satisfactory after the local TV station zips up its audience share with live shots from the latest gruesome crime scene. But 19 out of 20 of those prison inmates chilling in noisy, crowded, understaffed, over-brutalized prisons come out, typically after 25 months of soul-deadening punishment.

12    And they come back to live in our midst and try to pick up where they left off. Some go straight. Some have the gumption and IQ to get jobs, to overcome the stigma of a prison record, to renew family life, to get on with living. A lot don't. They were drunk or high when they did what they did to get in trouble in the first place, and most prisoners have done a lot more wrong than what they got sentenced for.

13    Drink and drugs gave a lot of them the false courage they needed to try something really crooked. And if they're a little light in the IQ department, as many prisoners are, if they had broken families, lousy schooling, and a predilection for dope, booze, or violent behavior, then over they go, and in they go. But every other industrial nation, save one, has devised smoother, calmer, more efficient, and less costly ways of dealing with malefactors.

14    Shorter, swifter sentences, more counseling and oversight on the street, intensive job-skill training and maximization of religious and psychological help, teaching reading and writing and basic social skills, all these would help. Prison too often makes hard and brutal men harder and more brutal. I write a similar column every summer when the numbers come out, usually picking two states whose population mirrors that in prison. Next year, I'm afraid. I may have to toss in Rhode Island.

### WRITING PROMPTS

1. Nyhan argues that prisoners would be better off with shorter sentences and better services. Why does he hold this belief?
2. What supporting data does he include?
3. How does he contrast the prisons of other countries with those of America?
4. What examples of humor do you see in Nyhan's essay?
5. Do you think shorter sentences would be cost effective?
6. Would you feel comfortable if prisoners were released from prison, given extended services, and then "relocated" to the community (where you live)?

## EXERCISE

Write a paragraph that examines the cause(s) and effect(s) of watching so much television. Make your topic sentence explain the effect, and support that sentence with the causes. If you have a younger sister or brother, make her or him your audience. If you have no siblings, write the paragraph to an eight-year-old child.

## DEFINITION

Good argument writing includes *definitions* of any ambiguous terms so the writer and reader share a common frame of reference. Defining abstract terms (words we cannot see or touch—words like *liberty*, *peace*, *honor*, or *justice*) is particularly important. Clearly, definition is often an important component of the other eight modes; however, it can also exist as a pattern of development in its own right. The following paragraphs, written by college freshmen, define abstract terms. Notice how in each case a personal example supports the definition.

### Love

Love is caring, sharing, and being there. It means that the person you love is there for you when you are sick or depressed. My husband showed me how much he loved me when he was willing to give up his favorite activity just to be with me when I was sick. He had gone skiing for the weekend but turned around and came home when he knew I was sick. He cared for me; he was there for me; he shared the pain of my illness with me. This sacrifice he made for me demonstrated just how much he loved me.

### Love

There can be many types of love, not necessarily just a boy and a girl relationship. Love as defined is a deep affection or liking for someone or something. A personal example of love is my love for my dog. My pet dog, Princess, a German Shepherd Alsatian, is very faithful, obedient, playful and gentle. She has never made me feel unhappy. Whenever she sees me, she will wag her bushy tail. Whenever I feel down, she behaves as though she can understand and share my feelings. She will lick me in my face or sometimes bite my hand playfully. Never ever has she disobeyed my commands. After several years of [her] being attached to me faithfully, my love and affection became very strong. I have surely missed her very much since I came to the United States for my studies. To show my love and care I am accelerating my studies and hope to complete them by next year so that I will be able to see her sooner.

### Prejudice

Prejudice means many things to many people. To me, the word *prejudice* means disliking someone before you even know him/her or know what he/she is like. A couple of years ago a friend and I were walking down the street, in a nearby town, doing some shopping. Well, we saw a group of girls who were black. Automatically my friend said, "Look at those niggers; they think they are so cool." I turned to her and said, "You don't know who they are or what they are like; how do you know they think they are cool?" I know at one time or another everyone is prejudiced about someone or something. But I also know that it's not fair to the people he or she is prejudiced against, and not fair to himself or herself. These girls we saw could have been very nice, but my friend didn't even give them a chance.

Two essays, "The Meanings of a Word" by Gloria Naylor and "Daddy Tucked the Blanket" by Randall Williams, illustrate ways to define two quite disparate terms.

## THE MEANINGS OF A WORD
### Gloria Naylor

1   Language is the subject. It is the written form with which I've managed to keep the wolf away from the door and, in diaries, to keep my sanity. In spite of this, I consider the written word inferior to the spoken, and much of the frustration experienced by novelists is the awareness that whatever we manage to capture in even the most transcendent passages falls far short of the richness of life. Dialogue achieves its power in the dynamics of a fleeting moment of sight, sound, smell, and touch.

2   I'm not going to enter the debate here about whether it is language that shapes reality or vice versa. That battle is doomed to be waged whenever we

seek intermittent reprieve from the chicken and egg dispute. I will simply take the position that the spoken word, like the written word, amounts to a non-sensical arrangement of sounds or letters without a consensus that assigns "meaning." And building from the meanings of what we hear, we order reality. Words themselves are innocuous; it is the consensus that gives them true power.

3    I remember the first time I heard the word *nigger*. In my third-grade class, our math tests were being passed down the rows, and as I handed the papers to a little boy in back of me, I remarked that once again he had received a much lower mark than I did. He snatched his test from me and spit out that word. Had he called me a nymphomaniac or a necrophiliac, I couldn't have been more puzzled. I didn't know what a nigger was, but I knew that whatever it meant, it was something he shouldn't have called me. This was verified when I raised my hand, and in a loud voice repeated what he had said and watched the teacher scold him for using a "bad" word. I was later to go home and ask the inevitable question that every black parent must face—"Mommy, what does *nigger* mean?"

4    And what exactly did it mean? Thinking back, I realize that this could not have been the first time the word was used in my presence. I was part of a large extended family that had migrated from the rural South after World War II and formed a close-knit network that gravitated around my maternal grand-parents. Their ground-floor apartment in one of the buildings they owned in Harlem was a weekend mecca for my immediate family, along with countless aunts, uncles, and cousins who brought along assorted friends. It was a bustling and open house with assorted neighbors and tenants popping in and out to exchange bits of gossip, pick up an old quarrel, or referee the ongoing checkers game in which my grandmother cheated shamelessly. They were all there to let down their hair and put up their feet after a week of labor in the factories, laundries, and shipyards of New York.

5    Amid the clamor, which could reach deafening proportions— two or three conversations going on simultaneously, punctuated by the sound of a baby's crying somewhere in the back rooms or out on the street—there was still a rigid set of rules about what was said and how. Older children were sent out of the living room when it was time to get into the juicy details about "you-know-who" up on the third floor who had gone and gotten herself "p-r-e-g-n-a-n-t!" But my parents, knowing that I could spell well beyond my years, always demanded that I follow the others out to play. Beyond sexual misconduct and death, every-thing else was considered harmless for our young ears. And so among the anecdotes of the triumphs and disappointments in the various workings of their lives, the word *nigger* was used in my presence, but it was set within contexts and inflections that caused it to register in my mind as something else.

6    In the singular, the word was always applied to a man who had distin-guished himself in some situation that brought their approval for his strength, intelligence, or drive:

7    "Did Johnny *really* do that?"

8    "I'm telling you, that nigger pulled in $6,000 of overtime last year. Said he got enough for a down payment on a house."

9    When used with a possessive adjective by a woman—"my nigger"—it became a term of endearment for her husband or boyfriend. But it could be more than just a term applied to a man. In their mouths it became the pure essence of manhood—a disembodied force that channeled their past history of struggle and present survival against the odds into a victorious statement of being: "Yeah, that old foreman found out quick enough—you don't mess with a nigger."

10    In the plural, it became a description of some group within the community that had overstepped the bounds of decency as my family defined it. Parents who neglected their children, a drunken couple who fought in public, people who simply refused to look for work, those with excessively dirty mouths or unkempt households were all "trifling niggers." This particular circle could forgive hard times, unemployment, the occasional bout of depression—they had gone through all of that themselves—but the unforgivable sin was a lack of self-respect.

11    A woman could never be a "nigger" in the singular, with its connotation of confirming worth. The noun *girl* was its closest equivalent in that sense, but only when used in direct address and regardless of the gender doing the addressing. *Girl* was a token of respect to a woman. The one-syllable word was drawn out to sound like three in recognition of the extra ounce of wit, nerve, or daring that the woman had shown in the situation under discussion.

12    "G-i-r-l, stop. You mean you said that to his face?"

13    But if the word was used in a third-person reference or shortened so that it almost snapped out of the mouth, it always involved some element of communal disapproval. And age became an important factor in these exchanges. It was only between individuals of the same generation, or from any older person to a younger (but never the other way around), that *girl* would be considered a compliment.

14    I don't agree with the argument that use of the word *nigger* at this social stratum of the black community was an internalization of racism. The dynamics were the exact opposite: the people in my grandmother's living room took a word that whites used to signify worthlessness or degradation and rendered it impotent. Gathering there together, they transformed *nigger* to signify the varied and complex human beings they knew themselves to be. If the word was to disappear totally from the mouths of even the most liberal of white society, no one in that room was naive enough to believe it would disappear from white minds. Meeting the word head-on, they proved it had absolutely nothing to do with the way they were determined to live their lives.

15    So there must have been dozens of times that *nigger* was spoken in front of me before I reached the third grade. But I didn't "hear" it until it was said by a small pair of lips that had already learned it could be a way to humiliate me. That was the word I went home and asked my mother about. And since she knew that I had to grow up in America, she took me in her lap and explained.

## WRITING PROMPTS

1. What does Naylor mean when she says, "Words themselves are innocuous; it is the consensus that gives them true power"?

2. What word does she use as an extended example, and how has this word changed in its connotation for Naylor?

3. Why does the author think written language is inferior to spoken language?

4. What were your connotations of the word *nigger* before you read this essay? Have they changed at all since your reading?

5. Can you think of any words whose meanings have changed for you? Are the meanings different for spoken and written language?

---

## DADDY TUCKED THE BLANKET

### Randall Williams

1    About the time I turned 16, my folks began to wonder why I didn't stay home any more. I always had an excuse for them, but what I didn't say was that I had found my freedom and I was getting out.

2    I went through four years of high school in semirural Alabama and became active in clubs and sports: I made a lot of friends and became a regular guy, if you know what I mean. But one thing was irregular about me: I managed those four years without ever having a friend visit at my house.

3    I was ashamed of where I lived. I had been ashamed of where I lived. I had been ashamed for as long as I had been conscious of class.

4    We had a big family. There were several of us sleeping in one room, but that's not so bad if you get along, and we always did. As you get older, though. it gets worse.

5    Being poor is a humiliating experience for a young person trying hard to be accepted. Even now—several years removed—it is hard to talk about. And I resent the weakness of these words to make you feel what it was really like.

6    We lived in a lot of old houses. We moved a lot because we were always looking for something just a little better than what we had. You have to understand that my folks worked harder than most people. My mother was always at home, but for her that was a full-time job—and no fun, either. But my father worked his head off from the time I can remember in construction and shops. It was hard, physical work.

7    I tell you this to show that we weren't shiftless. No matter how much money Daddy made, we never made much progress up the social ladder. I got out thanks to a college scholarship and because I was a little more articulate than the average.

8    I have seen my Daddy wrap copper wire through the soles of his boots to keep them together in the wintertime. He couldn't buy new boots because he

had used the money for food and shoes for us. We lived like hell, but we went to school well-clothed and with a full stomach.

9    It really is hell to live in a house that was in bad shape years before you moved in. And a big family puts a lot of wear and tear on a new house, too, so you can imagine how one goes downhill if it is teetering when you move in. But we lived in houses that were sweltering in summer and freezing in winter. I woke up every morning for a year and a half with plaster on my face where it had fallen out of the ceiling during the night.

10    This wasn't during the Depression; this was in the late 60's and early 70's.

11    When we boys got old enough to learn trades in school, we would try to fix up the old houses we lived in. But have you ever tried to paint a wall that crumbled when the roller went across it? And bright paint emphasized holes in the wall. You end up more frustrated than when you began, especially when you know that at best you might come up with only enough money to improve one of the six rooms in the house. And we might move out soon after, anyway.

12    The same goes for keeping a house like that clean. If you have a house full of kids and the house is deteriorating, you'll never keep it clean. Daddy used to yell at Mama about that, but she couldn't do anything. I think Daddy knew it inside, but he had to have an outlet for his rage somewhere, and at least yelling isn't as bad as hitting, which they never did to each other.

13    But you have a kitchen which has no counter space and no hot water, and you will have dirty dishes stacked up. That sounds like an excuse, but try it. You'll go mad from the sheer sense of futility. It's the same thing in a house with no closets. You can't keep clothes clean and rooms in order if they have to be stacked up with things.

14    Living in a bad house is generally worse on girls. For one thing, they traditionally help their mother with the housework. We boys could get outside and work in the field or cut wood or even play ball and forget about the living conditions. The sky was still pretty.

15    But the girls got the pressure, and as they got older it became worse. Would they accept dates knowing they had to "receive" the young man in a dirty hallway with broken windows, peeling wallpaper and a cracked ceiling? You have to live it to understand it, but it creates a shame which drives the soul of a young person inward.

16    I'm thankful none of us ever blamed our parents for this, because it would have crippled our relationships. As it worked out, only the relationship between our parents was damaged. And I think the harshness which they expressed to each other was just an outlet to get rid of their anger at the trap their lives were in. It ruined their marriage because they had no one to yell at but each other. I knew other families where the kids got the abuse, but we were too much loved for that.

17    Once I was about 16 and Mama and Daddy had a particularly violent argument about the washing machine, which had broken down. Daddy was on the back porch—that's where the only water faucet was—trying to fix it and Mama had a washtub out there washing school clothes for the next day and they were screaming at each other.

18   Later that night everyone was in bed and I heard Daddy get up from the couch where he was reading. I looked out from my bed across the hall into their room. He was standing right over Mama and she was already asleep. He pulled the blanket up and tucked it around her shoulders and just stood there and tears were dropping off his cheek and I thought I could faintly hear them splashing against the linoleum rug.

19   Now they're divorced.

20   I had courses in college where housing was discussed, but the sociologist never put enough emphasis on the impact living in substandard housing has on a person's psyche. Especially children's.

21   Small children have a hard time understanding poverty. They want the same things children from more affluent families have. They want the same things they see advertised on television, and they don't understand why they can't have them.

22   Other children can be incredibly cruel. I was in elementary school in Georgia—and this is interesting because it is the only thing I remember about that particular school—when I was about eight or nine.

23   After Christmas vacation had ended, my teacher made each student describe all his or her Christmas presents. I became more and more uncomfortable as the privilege passed around the room toward me. Other children were reciting the names of the dolls they had been given, the kinds of bicycles and the grandeur of their games and toys. Some had lists which seemed to go on and on for hours.

24   It took me only a few seconds to tell the class that I had gotten for Christmas a belt and a pair of gloves. And then I was laughed at—because I cried—by a roomful of children and a teacher. I never forgave them, and that night I made my mother cry when I told her about it.

25   In retrospect, I am grateful for that moment, but I remember wanting to die at the time.

## Writing Prompts

1. Williams had a difficult childhood and claims he felt shamed because he was poor. How does he define poverty, and what were some of his humiliating experiences?

2. Why does the author say he never stayed at home once he turned sixteen?

3. How does Williams say poverty affects a marriage? How does it affect the children in a family?

4. Have you ever known a family as poor as Williams's family was? How did they cope with their socioeconomic status?

5. What can teachers do to help students from impoverished backgrounds so these students do not feel inferior and humiliated at school?

## EXERCISE

What is *success?* What does the term mean to you?  Using specific examples, see if you are able to define what it means to be successful. You are writing this paragraph for your classmates who have been given the same assignment, so be prepared to discuss and argue for your definition.

# ARGUMENT AND PERSUASION

You have reached the last of the nine modes—*argument*. Keep in mind that any one of the first eight patterns just covered can be used to persuade readers, but good formal arguments must include the three major characteristics of argumentation we wrote about in Part II: *ethos*, *logos*, and *pathos*, Greek words that mean, loosely, facts, logic, and emotion. Further, a difference exists between argument and persuasion. Argumentative writing tries to persuade but with facts and logic. Authors of persuasive writing try to convince their readers to believe their values or to take some type of action. This writing is loaded with emotional language and tugs on the reader's heartstrings, but it is *not* necessarily logical. The two paragraphs that follow demonstrate the difference between the two terms.

### Restoration of a Terrestrial Environment

There is little doubt that surface mining almost always causes damage to the environment. Damage, in the form of degraded water quality, results in the water being unusable for domestic, industrial and recreational use. In addition, the aesthetic eyesore and the decreased real estate value of the useless land only contribute to more problems in the future. However, this does not have to be the outcome of surface mining. With proper pre-planning, mining, water control and reclamation projects, environmental damage can be held to a minimum. This is not to suggest it will be easy or inexpensive. It does suggest, however, that if we want to preserve our environment, this is the price we may have to pay.

From R. Hill's "Restoration of a Terrestrial Environment"

### People of the Ruined Hills

It is not committed with guns and knives, but with great, relentless bulldozers and thundering dump trucks, with giant shovels like mythological creatures, their girdered necks lifting massive steel mouths high above the tallest trees. And with dynamite. They cut and blast and rip apart mountains to reach the minerals inside, and when they have finished there is nothing left but naked hills, ugly monuments to waste, stripped of everything that once held them in place, cut off from the top and sides and dug out from the inside and then left, restless, to slide down on houses and wash off into rivers and streams, rendering the land unlovable and the water for miles downstream undrinkable.

Terracide. Or if you prefer, strip mining.

From Rosen's "People of the Ruined Hills"

In the two preceding paragraphs, the purpose of each author is the same: to persuade. Each wants to convince the reader that strip mining is harmful; however, in the first example we are able to base our opinion on facts. The paragraph is argumentative. With the second paragraph the author presents only emotional cries, no deeper thoughts, no facts on which to base our opinions. The writer touches us on the surface but isn't really convincing. John Fleeger's "Why Isn't Pete Rose in the Hall of Fame"? Ann Bookman's "Family Leave Act, Five Years Later," and Mariah Burton Nelson's "Who Wins? Who Cares?" all include ethos, logos, and pathos, making them fine examples of argument. "Drugs" by Gore Vidal and "I Have a Dream" by Martin Luther King, Jr. are both excellent examples of persuasive writing.

## WHY ISN'T PETE ROSE IN THE HALL OF FAME?

### John Fleeger

1    Nineteen ninety-two marked the first year Pete Rose would have been eligible for the National Baseball Hall of Fame. Not only was he not elected, his name did not even appear on the ballot. Why? Has he not established himself as the all-time best hitter in baseball? Was he not a member of two championship teams with the Cincinnati Reds and one with the Philadelphia Phillies? Did he not help build the foundation for the 1990 championship Reds team? Has he not set or tied several major-league and team records during his career? The answer to all of these questions is "Yes." His dedication to and enthusiasm for the game of baseball earned him the nickname "Charlie Hustle," but not his rightful place in the Hall of Fame. This is unfair and should be changed.

2    In the late summer of 1989, Pete Rose was banned from professional baseball. The legal agreement reached between major-league officials and Pete Rose does not offer any evidence that Rose bet on any baseball games, and Rose himself does not say that he did. Despite the lack of any confirmation, A. Bartlett Giamatti, Commissioner of Baseball at that time, publicly declared that Rose bet not only on baseball, but also on his own team. Betting on baseball is a violation of major-league rules and is punishable by lifetime banishment from baseball. This was the sentence Pete Rose received.

3    In 1991 the Hall of Fame Committee along with Fay Vincent, who was then Commissioner of Baseball, decided that as long as a player is banned from baseball, he is ineligible for Hall of Fame selection. This action was taken just

a few weeks before Rose's name could have been placed on the ballot, and many believe that Vincent encouraged it specifically to make sure Rose could not be considered for selection. Several of the baseball writers who voted for the Hall of Fame candidates voiced their disapproval of this policy by writing in Rose's name on the ballot. Unfortunately, write-in votes are not counted.

4    Rose's only hope of making the Hall of Fame depends on his being readmitted to baseball. The commissioner would have to review Rose's application and approve his reinstatement. Chances are not good, however, that the commissioner would reinstate Rose. Therefore, Rose will probably have to wait for a commissioner who is sympathetic to his situation before he applies for reinstatement.

5    Meanwhile, on the strength of circumstantial evidence and the testimony of convicted felons, baseball has convicted Pete Rose of betting on baseball. He has admitted to betting on horse races and football games but denies ever betting on the sport he loves. He has also admitted that his gambling was a problem and has spent time in counseling. Why is a player who once gambled any worse than the many players who have tested positive for drugs? Those players are suspended from the game for a period of time and are given one or more chances to recover and return to the major league. Why are gamblers not treated the same way as drug abusers?

6    Many people mistakenly believe that Pete Rose went to prison for betting on baseball and that, for this reason, he should be kept out of the Hall of Fame.

The fact is, however, that Rose went to prison for tax-law violations. He failed to pay income tax on his gambling winnings and on the money he made at baseball-card shows. Even so, when has the Hall of Fame ever been reserved for perfect people? Babe Ruth was an adulterer and a serious drinker, but he still holds a place in the Hall. Mickey Mantle and Willie Mays were barred from baseball for being employees of an Atlantic City casino (an obvious gambling connection), but even this decision was eventually overturned.

7    I have met Pete Rose and, granted, he does not have the greatest personality, but his personal shortcomings are no reason to keep him out of the Hall of Fame. His contributions to the game and his accomplishments as a player more than qualify him to occupy a place beside the greats of the game. Baseball should, in all fairness, let Pete Rose return to the game and allow him to take his rightful place in the Hall of Fame.

---

# FAMILY LEAVE ACT, FIVE YEARS LATER

### Ann Bookman

1    This week marks the fifth anniversary of the Family and Medical Leave Act, the ground-breaking law that enables workers at companies with at least 50 employees in order to take 12 weeks of job-protected, unpaid leave to care for a newborn baby, newly adopted child, care for an ill family member, or recover from a serious illness.

2    What has this act accomplished for working families in its first five years? A good deal, but not enough.

3    The story of Marie is a case in point. A second-generation American whose parents worked at manual jobs, she has a 9-to-5 office job she loves at a biotechnology company. She has a high school diploma, but takes community college courses whenever she can.

4    As a working mother with two young children, Marie finds it hard to work, be a parent, and attend school. In fact, she has had to put her career development on hold to struggle with pressing questions: Is her daughter's day care meeting her social and developmental needs? Did she stay home long enough with her son?

5    The Family Leave Act enabled Marie to stay home for three months after her second child was born. Her employer paid her for two of those months. She wanted to take more time, but one month without pay was all her family could afford.

6    Marie was lucky to work for a company whose policies go beyond the federal law and provide some wage replacement. She was unlucky because her husband is not covered by the act and had no time off with his new son. And because she worries about taking any more time off now, Marie recently refused an invitation to accompany her daughter's day-care class on a field trip.

7    When it was time for Marie to return to work, she discovered that child care for two children was prohibitive. "It would cost me as much as I make, my whole paycheck," she said. "If I didn't have my mother and mother-in-law to leave the baby with, I would have had to quit my job."

8    Marie's situation is typical of young families who hold jobs, have families, and want to upgrade their skills and education. Yet the policies that shape their options around parental leave and infant child care undermine their plans for a future of economic security. Many young families are forced to deplete their savings to fund unpaid leaves and cover costly child-care expenses. Some even quit their jobs when the math of working and child care does not add up.

9    The Family Medical Leave Act has helped more than 15 million working Americans. And it is not the burden to business that many feared. A 1996 report to Congress, issued by a bipartisan commission, found that more than 90 percent of employers said most aspects of the law were "very easy" or "somewhat easy" to administer, more than 89 percent found they incurred "no cost" or "small costs," and more than 86 percent reported "no noticeable effect" on productivity, profitability, and growth.

10    The act's anniversary is a good time to celebrate its accomplishments and to set goals for the future. Goals such as:
- It should be a universal law. It now covers only 55 percent of the work force. The other 45 percent who work for small businesses, including young fathers like Marie's husband need job-protected leaves, too.
- It should expand the reasons workers can take leaves. Specifically, it should cover parents, like Marie, who want to be involved in their children's education no matter what the child's age.
- It should provide for some wage replacement. While the mechanism for funding these leaves requires further study, we must find a way to financially support leaves for families who are raising our next generation of workers and caring for our retirees.

11    Finally, we should not expand the reach and scope of the law in a vacuum. We need to link it to public policies that affect the lives of young children—particularly child care for infants and toddlers. Unpaid parental leaves and the lack of quality infant care put parents in untenable positions.

12    We need to make staying home with an infant both more accessible and financially viable, and make infant day care more available and affordable to support the healthy development of children and the economic security of families.

## Writing Prompts

1. Bookman wrote this essay on the anniversary of a piece of legislation. Explain that act. What changes would she like to see now that it has been in place for five years?
2. What example does she use to show that this legislation is not sufficient?

3. Bookman includes statistics in several places. Do her figures help persuade you?

4. Have you, or has anyone in your immediate family, had to miss work and lose wages in order to stay home with a relative? What were the consequences?

5. Should private companies or the government pay for time off for employees who experience family emergencies? Why?

---

# WHO WINS? WHO CARES?

## Mariah Burton Nelson

1    Competition can damage self-esteem, create anxiety, and lead to cheating and hurt feelings. But so can romantic love. No one suggests we do away with love; rather, we must perfect our understanding of what love means.

2    So too with competition. "To compete" is derived from the Latin, "to seek together." Women seem to understand this. Maybe it is because we sat on the sidelines for so long, watching. Maybe it is because we are raised to be kind and nurturing. I'm not sure why it is. But I noticed it's not women who greet each other with a ritualistic, "Who won?"; not women who memorize scores and statistics; not women who pride themselves on "killer instincts." Passionate though we are, women don't take competition that seriously. Or rather we take competition seriously, but we don't take winning and losing seriously. We've always been more interested in playing.

3    In fact, since the early part of this century, women have devised ways to make sport specifically inclusive and cooperative. Physical educators in the 1920s taught sportswomanship as well as sport skills, emphasizing health, vigor, high moral conduct, participation, respect for other players, and friendship. So intent were these women on dodging the pitfalls of men's sports that many shied away from competition altogether.

4    Nowadays, many women compete wholeheartedly. But we don't buy into the "Super Bull" mentality that the game is everything. Like Martina Navratilova and Chris Evert, former "rivals" whose rapport has come to symbolize a classically female approach to competition, many women find ways to remain close while also reaching for victory. We understand that trying to win is not tantamount to trying to belittle; that winning is not wonderful if the process of playing isn't challenging, fair or fun; and that losing, though at times disappointing, does not connote failure. For women, if sports are power plays, they are not about power over (power as dominance) but power to (power as competence). Sports are not about domination and defeat but caring and cooperation.

5    "The playing of the game has to do with your feelings, your emotions, how you care about the people you are involved with," says University of Iowa basketball coach C. Vivian Stringer.

6      Pam Shriver has said of Steffi Graf, "I hope in the next couple of years that I get to be friends with her because it's just easier. It's more fun. I don't think that it affects the competitive side of things."

7      Friendship has been a major theme of my sporting life as well, along with physical competence, achievement, and joy. Though I have competed in seven sports from the high school to the professional level, I've few memories of victories or losses. I don't think winning taught me to be a gracious winner. I don't think losing readied me for the serious losses in my life. Rather, my nearly 30 years of competition have taught me how to play, with empathy, humor, and honesty. If another player challenges me to row harder, swim faster, or make more clever moves toward the basket, the games take on a special thrill. But the final score is nearly irrelevant. Chris Evert once said the joy of winning "lasts about an hour."

8      I'm choosy about whom I compete with, and how. I don't participate in games in which "losers" are no longer allowed to play. Monopoly, poker, musical chairs, and single-elimination tournaments are a few examples. If playing is the point, then exclusion never makes sense. I also eschew competitions that pit women against men; they only serve to antagonize and polarize. I no longer injure myself in the name of victory. Nor, as a coach, will I allow players to get that carried away.

9      Some women, scarred by childhood exclusion, shamed by early "defeats," or sickened by abuses such as cheating and steroid use, still avoid competition. They are right to be wary. Although these things are more visible in men's sports, female athletes and coaches also can succumb to the "winning is the only thing" myth, committing myriad ethical and personal offenses, from recruiting violations to bulimia, in the name of victory.

10     But once one understands the spirit of the game, it's not a matter of believing that winning and losing aren't important, it's a matter of noticing that they're not. Women seem to notice. Most women can play soccer, golf, or run competitively and enjoy themselves, regardless of outcome. They can play on the "losing" team and leave the court with little or no sense of loss. They can win without feeling superior.

11     I think it is the responsibility of these women—and the men who remain unblended by the seductive glow of victory—to share this vision with young players. Children, it seems to me, share this vision with young players. Children, it seems to me, naturally enjoy comparing their skills: "How far can you throw the ball? Farther than I can? How did you do it? Will you show me?" It's only when adults ascribe undue importance to victory that losing becomes devastating and children get hurt.

12     Adults must show children that what matters is how one plays the game. It's important that we not just parrot that cliché, but demonstrate our commitment to fair, participatory competition by paying equal attention to skilled and unskilled children; by allowing all children to participate fully in games, regardless of the score; and by caring more about process than results. This way, children can fully comprehend what they seem to intuit: that competition

can be a way to get to know other people, to be challenged, and to have fun in a close and caring environment. To seek together.

13    Some of my best friends are the women and men who share a court or pool or field with me. Together we take risks, make mistakes, laugh, push ourselves, and revel in the grace and beauty of sports. Who wins? Who cares? We're playing with, not against each other, using each other's accomplishments to inspire.

14    At its best competition is not divisive but unifying, not hateful but loving. Like other expressions of love, it should not be avoided simply because it has been misunderstood.

## WRITING PROMPTS

1. What does Nelson say is wrong with our current definition of "competition," and what is her preferred meaning?

2. In what ways do men and women differ in the way they compete? Which way does Nelson prefer?

3. What examples does the author include from professional sports for women?

4. What responsibilities does Nelson say adult athletes have to children regarding competition?

5. How do you define "competition," and do you consider yourself a competitive person?

6. Should children be encouraged to be competitive? Why or why not?

---

## DRUGS

### Gore Vidal

1    It is possible to stop most drug addiction in the United States within a very short time. Simply make all drugs available and sell them at cost. Label each drug with a precise description of what effect—good and bad—the drug will have on the taker. This will require heroic honesty. Don't say that marijuana is addictive or dangerous when it is neither, as millions of people know—unlike "speed," which kills most unpleasantly, or heroin, which is addictive and difficult to kick.

2    For the record, I have tried—once—almost every drug and liked none, disproving the popular Fu Manchu theory that a single sniff of opium will enslave the mind. Nevertheless, many drugs are bad for certain people to take and they should be told why in a sensible way.

3    Along with exhortation and warning, it might be good for our citizens to recall (or learn for the first time) that the United States was the creation of men who believed that each man has the right to do what he wants with his

own life as long as he does not interfere with his neighbor's pursuit of happiness (that his neighbor's idea of happiness is persecuting others does confuse matters a bit).

4    This is a startling notion to the current generation of Americans. They reflect a system of public education which has made the Bill of Rights, literally, unacceptable to a majority of high school graduates (see the annual Purdue reports) who now form the "silent majority"—a phrase which that underestimated wit Richard Nixon took from Homer, who used it to describe the dead.

5    Now one can hear the warning rumble begin: if everyone is allowed to take drugs everyone will and the GNP will decrease, the Commies will stop us from making everyone free, and we shall end up a race of Zombies, passively murmuring "groovy" to one another. Alarming thought. Yet it seems most unlikely that any reasonably sane person will become a drug addict if he knows in advance what addiction is going to be like.

6    Is everyone reasonably sane? No. Some people will always become drug addicts just as some people will always become alcoholics, and it is just too bad. Every man, however, has the power (and should have the legal right) to kill himself if he chooses. But since most men don't, they won't be mainliners either. Nevertheless, forbidding people things they like or think they might enjoy only makes them want those things all the more. This psychological insight is, for some mysterious reason, perennially denied our governors.

7    It is a lucky thing for the American moralist that our country has always existed in a kind of time-vacuum: we have no public memory of anything that happened before last Tuesday. No one in Washington today recalls what happened during the years alcohol was forbidden to the people by a Congress that thought it had a divine mission to stamp out Demon Rum—launching, in the process, the greatest crime wave in the country's history, causing thousands of deaths from bad alcohol, and creating a general (and persisting) contempt among the citizenry for the laws of the United States.

8    The same thing is happening today. But the government has learned nothing from past attempts at prohibition, not to mention repression.

9    Last year when the supply of Mexican marijuana was slightly curtailed by the Feds, the pushers got the kids hooked on heroin and deaths increased dramatically, particularly in New York. Whose fault? Evil men like the Mafiosi? Permissive Dr. Spock? Wild-eyed Dr. Leary? No.

10    The Government of the United States was responsible for those deaths. The bureaucratic machine has a vested interest in playing cops and robbers. Both the Bureau of Narcotics and the Mafia want strong laws against the sale and use of drugs because if drugs are sold at cost there would be no money in it for anyone.

11    If there was no money in it for the Mafia, there would be no friendly playground pushers, and addicts would not commit crimes to pay for the next fix. Finally, if there was no money in it, the Bureau of Narcotics would wither away, something they are not about to do without a struggle.

12    Will anything sensible be done? Of course not. The American people are as devoted to the idea of sin and its punishment as they are to making money—and fighting drugs is nearly as big a business as pushing them. Since the combination of sin and money is irresistible (particularly to the professional politician), the situation will only grow worse.

## WRITING PROMPTS

1. What solution does Vidal suggest for the drug problem the United States faces, and why does he assure readers it will work?

2. What are some other outcomes of his proposed solution?

3. Does Vidal believe the American public will buy into his solution? Why or why not?

4. The author argues his point using an analogy. What is it, and do you think this analogy is convincing? Why or why not?

5. What do you think the government should do about the drug problem?

6. Do you think we will ever win the war on drugs? Why or why not?

---

## I HAVE A DREAM

### Martin Luther King, Jr.

1    Five score years ago, a great American, in whose symbolic shadow we stand, signed the Emancipation Proclamation. This momentous decree came as a great beacon light of hope to millions of Negro slaves who had been seared in the flames of withering injustice. It came as a joyous daybreak to end the long night of captivity.

2    But one hundred years later, we must face the tragic fact that the Negro is still not free. One hundred years later, the life of the Negro is still sadly crippled by the manacles of segregation and the chains of discrimination. One hundred years later, the Negro lives on a lonely island of poverty in the midst of a vast ocean of material prosperity. One hundred years later, the Negro is still languishing in the corners of American society and finds himself an exile in his own land. So we have come here today to dramatize an appalling condition.

3    In a sense we have come to our nation's capital to cash a check. When the architects of our republic wrote the magnificent words of the Constitution and the Declaration of Independence, they were signing a promissory note to which every American was to fall heir. This note was a promise that all men—yes, black men as well as white men—would be guaranteed the unalienable rights of life, liberty, and the pursuit of happiness.

4    It is obvious today that America has defaulted on this promissory note insofar as her citizens of color are concerned. Instead of honoring this sacred

obligation, America has given the Negro people a bad check, a check which has come back marked "insufficient funds." But we refuse to believe that there are insufficient funds in the great vaults of opportunity of this nation. So we have come to cash this check—a check that will give us upon demand the riches of freedom and the security of justice. We have also come to this hallowed spot to remind America of the fierce urgency of *now*. This is no time to engage in the luxury of cooling off or to take the tranquilizing drugs of gradualism. *Now* is the time to make real the promises of Democracy. *Now* is the time to rise from the dark and desolate valley of segregation to the sunlit path of racial justice. *Now* is the time to open the doors of opportunity to all of God's children. *Now* is the time to lift our nation from the quicksands of racial injustice to the solid rock of brotherhood.

5    It would be fatal for the nation to overlook the urgency of the moment and to underestimate the determination of the Negro. This sweltering summer of the Negro's legitimate discontent will not pass until there is an invigorating autumn of freedom and equality; 1963 is not an end, but a beginning. Those who hope that the Negro needed to blow off steam and will now be content will have a rude awakening if the nation returns to business as usual. There will be neither rest nor tranquility in America until the Negro is granted his citizenship rights. The whirlwinds of revolt will continue to shake the foundations of our nation until the bright day of justice emerges.

6    But there is something that I must say to my people who stand on the warm threshold which leads into the palace of justice. In the process of gaining our rightful place we must not be guilty of wrongful deeds. Let us not seek to satisfy our thirst for freedom by drinking from the cup of bitterness and hatred. We must forever conduct our struggle on the high plane of dignity and discipline. We must not allow our creative protest to degenerate into physical violence. Again and again we must rise to the majestic heights of meeting physical force with soul force. The marvelous new militancy which has engulfed the Negro community must not lead us to a distrust of all white people, for many of our white brothers, as evidenced by their presence here today, have come to realize that their destiny is tied up with our destiny and their freedom is inextricably bound to our freedom. We cannot walk alone.

7    And as we walk, we must make the pledge that we shall march ahead. We cannot turn back. There are those who are asking the devotees of civil rights, "When will you be satisfied?" We can never be satisfied as long as the Negro is the victim of the unspeakable horrors of police brutality. We can never be satisfied as long as our bodies, heavy with the fatigue of travel, cannot gain lodging in the motels of the highways and the hotels of the cities. We cannot be satisfied as long as the Negro's basic mobility is from a smaller ghetto to a larger one. We can never be satisfied as long as a Negro in Mississippi cannot vote and a Negro in New York believes he has nothing for which to vote. No, no, we are not satisfied, and we will not be satisfied until justice rolls down like waters and righteousness like a mighty stream.

8       I am not unmindful that some of you have come here out of great trials and tribulations. Some of you have come fresh from narrow jail cells. Some of you have come from areas where your quest for freedom left you battered by the storms of persecution and staggered by the winds of police brutality. You have been the veterans of creative suffering. Continue to work with the faith that unearned suffering is redemptive.

9       Go back to Mississippi, go back to Alabama, go back to South Carolina, go back to Georgia, go back to Louisiana, go back to the slums and ghettos of our northern cities, knowing that somehow this situation can and will be changed. Let us not wallow in the valley of despair.

10      I say to you today, my friends, that in spite of the difficulties and frustrations of the moment I still have a dream. It is a dream deeply rooted in the American dream.

11      I have a dream that one day this nation will rise up and live out the true meaning of its creed: "We hold these truths to be self-evident, that all men are created equal."

12      I have a dream that one day on the red hills of Georgia the sons of former slaves and the sons of former slaveowners will be able to sit down together at the table of brotherhood.

13      I have a dream that one day even the state of Mississippi, a desert state sweltering with the heat of injustice and oppression, will be transformed into an oasis of freedom and justice.

14      I have a dream that my four little children will one day live in a nation where they will not be judged by the color of their skin but by the content of their character.

15      I have a dream today.

16      I have a dream that one day the state of Alabama, whose governor's lips are presently dripping with the words of interposition and nullification, will be transformed into a situation where little black boys and black girls will be able to join hands with little white boys and white girls and walk together as sisters and brothers.

17      I have a dream today.

18      I have a dream that one day every valley shall be exalted, every hill and mountain shall be made low, the rough places will be made plain, and the crooked places will be made straight, and the glory of the Lord shall be revealed, and all flesh shall see it together.

19      This is our hope. This is the faith with which I return to the South. With this faith we will be able to hew out of the mountain of despair a stone of hope. With this faith we will be able to transform the jangling discords of our nation into a beautiful symphony of brotherhood. With this faith we will be able to work together, to pray together, to struggle together, to go to jail together, to stand up for freedom together, knowing that we will be free one day.

20      This will be the day when all of God's children will be able to sing with new meaning

My country, 'tis of thee,
Sweet land of liberty,
   Of thee I sing:
Land where my fathers died,
Land of the pilgrim's pride,
From every mountainside,
   Let freedom ring.

21    So let freedom ring from the prodigious hilltops of New Hampshire. Let freedom ring from the mighty mountains of New York. Let freedom ring from the heightening Alleghenies of Pennsylvania. Let freedom ring from the snowcapped Rockies of Colorado. Let freedom ring from the curvaceous peaks of California.

22    But not only that. Let freedom ring from Stone Mountain of Georgia. Let freedom ring from Lookout Mountain of Tennessee. Let freedom ring from every hill and molehill of Mississippi. From every mountainside, let freedom ring.

23    When we let freedom ring, when we let it ring from every village and every hamlet, from every state and every city, we will be able to speed up that day when all of God's children, black men and white men, Jews and Gentiles, Protestants and Catholics, will be able to join hands and sing in the words of the old Negro spiritual, "Free at last! Free at last! Thank God almighty, we are free at last!"

## WRITING PROMPTS

1. What is King's dream for the future?

2. Is there any evidence in this piece of writing (which was originally a speech) that King is a religious person? Are there parts that you can "hear" as spoken language? Which parts?

3. Do you think King's use of repetition is effective as a persuasive technique? What are some examples of this repetition?

4. What are some examples of metaphor? Do such comparisons help you visualize King's message?

5. From what you know about the civil rights movement in America, why do you think this speech was so well received at the time? Why do you think it has been labeled by critics as one of the best speeches ever given?

6. Do you think King's dream has come true? If not fully true, has any part of his dream been realized?

---

You've seen the definition of rhetorical modes (organization patterns) and many examples of paragraphs and essays that capture the essence of those patterns. Now it's time to try your hand/pen at writing an essay. To refresh your memory, here is a very brief description of those modes:

- You use *narration* to tell someone a joke or to talk or write about an event in your life that made a difference—your first kiss, your senior prom.
- You use *description* to detail with sensory words (those words that derive from the senses: sight, smell, sound, taste, touch) some person, place, or thing—your dorm room, your grandmother.
- You use *exemplification* to support your statements. For example . . .
- You use *process* when you give directions—how to boil water, how to fix a drippy faucet, how to get to my house.
- You use both *comparison* and *contrast* when you explain the similarities and differences between two persons, places, or things—a Ford Mustang and a Chrysler LeBaron; your two sisters.
- You use *classification* and *division* to break down or to put together different items—classify horses into Arabians, mustangs, and quarter horses; divide cars into sports cars, vans, and utility vehicles.
- You use *cause* and *effect* to explain how you earned an "A" in a particular course and then used that "A" to claim expertise in that course to someone else.
- You use *definition* to make sure that anyone reading your work understands what you mean when you use the term.
- You use *argument* to present a rational logical reason for accepting your point of view, and you use *persuasion* to appeal to the reader's emotion.

In the following examples, the controlling idea is *fast food*. Each of the rhetorical devices is used as a way to develop the thesis. Remember, a thesis must have two parts: a topic and the author's point of view (the "because" clause).

*Narration:* "Ray Kroc was a clever entrepreneur who saw McDonald's potential."

This thesis lets a writer tell the story about Ray Kroc and his business ideas. Note the author's point of view through words, *clever entrepreneur*, which focus the narrative. Every body paragraph used in an essay with this thesis *must* help the reader see Kroc as a *clever entrepreneur*. The conclusion will make the point that the clever entrepreneur must be multitalented.

*Description:* "The fast-food chains in America have unique characteristics in their architecture."

This thesis lets the writer describe the various establishments and the *unique characteristics* of their architectural styles. Each body paragraph will describe a particular restaurant and what makes it different from the other chains as well as what makes it unique.

*Exemplification:* "The food at Burger King is much more interesting than that at McDonald's."

Here the author will use examples to show why Burger King has more interesting food. She may write about flame broiling, the ability to choose toppings, the variety in the menu. And she will probably define the term *interesting!*

*Process:* "There is a way to order a healthful meal at McDonald's."

In this sentence, the writer makes an assumption: much of McDonald's food is unhealthful—that is the point of view. The process of ordering a healthful meal can be explained in the body of the essay after the writer looks at the unhealthful aspects. This conclusion can encourage readers to be selective when they visit a McDonald's.

*Comparison:* "Although fast-food chains like Wendy's and Burger King feed America's passion for fast food, Wendy's menu choices are better than those offered by Burger King."

Here the writer must first show that *passion for fast food.* What rhetorical mode would you use to support that statement? Next, you must decide if you will compare and contrast by using point by point or by using the block method. The body paragraphs could consider how the menus of these fast-food restaurants are similar in their limited food offerings; they are alike in that they feed huge numbers of Americans every day; they are alike because they offer consistent quality all across the country. The writer must also determine the standards by which to judge the menus before identifying both menus and how they meet those standards. The standards might be variety, cooking method, freshness, taste, and nutrients. The conclusion could speculate about why these chains appeal to such a broad group of people and sum up why one is better than the other.

*Classification and division:* "If you work in a fast-food restaurant, you will see three negative types of fast-food eaters: the gorger, the French fry lover, and the slob."

Within this type of organization, the essay's introduction contains the thesis, and body paragraphs are descriptive of each type of diner. The conclusion could consider how these three might behave in a fine-dining establishment.

*Cause and effect:* "Why have hamburger chains become such successes in America?"

With this thesis, the writer must show the success of this type of business. Then the essay would look at the reasons for this success: Americans like consistency in their products, Americans like quick service and imme-diate gratification, and Americans have the income to eat at these types of restaurants. Each reason can be the topic of each body paragraph and be supported with statistics, personal experience, and observation. The con-clusion can restate the thesis.

> *Definition:* "Fast food in America means too much fat in the food and on our bodies."

Here the writer identifies the fast-food restaurants that are found just about everywhere and then divides the body of the essay into two parts, *fat in the food* and *fat on our bodies*, to provide an extended in-depth look at what the term means. The conclusion can speculate about future conse-quences if this definition is true.

> *Argument:* "We can cure Americans' addictions to unhealthful fast food by changing the menus, advertising diet and health concerns with present fast foods, and opening alternative fast-food restaurants that cater to health food addicts."

Although this thesis statement does not have a "because" clause, the direction of the writing is clear. The thesis statement will appear in the introduction and will be followed by three body paragraphs supporting the three parts of the thesis and followed by a conclusion that might call for Americans to wake up and demand better food in fast-food restaurants.

## EXERCISE

You've now become familiar with the organization patterns most com-monly used in writing. Now it's time for you to try them out. Before writing a full essay, try the following exercise: Write a thesis statement using each of the rhetorical modes that will demonstrate how you would organize a complete essay on the topic of "A Holiday in My Country."

Narrative and the point to be made (tell a story):
Description (describe a person, place, or thing):
Exemplification (give an example):
Process (how to):
Compare (similarities):
Contrast (differences):
Classification (types of):
Division (parts of):
Cause (why does_____happen?):
Effect (the results of _____are):
Definition (what does it mean?):
Argument:

**Tips for Drafting on the Computer**

- Typing your first draft on a computer gives you the chance to add new ideas, to move ideas as you write, and to have a clean copy of your thoughts.
- Triple-space your drafts, print them, and, as you read your work, make notes for revision.
- Save your drafts as you write new ones. You can then compare them for organizational patterns, details, and direction.
- When you have finished your draft, you can pull the first sentences of paragraphs to form an outline that will show how your essay is supporting your thesis.
- Pay attention to the messages your computer gives you. Many programs will question stylistic usage and spelling as you work, and other programs will give you analyses of areas that can be improved.
- The Search and Replace function is a wonderful way to get rid of words or phrases you should be trying to delete in your writing (very, it is, there is, a lot, etc.).
- Use the spell checker, but be aware it will not correct homonyms, words that are wrongly used (except in place of accept), missing plurals, or verb endings. You must proofread your final version.

## EXERCISE

Taking the controlling ideas and the topic, "A Holiday in My Country," write a paragraph for each of the rhetorical devices.

Using the work you have already done for the topic "A Holiday in My Country," write an essay developing a thesis statement, writing an introductory paragraph, using three or more of the rhetorical modes as development paragraphs for your thesis statement, and finishing with a concluding paragraph.

# CHAPTER 12

# Responding to Text

As we have suggested before, most of the writing you do in college involves responding to material you have read and/or has been lectured about in class. In Part II we discussed the five levels of reading. The fifth level, the creative level, involves responding to text. Here we introduce you to the methods most commonly used when responding to the writing of others: summary, paraphrase, quotation, analysis, and response.

## SUMMARY

*Summarizing* is the process of shortening or condensing a reading selection. Because summary will always be a part of analysis (the writer must assume the reader has not read the piece being analyzed), let's take a look at the six steps necessary for writing a summary:

1. Read the passage carefully.
2. Reread. This time divide the passage into sections or stages of thought and label each one. Underline key ideas and terms.
3. On a separate sheet of paper, write one-sentence summaries of each stage of thought or, if appropriate, of each paragraph.
4. Write a topic sentence—a one-sentence summary of the entire passage. The topic sentence should express the central idea of the passage as you have determined it from the preceding steps. You may find it useful to keep in mind the information contained in the lead sentence or para-graph of most newspaper articles—the *what, who, why, where, when,* and *how* of the matter. In the case of persuasive passages, summarize in a sentence the author's conclusion. For descriptive passages, indicate the subject of the description and its key feature(s).
5. Write the first draft of your summary by combining the topic sentence with the information from step 3. Eliminate repetition and combine sentences for a smooth and logical flow of ideas.

6. Revise your summary, inserting transitional words and phrases where necessary to ensure coherence. Check for style. Avoid a series of short, choppy sentences. Check for grammatical correctness, punctuation, and spelling.

When you summarize an entire reading selection, you are expected, first, to identify the author and the title of the selection. You can choose from among many different introductions to indicate the author and title:

- (The author) states in (title of essay) that . . .
- (The author), in (title of essay), shows that . . .
- In (title of essay), (the author) writes that . . .
- As (the author) says in (title of essay) . . .
- The main idea of (the author's essay) is that . . .

Many verbs can introduce an author's idea depending on the author's intention and your emphasis. "The author says (or writes) . . ." after the second sentence becomes boring. Consider the following verbs as you write a summary:

## Some Verbs to Consider When Summarizing

| | | | |
|---|---|---|---|
| acknowledge | contend | imply | recommend |
| admit | emphasize | indicate | remark |
| advise | endorse | insist | reveal |
| advocate | establish | intimate | show |
| affirm | examine | maintain | state |
| argue | explain | note | stress |
| ask | explore | observe | suggest |
| assert | expose | point out | uncover |
| assume | express | proclaim | underline |
| believe | find | propose | underscore |
| claim | focus on | question | unveil |
| concede | highlight | reason | voice |
| conclude | identify | recognize | write |
| confess | illustrate | | |

You read the essay, "Why Isn't Pete Rose in the Hall of Fame?" by John Fleeger in Chapter 11. Here is a student's summary of Fleeger's essay. Note that she names the author and the title of the essay in her first sentence:

In John Fleeger's essay, "Why Isn't Pete Rose in the Hall of Fame?" Fleeger expresses his opinions about Pete Rose not being allowed in the National Baseball Hall of Fame. Fleeger argues that Pete Rose had dedication and enthusiasm for the game of baseball, established himself as the all-time best batter, established himself as the all-time best hitter in baseball, was a member of two championship teams, and set and tied several major league and team records. The author believes that Pete Rose is being treated unfairly by not being put into the National Baseball Hall of Fame.

The writer uses the present tense when she writes about Fleeger, which acknowledges that Fleeger's ideas continue to exist even though the essay is finished. Also note that when the writer first names the author, she includes the full name. After that, you can refer to the author by last name only. (*Never* refer to authors by their first names unless you are personally acquainted with them.)

## EXERCISE

Read the following essay, "A Polish American Speaks Up: The Myth of the Melting Pot" by Barbara Mikulski. Following the six-step process just outlined, write a short paragraph summarizing Mikulski's essay. Be sure to include the essay title (enclosed within quotation marks) and the author's full name in your first sentence, which will also include the thesis. Be prepared to read your summary to your classmates and see how they have summarized the article.

### A POLISH AMERICAN SPEAKS UP: THE MYTH OF THE MELTING POT
#### Barbara Mikulski

1    America is not a melting pot. It is a sizzling cauldron for the ethnic American who feels that he has been politically extorted by both government and private enterprise. The ethnic American is sick of being stereotyped as a racist and dullard by phoney white liberals, pseudo black militants and patronizing bureaucrats. He pays the bill for every major government program and gets nothing or little in the way of return. Tricked by the political rhetoric of the illusionary funding for black-oriented social programs, he turns his anger to race—when he himself is the victim of class prejudice. He has worked hard all of his life to become a "good American"; he and his sons have fought on every battlefield—then he is made fun of because he likes the flag.

2    The ethnic American is overtaxed and underserved at every level of government. He does not have fancy lawyers or expensive lobbyists getting him tax breaks on his income. Being a home owner he shoulders the rising

property taxes—the major revenue source for the municipalities in which he lives. Yet he enjoys very little from these unfair and burdensome levies. Because of restrictive eligibility requirements linked either to income or "target areas," he gets no help from Federal programs. If he wants to buy in the "old neighborhood" he cannot get an FHA loan. One major illness in his family will wipe him out. When he needs a nursing home for an elderly parent, he finds that there are none that he can afford nor is he eligible for any financial assistance. His children tend to go to parochial schools which receive little in the way of government aid and for which he carries an extra burden. There is a general decline of community services for his neighborhood, e.g., zoning, libraries, recreation programs, sanitation, etc.

3      His income of $5,000 to $10,000 per year makes him "near poor." He is the guy that is hurt by layoffs, tight money that chokes him with high interest rates for installment buying and home improvements. Manufacturers with their price fixing, shoddy merchandise and exorbitant repair bills are gouging him to death. When he complains about costs, he is told that it is the "high cost of labor" that is to blame. Yet he knows he is the "labor" and that in terms of real dollars he is going backwards.

4      The ethnic American also feels unappreciated for the contribution he makes to society. He resents the way the working class is looked down upon. In many instances he is treated like the machine he operates or the pencil he pushes. He is tired of being treated like an object of production. The public and private institutions have made him frustrated by their lack of response to his needs. At present he feels powerless in his daily dealings with and efforts to change them.

5      Unfortunately, because of old prejudices and new fears, anger is generated against other minority groups rather than those who have power. What is needed is an alliance of white and black; white collar, blue collar, and no collar based on mutual need, interdependence and respect, an alliance to develop the strategy for a new kind of community organization and political participation.

## WRITING PROMPTS

1. What does Mikulski claim needs to happen politically for all racial and ethnic groups together?
2. For what reasons does she believe ethnic Americans are unfairly treated?
3. Why is the ethnic American "near poor"?
4. Do you agree with Mikulski that white-collar workers are in worse shape politically and economically than new immigrants and members of various minority groups? Why or why not?
5. What solutions can you suggest so that everyone gets a fair share of federal and state government assistance?

# PARAPHRASE

*Paraphrasing* restates a reading passage in your own words while preserving the writer's intended meaning and tone. When you paraphrase, you translate the author's ideas into your own words. Whereas summarizing is a shortened version of the original passage, paraphrasing may be as long as (or even longer than) an author's words if a student paraphrases an entire work. You might want to paraphrase to clarify an author's ideas, to refer to the essay at different points in your writing, to indicate to your readers exactly which of the author's ideas you are responding to, or to introduce or support an idea you want to discuss in your paper.

The following guidelines will help you:

1. Once you have read the passage, think carefully about what the author means.
2. Check the definitions of any words you don't know.
3. Rephrase the passage by taking notes and then closing the book and writing what you remember.
4. Rewrite the passage substituting synonyms for each word. Make sure your rewritten passage makes sense to you.

Here is a paragraph written by Brent Staples from his essay "Role Models, Bogus and Real":

### Role Models, Bogus and Real

Why then the constant "role model" morality play? Partly it's the archaic notion that athletes need to be paragons of virtue and temperance, exempt from moral flaw. Beyond that, I think, lies a deeper and more unfortunate presumption: that only stars can affect children's lives for the better, that the mere mortals among us are powerless to guide, shape, or enlighten. The sadness here is that the reverse is true. The only legitimate "role model" is the person whom children can see, feel, and interact with in their daily lives.

Brent Staples, "Role Models, Bogus and Real"

And here is a paraphrase of that paragraph:

Why do we continue to think of role models as "perfect" people? We still believe in the ancient idea that athletes must represent the ideal hero who makes no mistakes. And even worse, we continue to believe that only famous people can positively influence children and that we "normal" people are incapable of influencing our offspring. In reality, the only true "role models" are those with whom children come in contact all the time.

## EXERCISE

Read the following paragraph and see if you can write a paraphrase, following the guidelines given.

### The Fashionable Body

One of the boldest ways to interfere with human anatomy is to mold the skull. Among tribes who practice this art, it is part and parcel of a child's upbringing. It calls for special skills and has traditionally been a mother's duty and, we may presume, pleasure. The first provocation for a mother's pinching and kneading her baby's skull was perhaps its yielding softness. Playful handling developed into more conscious efforts to deform, and racial and aesthetic concepts were added later. Thus, broad heads were broadened, flat noses flattened closer to the face, a tapering occiput sharpened to a point—a shape associated today with humanoids from outer space. These spectacular forms were achieved with the aid of contraptions no more ingenious than a common mousetrap.

From Bernard Rudolfsky's "The Fashionable Body"

# QUOTATION

*Quoting* involves taking direct words from the author's work, enclosing those words in quotation marks, and crediting the author for his words. The following guidelines will help you decide when a direct quote is more appropriate than a paraphrase:

- The author's words are so impressive or so clever that to put them in your own words would lessen their impact.
- The author's words are so precise that to put them in your own words would change their meaning.
- The author's words are so concise that you would need twice as many words to paraphrase the passage.

If you choose to quote from an essay, you will want to incorporate the quote into your writing. To do that you may introduce or in some way lead into the quotation so readers know whose words are being quoted or can understand why the quotation is important. You can comment on the quotation after you have included it so readers understand its connection to other points you made in the paper.

When you are working with only one source (in other words, responding to one piece of writing), you have been told to name the author and the name of the work in the first sentence of your response. When you are working with more than one source, be sure to cite (or give credit to) the source from which you got the material.

The general rule governing when you should cite is to give credit for *any* information that does not come from your own head (except when the information is general or common knowledge). You must cite the source when you quote material (and you must quote the material *exactly* as it appears in the text from which you get it). You must cite the source when you paraphrase material from another source. And you must cite the source when you summarize material from another source. In fact, you must cite the source whenever you take *any* idea from another source.

In the following assignment, we ask you to cite the source from which you have gotten the information. If you do not name the author and title in the first body of your response, you must name the author and the page number at the end of the cited material. You will then include the complete source—author, title, and publishing information—at the end of the paper in a list of works used.

# EXERCISE

Read the following excerpt from Rachel Carson's *The Sea Around Us:*

### The Sea Around Us

Nowhere in all the sea does life exist in such bewildering abundance as in the surface waters. From the deck of a vessel you may look down, hour after hour, on the shimmering disks of jellyfish, their gently pulsating bells dotting the surface as far as you can see. Or one day you may notice early in the morning that you are passing through a sea that has taken on a

brick-red color from billions upon billions of microscopic creatures, each of which contains an organic pigment granule. At noon you are still moving through red seas, and when darkness falls the waters shine with an eerie glow from the phosphorescent fires of yet more billions and trillions of these same creatures.

And again you may glimpse not only the abundance but something of the fierce uncompromisingness of sea life when, as you look over the rail and down, down into water of a clear, deep green, suddenly there passes a silver shower of finger-long fishlets. The sun strikes a metallic gleam from their flanks as they streak by, diving deeper into the green depths with the desperate speed of the hunted. Perhaps you never see the hunters, but you sense their presence as you see the gulls hovering with eager, mewing cries, waiting for the little fish to be driven to the surface.

Rachel Carson, *The Sea Around Us*

1. Write a one- or two-sentence summary of the passage. Do not quote any of the passage directly. At the end of your summary, include a citation.

2. Write a paraphrase of the passage—again, do not quote directly—and include the same citation.

3. Write a brief passage that does quote Carson and use the citation.

# ANALYSIS

You've learned how to read analytically. You've learned how to mark texts; you've learned how to question the text; you've learned how to outline, to map, and to summarize—all methods involved in analyzing text. You've learned how to summarize, to paraphrase, and to quote material from text. Now it's time for you to learn how to write this information in a coherent manner. The following information will show you different ways to write about what you read.

To *analyze* means "to separate into basic parts or basic principles so as to determine the nature of the whole; [to] examine methodically" (*The American Heritage Dictionary*, 48). When you read and break apart a piece of writing, you are analyzing that passage. When you summarize, you are simply giving an account of material read, but when you analyze you try to teach your readers how authors achieve their effects or how well the authors have used evidence, or what evidence they have omitted, or what initial assumptions their arguments are based on. Similarly, writing an essay about what you did on your summer vacation or writing an essay defining the gasoline tax, would constitute a report and would not involve analysis. But when you write an essay about the function of school vacation or on the purposes of the gasoline tax, you are writing an analysis. Summary, paraphrase, and quotation are all devices that can be used in your analyses, but they become a part of the analysis.

Next let's look at two essays: "The Voyage Continues" and "In Defense of Deer Hunting and Killing." Read the two essays and then see how two writers summarized those essays. Then take a look at how they analyzed the same essays and note the differences between the summaries and the analyses.

## THE VOYAGE CONTINUES

### *Boston Globe* editorial

1    The epic film "Titanic" has heightened interest in what should happen to the artifacts strewn about the world's most famous watery grave. The man who found the Titanic 12 years ago, Robert Ballard, has long held that the wreck should be left alone in the silence of the deep. To salvage the wreck, Ballard argues, is akin to grave robbery.

2    Not so, says Ballard's nemesis, George Tulloch, who has been down to the Titanic four times and has brought up innumerable plates, cups, glasses, bits of luggage, and mail, all of which are being shown at exhibitions around the world.

3    Their quarrel, Ballard says, is between the salvager and the scientist. It is a quarrel that does not begin and end with the Titanic. There is a court battle pending on who has the right to salvage material from the torpedoed Lusitania, another famous Ballard find, and there are other challenges in court to determine who can exploit the lost treasures of the sea.

4    The Titanic is so famous that it would be shocking to see its contents auctioned off to the highest bidder—which, except for some lumps of Titanic coal, Tulloch has not done. But huge shipments of Chinese porcelain—some of considerable value from the Ming Dynasty—are regularly brought up from centuries-old wrecks in the China seas and sold at auction houses around the world. Coins, jewels, gold crosses from the Spanish Main also find their way onto world markets. No one seems to mind.

5    Supreme Court Justice Stephen Breyer, referring to a California sunken ship case, asked the key question: "When does the passage of time in and of itself become an abandonment?" If some hooligans dig up a freshly dug grave, it is a shocking and vile act of desecration. If learned scientists do the same thing to a pharaoh's crypt in the Egyptian desert, it is called archeology. Of course, there is a difference of motive, but it is time that distinguishes desecration from science.

6    A shipwreck is not, strictly speaking, a grave in the sense that anyone planned it as a final resting place. Shipwrecks have from time immemorial given back to the land lost artifacts—whether they be strewn on some leeward shore or carefully brought up and preserved, like Cyprus's Kyrema ship, which sank 2,300 years ago, or Stockholm's 17th century "Vasa," which was dredged from the harbor remarkably intact. On both, lives were undoubtedly lost.

7    It would be to everyone's benefit if Tulloch, after some tacky commercial fits and starts, kept to his stated purpose of preserving Titanic artifacts in a dignified manner. It might even have been best of all if Ballard's dream of an undisturbed resting place were preserved so many fathoms down. But mankind's curiosity will lead to hidden spaces behind the moon and down into the darkest deeps, and what will be found there will be brought back, sometimes for the sake of knowledge, sometimes for commercial gain, as it has always been and always will be.

### Summary of "The Voyage Continues"

The January 4, 1998, *Boston Sunday Globe's* editor claims in "The Voyage Continues" that people are curious and will always be fascinated with what might be hidden in space or at the bottom of the ocean—specifically in sunken ships—and these individuals will always find a way to retrieve their treasures. The editor refers to an ongoing argument between two men involved with one particular sunken ship, the *Titanic.* He/She urges one of these men, George Tulloch, to adhere to his original purpose in the retrieval of *Titanic's* artifacts—for preservation and display, not for commercial gain. Mr. Tulloch has made four dives so far and up until now has merely displayed his finds; however, he is being criticized by the person who discovered this ship twelve years ago, Robert Ballard, who wants the wreck and its contents to be left untouched. The editor tells us that similar quarrels between a "scientist" and a "salvager" have occurred over the contents of other sunken ships, and a court decision is pending over the *Lusitania,* another ship Ballard located. Valuable items from other ships' remains have been auctioned off, and no one has protested; in addition, items from ships that sank centuries ago have been preserved as a means of learning about the past. The editor states that time seems to make the difference in our acceptance of hauling belongings out of ocean crypts: "Time . . . distinguishes desecration from science." This same writer suggests that Tulloch should preserve the *Titanic's* contents in order to provide the dead passengers with dignity.

### Analysis of "The Voyage Continues"

Beginning with the contrasting views between a "scientist" and a "salvager" over the retrieval of items from the sunken ship *Titanic,* an editor for the January 4, 1998, *Boston Sunday Globe* admits in the final lines of "The Voyage Continues" that people will always want to explore space and ocean floors, with many individuals wanting to bring back their treasures. Then moving from this general concept, this editor urges the "salvager" of the *Titanic,* George Tulloch, to adhere to his original purpose "of preserving Titanic [sic] artifacts in a dignified manner" rather than seeking commercial gain from what he finds during his dives. To be convincing, the editor includes the views of both Tulloch, who so far has displayed rather than auctioned off most of the items retrieved during his four explorations of the *Titanic,* and Robert Ballard, the scientist who discovered this ship twelve years ago. Initially the editor seems to side with Ballard: By reminding us that the *Titanic* is really a grave, he/she appeals to our emotions and makes us aware of Ballard's respect for the deceased. Use of the terms "scientist" for Ballard and "salvager" for Tulloch also implies favoritism of Ballard's beliefs. But beginning with paragraph 3, we realize that the editor's view is more liberal. By drawing comparisons with other sunken vessels, this writer shows that people seldom care if items are retrieved from ocean-bottom ships; even in cases in which priceless possessions from Spanish and Chinese ships have been sold, no one objected. The passage of time seems to cause the difference in attitude, according to the editor, and by including a quotation from Supreme Court Justice Stephen Breyer, he/she demonstrates the difficulty in deciding the appropriate time to begin searching an unplanned ocean grave, thus helping us to understand Tulloch's argument. If a respected scholar such as Justice Breyer wonders when the time is right to touch these submerged belongings, how can anyone else be expected to make the proper decision? This editor saves his/her major claim (in the form of a request) for the final paragraph. Although admitting Ballard's argument is perhaps the preferred of the two, as previously mentioned, the writer shows acceptance of the retrieval of items from the *Titanic* but urges Tulloch to preserve those items for educational purposes rather than making a profit from them.

# IN DEFENSE OF DEER HUNTING AND KILLING

## Arthur C. Tennies

1    "You hunt deer?" When I nodded, my shocked colleague went on to say, "Why my whole image of you has been shattered. How can you kill such beautiful creatures?"

2    And so would many others who view the deliberate killing of deer as brutal and senseless. Such people look upon the hunter as a barbaric hangover from the distant past of the human race. To my colleague, the incongruity between the barbarism of hunting and normal civilized conduct was made more intense because I was a minister. How could I as a minister do such a thing?

3    I thought about that as I drove through the early morning darkness toward the southeastern part of Chenango County. It was a little after 5 A.M. I had gotten up at 4, something I do only in the case of an emergency or when I am going deer hunting. It was cold, the temperature in the 20s. With the ground frozen, it would be too noisy for still hunting until the sun had had a chance to thaw the frost. So it would be wait and freeze. My first thoughts about why I would hunt deer had nothing to do with the supposed barbarism of it. I thought of the foolishness of it. Wait hour after hour in the cold, feet numb, hands numb, and small chance of getting a deer.

4    I was going to hunt on Schlafer Hill on the farm of Pershing Schlafer. My choice of a place to hunt had been determined by the party permit that three of us had, which allowed us to kill one other deer of either sex besides the three bucks that we were allowed.

5    I thought about the party system in New York, the way the state controlled the size of the deer herd. The state is divided into about 40 deer-management areas. The state biologists know how many deer each area can handle, how many deer can feed on the browse available without destroying it. If there are too many deer, they will kill the plants and bushes upon which they depend. The next step is starvation for large numbers. Since the deer's natural preda-tors were wiped out by the first settlers, the only control over their numbers now is starvation or hunting. Thus, so many deer must be killed in a deer-management area. A certain number will be killed by motor vehicles. The biol-ogists can estimate how many will be killed on the highways and also the number of bucks that will be killed. The surplus is taken care of by issuing a set number of party permits.

6    I have often marveled at the state biologists, their skill and knowledge in managing the deer herd. As I have pondered the problems of people—poverty, starvation, injustice, and all the others—and our frantic and often futile efforts to solve these problems, I have thought, "If only we could manage the problems of people as well as we can manage a deer herd."

7    Then I realize the great difference between the two. People are not for being managed. We manage people only by robbing them of the right to choose—and the most brutal attempts to manage are ultimately frustrated by the obsti-nacy of human nature, its refusal to be managed. A handful of biologists may

manage a deer herd and a handful of scientists may be able to put a man on the moon, but no handful of planners will ever manage the human race. And so I thought again, as the car rushed through the dark, that all of our modern management techniques would fail to come up with quick and perfect solutions to the problems of people.

8      While the darkness was still on the land, I reached the bottom of the hill. I parked the car, put on my hunting shirts, took my gun, and began the long climb up the hill. For a few minutes I could hardly see the old road. Slowly my eyes adjusted to the dark. The trees in the woods on my right took shape and the road became clearly visible. I walked with greater confidence. As I climbed, the sun climbed toward the horizon to drive away the night. By the time I reached the top of the hill, the half-light of dawn had arrived.

9      Off to my left in the valley were lights and people, but on the hill I was alone. It had not always been that way. Once long ago the hilltop had been filled with people. Following the Revolution, white settlers came into Chenango County, and some had chosen that hilltop. I stopped and tried to picture in my mind their struggles to turn the forest into farms. I looked at the stone fence off to my right and wondered how many days it had taken to clear the stones from the fields and pile them into a fence. The fence ran into the woods. Woods again where there had been fields or pasture.

10      I looked on down the road. I could not see the old barn down farther on the left, the only structure from the past still standing. All of the others were gone. I had seen before the crumbling stone foundations where once houses had stood. A half century or more ago, if I had stood there, I could have seen a half-dozen houses. Smoke would have been rolling out of chimneys as fires were started to chase away the cold. Men and boys would have been outside and in the barns getting the chores done. Women and girls would have been busy in the kitchen getting breakfast. The hill would have been full of people and empty of deer. Now it was empty of people and full of deer.

11      On that hill and on many others, like Bucktooth Run, is a story of the hand of a man upon the land. Before the settlers came, only a few deer lived on that hill, far fewer than there are now, because the forests provided little food for the deer. The few were soon killed off. While the disappearance of the deer was the fault of the early hunters, there was more to it than that. There was no room for deer on the hill. As my Dad, who was born on Bucktooth Run, has pointed out:

12      *These farms were worked over morning and evening by the farmers and their sons and their dogs going after the cattle. The wood lots were worked over during the winter for wood. The larger tracts of woodland were worked over by the lumbermen.*

13      *Then came World War I and the years following. Large areas of land were abandoned. Where once the woods resounded to the call of "Come, boss'" and in the winter the woods echoed the ring of the ax and whine of the saw, the sylvan stillness, for months on end, was unbroken by the human voice. Where once the deer had no place to rest from the constant activity of the*

*busy farmer and lumberman, there was now a chance for the deer to carry on its life in solitude.*

14   *In 1900 there were no deer in much of New York. The state did some stocking shortly after that, and deer came across the border from Pennsylvania. The abandoned land provided a perfect setting for the deer and there were no natural enemies to stay their march. By the late 1930s, most of the state had a deer season.*

15   So as the farmers retreated from the hill, the deer returned. Now the hill is perfect for deer . . . some fields used by farmers, like Pershing, for pasture and hay, good feed for deer most of the year . . . brush for browse during the winter . . . woods, old and new, mixed with evergreen for cover. And most of the year, except during the hunting season, only a few people make their way to the top of the hill.

16   Let nature have her way and in another century nature's hospitality to the deer will be withdrawn as large trees again cover the hill as they did before the first white settlers came.

17   I started to walk again and felt like I had left one world, the world of technology and entered another one, the world of nature. The rush to get things done had to give way to waiting and patience, for nature does not live at our frantic pace. The noise had to give way to quietness, for only in silence can one get close to a deer.

18   But the ground crunched beneath my feet, so I walked to a likely spot and waited. Two hours and nothing, except a few small birds. Finally the cold forced me to move. I walked and found some fresh tracks in the snow. I followed them for an hour, trying to get close enough to the deer wandering in the woods ahead of me. But I was too noisy. All I saw was the flash of brown bodies and white tails too far ahead. I waited some more. No luck. I walked to another spot where deer cross.

19   I waited another hour. It was warmer now. Finally a deer appeared, a head above a rise. It started to come nearer. Then it stopped. Something was wrong. It decided to leave. As it turned, my gun came up and I shot. It lurched sideways, kicking and thrashing, disappearing under a pine tree. I walked to the spot. No deer. I went around the tree and there it lay. In a second it was dead.

20   I looked down at the deer, a button buck, and I thought: This is the way of nature, one creature feeding on another. Thousands of years ago our forebearers survived in just this way. They killed, gutted, butchered, and ate. Now we buy in a supermarket or order in a restaurant.

21   The first task was to gut the deer, kind of a messy process. I got my knife out, turned the deer on his back, and slit him open. I spilled the guts out on the ground. I saved the liver and heart: even though the heart had been mangled by the bullet. I cut through the diaphragm and pulled the lungs out.

22   Then I was ready to pull the deer back to the car. It was 3 P.M. when I got to the car. Time yet to hunt for a buck, so I dumped the deer into the trunk. Back up to the hill, but no luck. As night came on, I got back to the car. I tied the deer on the top of the trunk and started for home.

23   As I drove toward home, I had a sense of satisfaction. I had fitted myself to nature's way and had been successful. For a few short hours, I had marched to the beat of nature's drum, not that of our modern world. At least for me, the barrier that we had built between nature and us could still be breached.

24   Back in suburbia, I parked the car in the driveway and went into the house. Jan and the kids were eating supper.

25   "Any luck?" Jan asked.

26   "Not much."

27   "Did you get a deer?" one of the kids asked.

28   "Yup, a button buck."

29   Then the excited rush to see the deer, and the thrill of shared success.

30   After that there was the tedious job of butchering. I hung the deer in the garage. Then I began the task of skinning it. Once skinned, I cut the deer in half, then in quarters. Jan washed the blood and hair off of each quarter. I then cut the quarters into smaller pieces, and then Jan sliced it up into roasts, steaks, and stew meat.

31   "Can you get the brains out?" Jan wanted to know.

32   "I can try, but why the brains?"

33   "We always had brains when we butchered."

34   So I went to work to cut the skull open and get the brains out. When I got back into the kitchen, Jan had a skillet on.

35   "Let's have some venison," she said.

36   "At this hour?"

37   "Sure."

38   So she had some brains and I had some liver. As I sat there weary, eating the liver, I thought, "This meat is on the table because I put it there." By our efforts, and ours alone, it had gone from field to table.

39   "Don't you want some brains?" Jan asked.

40   "No."

41   "But they are a delicacy."

42   "That may be, but I'll stick to the liver."

43   As I went to sleep that night I thought: "I suppose that no matter what I say, a lot of people will never understand why I hunt deer. Well, they don't have to, but let only vegetarians condemn me."

### Summary of "In Defense of Deer Hunting and Killing"

Thesis: In his essay "In Defense of Deer Hunting and Killing," author Arthur C. Tennies argues that deer hunting is not brutal and senseless, but is a pastime which is environmentally sound because it controls surplus growth and fits in with the *natural cycle*, and sensible because it is an inexpensive way to provide for oneself.

### Summary

At the beginning of the essay, Tennies indicates that he is a minister. This fact surprises a colleague, who could not understand how a person in such a civilized role could be engaged in an act as barbaric as hunting. Tennies describes how uncomfortable it is to go deer hunting on a frosty morning at 5 A.M., and the last thing he is thinking about is the barbarism of his activity.

Tennies mentions a party system in his hunting area under which a limited number of hunting permits are distributed, depending on the surplus deer in the area. Tennies adds that since the deer's natural predators in the area have been killed off, a certain number of deer actually need to be hunted or else the surplus deer will simply die off through starvation in competition for limited food. According to Tennies, human beings, with their overpopulation, could take a lesson from the efficient way in which deer populations are managed through hunting.

Tennies describes the peacefulness of the hill on which he is hunting. He thinks about how the hill, which used to be full of settlers, is now absent of people and beginning to be overtaken by trees. The hill now has a balance between pasture for feeding and trees for shelter, just right for deer. Tennies feels he is part of a natural cycle of creatures surviving off one another.

Tennies is successful in hunting the deer. He talks about how he uses all parts of the deer for food. His wife even eats the brains. Tennies feels that his deer hunting is essentially no different from picking up meat in the supermarket and that for this reason only vegetarians have a right to condemn his hunting.

### Analysis of "In Defense of Deer Hunting and Killing"

Arthur C. Tennies, author of "In Defense of Deer Hunting and Killing," begins his defense of deer hunting by presenting the opposing viewpoint—that the hunting of such beautiful animals is brutal and senseless. But in the same paragraph, he mentions that he is a minister. This fact makes the reader, who might agree with the opposition, to be at least more open to what Tennies has to say. If someone as "good" as a minister can hunt, then it might be acceptable after all. Tennies also stresses how uncomfortable it is to get up to go hunting at 5 A.M., as if to suggest that if all he really wanted to do was to perform a cruel act, he would not go to such trouble as he does.

Tennies provides evidence that his practice of deer hunting is, in fact, a sensible, environmentally sound one. He describes a party system in his hunting area under which a limited number of hunting permits are distributed depending on the surplus deer in the area. Tennies adds that since the deer's natural predators in the area have been killed off, a certain number of deer actually need to be hunted or else the surplus deer will die off through starvation in competition for limited food. In order to strengthen this argument, he points to his fellow human beings, a species for whom things are going badly through lack of management.

Tennies describes the peacefulness of the hill on which he's hunting. By thinking about this hill, which was once covered with settlers but is now returning to forest, he seems to be arguing in an indirect way that there is a very natural order to his being on the hill hunting at this time. A balance between pasture left behind by the settlers, now to be used for food by the deer, and just the right number of trees for shelter, has created a situation on the hill where the deer are thriving. Tennies seems to feel that he plays a very natural role in this picture by keeping the delicate balance under control with the hunting of an occasional deer. The author even states that he is part of a natural cycle of creatures surviving off one another.

Tennies is successful in hunting the deer. He talks about how he uses all parts of the deer for food, with even the brains being used. This incident impresses upon the reader how much cheaper it must be to hunt a deer than to buy meat in a supermarket. Tennies argues that hunting deer is an all-around more natural, normal way to provide for oneself than going to a market. The fact that so much of the deer is used demonstrates that there is a purpose to hunting deer, that it is not a purely cruel act.

---

Remember Fleeger's essay about Pete Rose? Take a look at how our student analyzed that essay. After her opening paragraph of summary, she continues:

Fleeger writes that the reason why Pete Rose is banned from professional baseball is because Pete Rose bet on baseball. Even though betting on baseball is a violation of major-league rules and is punishable by lifetime banishment from baseball, Rose did not offer any evidence that he bet on any baseball game. The author also writes that in 1991, the Hall of Fame Committee, along with Fay Vincent, the commissioner of baseball, decided that as long as a player is banned from baseball, he is ineligible for Hall of Fame selection. Fleeger states that many people disapproved of the new rule and believed that Vincent encouraged the new rule specifically to make sure Pete Rose could not be considered for selection.

The author writes that Rose's only hope of making the National Baseball Hall of Fame depends on his being readmitted to baseball by the commissioner. Fleeger states that Rose has admitted to gambling on football and on horse races, but never on the game Rose loves. Rose has spent time in counseling to help deal with his betting problem. Fleeger writes that he doesn't understand why a player who once gambled is any worse than the many players who have tested positive for drugs. The players who tested positive for drug use are only suspended from the game for a period of time and given a chance to recover. The author also mentions how Babe Ruth was an adulterer and a serious drinker, but still holds a place in the Hall of Fame. Mickey Mantle and Willie Mays were barred for

## Formula for Writing a Successful Essay

- Read the essay once for the general idea; write the author's claim (thesis statement) when you finish.

- Read the essay a second time—this time analytically.
  Mark your text—write between the lines.
  Make notes that answer "the journalist's six."
  Who is the author? (his/her background)
  Why does he/she believe what he/she does (his/her biases)?
  When was the essay written (Is the message still true today?)?
  What is the main point? (the thesis)
  How does the author support his thesis? (examples, reasons, statistics, testimony, definitions, or analogies)
  Where in the essay do the thesis statement and different types of support appear?

  Note anything pertinent about the level of language, sentence structure, or tone.

- Write a scratch outline of your analysis, including answers to the above questions.

- Write your opening paragraph. Include in this paragraph the following:
  Author's full name
  Title of essay (in quotation marks)
  Original source (if known)
  Date first published
  Author's thesis
  Summary of article
  General evaluative comment (What do you think of his argument? Does she convince you?)
  Your thesis (your opinion about the topic and why)

- Write your successive paragraphs.
  Refer to the author by last name, use pronouns, or occasionally "this author" or "the writer."
  Use present tense verbs unless referring to a particular historical incident.
  Include analysis verbs (i.e., says, states, claims, believes, cites, informs, expresses, presents, points out, discusses, describes, illustrates, examines, suggests).
  Include a restatement of the claim before your evaluation (a transition paragraph).
  Evaluate the argument. (An alternate method of analysis would be to evaluate each point you make throughout your essay.)

being employees of an Atlantic City casino, but even this decision was eventually overturned.

Now it's time to try a full analysis of an essay. The following article, "The Hall Is Now Ready for Rose" by Phil Mushnick, appeared in *TV Guide*, (August 29, 1998). Following all the directions you've been given in this chapter, write an analysis. For additional guidance, refer to the *Formula for Writing a Successful Essay*.

## THE HALL IS NOW READY FOR ROSE
### Phil Mushnick

1     The time has come to induct Pete Rose into the Baseball Hall of Fame. Right now. Before the wind shifts to cleanse the air. The "character" issue—weighing a man's integrity in addition to his statistics—apparently no longer applies.

2     Several weeks ago, New York Yankees owner George Steinbrenner, who has pleaded guilty to felonies and was twice suspended from baseball, was elected to the board of the Hall of Fame. So much for standards. Pete Rose belongs in the Hall, effective immediately.

3     Not long ago in this space, I stated the case against Rose's inclusion. I cited examples of how his lifestyle had not changed from one that made him a problem gambler, an associate of scam artists in the sports collectibles industry and a fellow who would eventually do time for tax evasion while serving an open-ended ban from baseball.

4     The former Charlie Hustle has sustained his image as Charlie the Hustler. He has appeared on a TV show that primarily promotes sports gambling. He is still eager to sell his autograph on shopping networks that push dubious "limited edition" junk. His actions suggest, at least, "Sleazy, as charged."

5     But Steinbrenner's election to the Hall's board is such an outrage, such a contradictory declaration from a shrine that claims to place a premium on integrity, that Rose's sins are rendered irrelevant.

6     Let us not forget that Steinbrenner's first suspension from baseball came after he pleaded guilty to two felony counts, one for trying to buy influence in the Richard Nixon White House, the other for obstructing an investigation into his illegal donations to Nixon's reelection campaign.

7     Steinbrenner's second suspension came eight years ago when, in his haste to discredit Yankee outfielder Dave Winfield, he enlisted the help of Howard Spira, a self-described gofer of Winfield's and a young man quickly identified as a pathetic soul with emotional problems.

8     You or I might have extended Spira five bucks for a sandwich and sent him on his way. Steinbrenner extended Spira a check for $40,000 in exchange for dirt on Winfield. When Spira pressured him for more, Steinbrenner called some friends at the FBI. The feds put Spira away for two years. Former MLB commissioner Fay Vincent considered the situation and ordered Steinbrenner to go away for two years, too.

9    And now Steinbrenner—the bully, the braggart, the ex-criminal—sits on the board of baseball's Hall of Fame, making this the proper time to induct Pete Rose.

10   But do us a favor, will ya, Pete? Leave your Hall of Fame plaque in Cooperstown, no matter how much it might fetch on the Home Shopping Network.

---

# RESPONSE

This level is fun. Up to this point, you have been asked to summarize and analyze essays. Now you have the chance to respond to the author and to what the author has had to say. Up to this point, you have referred only to the author using his name or third-person pronouns. Now you can have your say based on your own experience (personal or that of friends), books and articles you've read, movies you've seen, or shows you've watched on television. Now you have the chance to agree or disagree with, criticize, or evaluate the author's thesis.

This response requires that you create your own thesis statement and then support it with your experiences, stories, or criticisms. The purpose of this part of the analytical essay is to show your reader that you have understood the essay. You understand the author's thesis, and you are able to relate to it by providing examples from your own life experience.

You've read two essays about Pete Rose. You've seen how one student summarized and analyzed John Fleeger's essay, "Why Isn't Pete Rose in the Hall of Fame?" Now look at how that student responded critically to this essay:

When Fleeger writes, "Why is a player who once gambled any worse than the many players who have once been tested for drugs? He makes a good point. I can remember back to high school when some football players were caught drinking alcohol in school. These players were only suspended from playing one football game. Then there was another group of football players who tested positive for drugs and got kicked off the team. I don't understand because alcohol and drugs are illegal for these high school football players. What makes alcohol drinking so different from doing drugs? I think that the football players who were caught drinking deserve to be kicked off the team like the football players who tested positive for drugs. I clearly understand Fleeger's question.

I also believe that Pete Rose should be put into the Hall of Fame because like Fleeger said, Babe Ruth was a serious drinker and adulterer. Ruth still holds a place in the Hall of Fame. Mickey Mantle and Willie Mays worked for a casino. Both of these players still hold a place in the National Baseball Hall of Fame too. Since there has been no proof of Rose gambling on a baseball game, then Rose should be also put into the Hall of

Fame with the other players who were put there but convicted for something like Babe Ruth, Mickey Mantle, and Willie Mays.

Overall I like Fleeger's essay. Fleeger gave a lot of supporting details to back up his opinion about Pete Rose not being in the Hall of Fame. The part of the author's essay that convinced me that Rose should be put in the Hall of Fame was when the author wrote about Babe Ruth, Mickey Mantle, and Willie Mays. Pete Rose is no more guilty than Babe Ruth, Mickey Mantle or Willie Mays. Therefore I believe that Pete Rose should be put in the National Baseball Hall of Fame.

## EXERCISE

Reread John Fleeger's and Phil Mushnick's essays. You've written an analysis of "The Hall Is Now Ready for Rose." Now write a critical (or evaluative) response to that essay, given the material in Fleeger's essay and the student's response to that essay. It's your turn to speak!

# CHAPTER 13

# Revising and Editing

Y ou've learned the writing process. You've written a complete analysis and response to the Mushnick essay. You're now at the point where you're ready to examine your draft. Using the work you've written thus far on the Mushnick article, the summary, the analysis, and the response, let's take a look at how to begin the revision process.

## REVISING

The word *revise* stems from the Latin—*re-*(again) and *videre* (see). Thus, when you begin the process of revision, you are, in fact, looking again at your work in progress. At the beginning of Part III, we outlined the considerations that every writer must address when preparing to write. Those same considerations must now be readdressed at the revision stage. Most students think of revision simply as proofreading. But the revision process involves "re-seeing" two levels of concerns that we call high-order and low-order priorities. The four priority issues are thesis or focus, voice or audience, organization, and development.

### Thesis or Focus

Try writing a one-sentence summary of your work. What is the purpose of your essay? What is its essence? Does your paper have a clear focus and a central thesis? If so, move on to the next priority.

### Voice or Audience

To whom are you writing and is the level of language you are using appropriate to that audience? Remember, the level of diction you use when you write to your peers will differ from the level you use when you write to your little sister or brother and will differ from the level you use when you write to your professor. The ideal voice is universal; it is the voice that can be understood easily by everyone.

## Organization or Structure

Recall three terms as you begin the revision process at this level: *unity, coherence*, and *diction*. You've learned that each paragraph of a piece of work should contain a topic sentence and supporting material. You've also learned that each paragraph's topic sentence should relate directly to the thesis.

***Unity***   First check the *unity* of your essay. Does your first paragraph name the thesis? In fact, the first paragraph of an analysis/response essay should name two theses: the author's and yours. Do the topic sentences of the paragraphs that follow relate directly to or support the thesis? Now go one step farther. Examine each paragraph separately. Does each paragraph contain material that supports its topic sentence? An easy way to check the unity of your essay is to complete the following exercise.

## EXERCISE

*Unity and Coherence Outline*   At the top of a piece of paper, write your thesis statement. Under your thesis statement, write, in order, the topic sentences from each paragraph in your essay. Each topic sentence should support, in some way, the thesis statement, and each topic sentence should be a logical step forward in your argument. If a sentence seems out of place, either move it or take it, and the paragraph from which you took it, out of the essay. Once you have finished that exercise, go through your essay again, paragraph by paragraph, doing the same thing with the sentences in each paragraph. Does each sentence support the topic sentence? If not, take it out.

***Coherence***   The next step in the revision process involves the *coherence* of the writing. Does the writing flow? Are there smooth transitions between paragraphs? Notice that in the last paragraph, I say, "First . . ." I then begin this paragraph with "The next step . . ." I am trying to lead you through this piece of writing by giving you stepping-stones. (And you should be looking for "And finally . . ." when you will know we're almost through!)

**Transitional words** and ideas fall into the following categories:

- Linking similar ideas: *and, again, also, another, besides, for example, in other words, similarly, too*
- Linking dissimilar or contrasting ideas: *although, but, however, conversely, on the contrary, yet, still*
- Indicating cause and effect: *as a result, because, consequently, for this reason, since, so, therefore*

- Indicating time and place: *across, at present, before, eventually, finally, first, here, next, second, lastly*
- Indicating example or summary: *as a result, for example, in conclusion, in other words, to sum up*

**Diction**  Now look at the *diction*, or word choice, in your writing. Remember that you are not writing for yourself; you are writing for an audience that might not share the same meanings of words that you do. Does your writing contain precise, specific words rather than vague words that might be misunderstood? Does your writing contain verbiage—too many words to express an idea? Do not write "In my opinion, I think . . ." Clearly, what you write is your opinion and you think it! You needn't be redundant, and you needn't use four words to express one. "Due to the fact that" means "because" or "since." "In the near future" means "soon." "At the present time" means "now."

## Development

The revision you do at the organizational level may suggest further development of some main ideas. Here you might want to return to freewriting for five to ten minutes to record everything that comes to mind about a particular aspect of your paper. (Do you see how the writing process can be recursive?)

# EDITING

After addressing the global issues in your paper, your emphasis will shift from the draft as a whole to lower order concerns that include sentence structure, punctuation, and usage. Does the paper contain incomplete or incorrect sentences? Are the sentences too long or too choppy? Try writing awkward sentences another way.

Get rid of tag statements, sentences that begin with "it is," "there is," and the like. Starting a sentence with a tag tells the reader that the two most important words in the sentence are the subject "it" and the verb "is" rather than putting the true subject at the beginning, followed by a strong verb. For example, "It is very probable that the intimidation of witnesses will result from such threatening remarks" becomes a much stronger sentence when written "Intimidation of witnesses probably will result from such threatening remarks" or, even better, "Such threatening remarks will probably intimidate witnesses." Remember that subject-verb-object is the most direct and clearest sentence pattern. Name the subject, use a complete and active verb, and state the obvious!

Most nouns that end in *-ment, -ion,* or *-ism* are words that can be more vigorously expressed as verbs, and changing those nouns to verbs will enliven your sentences. For example, "A conscientious teacher's satisfaction is incomplete unless she reaches a full realization of her goals" becomes much more readable and interesting if rewritten as "A conscientious teacher is dissatisfied unless she reaches her goals."

Once you've accomplished the steps we've outlined, you're ready for the final editing of your work. Refer to the Editing Checklist in Chapter 20 of the handbook (Part IV) for the steps you should take to ensure that your paper is free of the most common errors we find in college writing.

# PEER REVIEW

We have not written much about peer review, but we believe it is a major component of the writing process. Whether your classmates, spouse, roommate, significant other, or someone on the dorm floor reads your paper, peer review can be extremely valuable. Remember, usually you are writing for a universal audience; thus your peers can often offer insights you might not consider. (We, the authors, *never*—well, hardly ever—allow work to leave our desks until someone else has read over the piece, both for content and grammar.) We include a Peer Review Sheet on the next page as an example of the kinds of issues you should address when reading another's work. Note that we have included boxes for you to check regarding grammar, spelling, typing errors, and sentence clarity. We suggest you tell the author that those errors exist, but we do not recommend that you edit or proofread the paper; that is the job of the writer. Your instructor may have his or her own form for you to follow; if not, here's one for you to try.

# PROOFREADING

The very last step before you turn in your final paper is to proofread for typing errors. Try reading your paper backward, from end to beginning, word for word, to pick up any typing errors you might have made on your final draft.

Finally, most of the writing you will do for your college courses, with the exception of reports, will consist of summarizing and analyzing works that you will read for those courses. We firmly believe that if you follow the directions we've laid out for you, you will not only do well in this course, you will succeed in all your college courses that require writing of any kind.

## Peer Review

Note: Leave revising to the writer. Do not mark up the draft unless the writer approves. Rather, put your comments on this page or use additional paper if necessary.

WRITER:

TITLE OF PAPER:

CRITICAL READER (Print name):

DATE:

Write down what you understand the thesis (arguing for or against what) to be. Is the thesis clearly stated? If not, what do you suggest?

Which terms should the writer more clearly define? Is there any ambiguity about the writer's meaning? If so, where?

Write down additional opposing views or concessions the writer should consider addressing.

Follow the writer's logic by writing down the main points of the argument.

Point to any place where evidence is insufficient to back up the main points. In other words, which part of the argument is weak?

What seems particularly good?

Write down the conclusion. Does it follow logically from the argument and evidence?

_____

❏ Grammar ❏ Spelling ❏ Typos ❏ Sentence Clarity

## Common Revision Symbols

| | | | |
|---|---|---|---|
| ABB | abbreviation | // | faulty parallelism |
| AD | adjective/adverb | PARA | paraphrase |
| AGR | agreement | REF | unclear pronoun reference |
| AWK | awkward | RUN-ON | run-on (fused) sentence |
| CAP | capitalization | SLANG | slang |
| CASE | pronoun case | SP | spelling |
| CLICHÉ | cliché | SUB | subordination |
| CO | coordination | SUM | summarize |
| COH | coherence | T | tone |
| CS | comma splice | TRANS | transition |
| D | diction | U | unity |
| DEF | define | VERB | verb form |
| DM | dangling modifier | VT | verb tense |
| FRAG | sentence fragment | WV | weak verb |
| INTRO | weak introduction | .?! | period, question mark, exclamation point |
| LC | lowercase letter | , | comma |
| MM | misplaced modifier | ; | semicolon |
| NO , | no comma | ' | apostrophe |
| ¶ | paragraph | " " | quotation marks |
| | | ^ | insert |

# PART IV
# A Handbook for Writers

Why do we include a fundamental review of grammar and mechanics in a college textbook? By now, you must have recognized that the teaching of English is cumulative but also redundant. You are always improving your skills, but you are finding that the way in which you are being taught seems repetitive. The basic rules of writing are, in reality, fairly simple. Perhaps the most famous book on writing, Strunk and White's *Elements of Style*, is only eighty-five pages long. The study of grammar is the study of the language of English; without knowledge of the words that govern language, we are unable to communicate the knowledge you need to improve your writing.

No doubt you were taught grammar early, in elementary school. You were taught that nouns named persons, places, and things. You were taught that verbs represented action. And you were taught that a sentence had to have a subject, a verb, and a complete thought. You were taught the principal parts of speech, and you were probably taught their functions in a sentence. But notice that I have purposely used the verb *taught*, and I have used the passive voice. You were taught; the action was done to you: I purposely did not say that you learned; you performed little or no action. We learn when we are ready to learn, when we are motivated to learn. We teach grammar in college because we believe many of you, by the time you come to college, want to improve your communication skills; thus you are ready to communicate with the faculty about writing, and in order to do that you must be able to speak the language. So, let's get to it!

Your instructor will give you a diagnostic pretest to see how much you remember from the teaching you received in elementary, middle, and high school. After you've finished the grammar section of the book, you'll take a posttest to see how much you've learned this time. We suspect you'll be pleasantly surprised at your progress.

# CHAPTER 14

# Parts of Speech: Form and Function

Parts of speech refer to the forms of words in a sentence. Can you name them? There are eight parts of speech:

_____        _____

_____        _____

_____        _____

_____        _____

Let's briefly review them.

## NOUNS

Can you name the nouns in this sentence?

Mary bought clothes when she went to New York.

_____        _____        _____

*Mary* names a person; *clothes* name a thing; *New York* names a place. Thus nouns are naming words that name persons, places, and things (and ideas like truth, beauty, love).

Try writing three sentences with three nouns in each sentence.

1. _____

2. _____

3. _____

With a partner, each of you take a paragraph that you've written, either in class or as homework, and underline all the nouns that appear in your paragraph. Then trade papers with your partner and see if your partner agrees with the underlinings you've made.

# PRONOUNS

What are the pronouns in this sentence?

Mary bought clothes for herself, her brother, his wife, and their children.

_____  _____  _____  _____

*Herself* renames Mary; *her* renames Mary; *his* renames brother; *their* renames brother and wife.

Thus pronouns are renaming words that take the place of the nouns for which they stand. Think how ridiculous this sentence would sound if no pronouns existed:

Mary bought clothes for Mary, Mary's brother, Mary's brother's wife, and Mary's brother's and his wife's children!

Pronouns are classified as personal, possessive, reflexive, relative, interrogative, demonstrative, and indefinite. But you don't need to remember those names. You do need to familiarize yourself with the following list of pronouns, so you will recognize them:

- Personal: *I, me, you, he, him, she, her, it, we, us, they, them*
- Possessive: *My, mine, your, yours, his, her, hers, its, our, ours, their, theirs*
- Reflexive: *Myself, yourself, himself, herself, itself, ourselves, yourselves, themselves*
- Relative: *Who, whom, which, that, whose, what*
- Interrogative: *Who, whom, which, whose, what*
- Demonstrative: *This, these, that, those*
- Indefinite: *All, another, any, anybody, anyone, both, each, either, everybody, everyone, few, many, most, neither, nobody, none, no one, one, other, several, some, somebody, someone, such*

# ADJECTIVES

Can you name the nine adjectives in this sentence?

For herself, Mary bought a lime green linen dress, white canvas sandals, and a white cashmere sweater.

_____  _____  _____

_____  _____  _____

_____  _____  _____

*A, lime, green,* and *linen* all describe dress; *white* and *canvas* describe sandals; and *a, white,* and *cashmere* describe (or modify) sweater.

Adjectives tell *what kind, which one,* or *how many* and usually precede the noun or pronoun they describe.

*A, an,* and *the,* usually called articles or determiners, are also adjectives. They signal that a noun will follow.

# VERBS

Find the four verbs in this sentence:

> Mary spent all her money in two days while she was in New York, so she drove home sooner than she expected.

_____    _____    _____    _____

Most verbs explain what the subject of the sentence does or has. These words are called *action verbs* because they express physical actions like *spent, drove,* and *expected.* Action verbs may also express mental actions like *think, believe,* or *know.* We will explain the fourth verb in this sentence momentarily.

Action verbs are easy to spot because they tell what is being done and are really the heart of the sentence. If you can *do* it, the word will be an action verb.

> Mary is very tall, and she is overweight.

_____    _____

Did you find two verbs?

*Linking verbs* do not show action; they specify what the subject is. They link the subject to another word or words that rename or describe the subject. Thus *is* links Mary with *tall* (an adjective that describes Mary) and *overweight* (another adjective). *Is, are, was, were, am, be, being,* and *been* are linking verbs. *Appear, become, feel, grow, look, remain, seem, smell, sound, stay* and *taste* are action or linking verbs depending on how they are used in a sentence:

Active:    Buds *appear* quickly on the trees after a good rain.

Babies *feel* objects as a way of learning what the objects are.

Did you *smell* those lilies?

Come here and *taste* this fudge; it's delicious.

Linking:    Diane *appeared* nervous when she walked to the podium to give her speech.

John *feels* sick every time he eats peanut butter and banana sandwiches.

You *smell* good; what perfume are you wearing?

Diet candy *tastes* awful.

Remember what we said about the difference between active and linking verbs? Can you explain the difference between the use of the verbs in these two sets of examples?

Mary *had worn* a size 10 when she was a teenager. Now she *is wearing* a size 14.

Finally, *helping verbs* help the main verb by establishing the time of the action. That time—present, past, or future—is called *tense*. Helping verbs are used with main verbs to establish the tense of the sentence. They include the *to be* linking verbs as well as *can, will, shall, should, could, would, may, might,* and *must, do, does, have, has,* and *had*.

Caution: Any word ending in *-ing* must have a helping verb in order to be a verb. (The *-ing* form of a word functions as a noun if it is *not* preceded by a helping verb. When *-ing* words function as nouns, they are called *gerunds*.)

Buying clothes is Mary's favorite pastime.

Here *buying clothes* is the subject of the sentence and acts as the verb. Mary is buying a lot of clothes shows *buying*, an *-ing* word, with a helping verb; *buying*, therefore, is a verb.

A verb form preceded by *to* is called an *infinitive* and functions as a noun, adjective, or adverb. It cannot function as the verb in a sentence.

I love to write.

*To write* is the object of the sentence.

# ADVERBS

We have two hints about adverbs. Because they already contain the word *verb*, their definition should be easy to remember. They describe verbs, adjectives, and other adverbs. And they often end in *-ly*. They answer the questions How? Where? When? Why? To what extent? and On what condition? Finally, *not* is an adverb.

Mary dresses beautifully; she always looks like a model.

_____    _____

Did you recognize the two adverbs that answer how and when?

# PREPOSITIONS

Find the four prepositional phrases and see what the sentence says without them.

On the way to New York, Mary drove through New Jersey and along the Hudson River.

_____        _____

_____        _____

Prepositions show the relationship between one noun or pronoun and another word in the sentence. Prepositional phrases (a preposition followed by a noun or pronoun) function as adjectives or adverbs, thus answering the same questions that adjectives and adverbs answer. In the sample sentence the phrases answer the questions When? and Where?

When we were in school (back in the Middle Ages), we had to memorize a list of prepositions. Here they are:

## Prepositions

| | | |
|---|---|---|
| about | between | past |
| above | beyond | since |
| across | by | through |
| after | concerning | throughout |
| against | down | to |
| along | during | toward |
| amid | except | under |
| among | for | underneath |
| around | from | until |
| at | in | unto |
| before | into | up |
| behind | like | upon |
| below | of | with |
| beneath | off | within |
| beside | on | without |
| besides | over | |

Hint: Many of these words will answer the question, What does a plane do to a cloud? Try it! Another hint: When asked to find subjects and verbs in a sentence, crossing out the prepositional phrases first will make your life much easier.

A final word of caution: Prepositional phrases _never_ (for your intents and purposes) function as subjects of sentences. For example:

Some of my brothers are doctors.

The subject is *Some*, not brothers, because brothers is the object of the preposition *of*.

# CONJUNCTIONS

Can you locate the three coordinating conjunctions in this sentence?

Mary and her brother met for lunch, and they had steamed shrimp, Caesar salad, and boiled lobster.

———————————  ———————————  ———————————

Coordinating conjunctions are easy. Just remember FANBOYS—For, And, Nor, But, Or, Yet, and So. These words join words or groups of words.

Correlative conjunctions are always used together: *either . . . or, neither . . . nor, both . . . and, not only . . . but also.*

Subordinating conjunctions are tough. We call them weasel words because they cause more trouble in student writing than any other part of speech. You really need to recognize and know these words because they lead to *fragments*, a major writing error. We'll talk much more about these conjunctions later, but for now, learn them:

## Conjunctions

| | | |
|---|---|---|
| after | inasmuch as | what |
| although | provided | when |
| as | since | where |
| as much as | than | which |
| because | that | while |
| before | though | who |
| how | unless | whom |
| if | until | whose |
| in order that | | |

Note that *after, before, since,* and *until* can also be prepositions depending on their use in the sentence; *how, when,* and *where* can be adverbs; and *that* can be a relative pronoun.

# INTERJECTIONS

Finally! Words or groups of words that express emotion are called interjections; they are interjected into the sentence to give emphasis. *Oh, hey, ouch,* and *ah* are all examples of interjections.

## Summary of Parts of Speech

| Noun | names a person, place, or thing | Mary, New York, clothes |
|------|--------------------------------|-------------------------|
| Pronoun | renames a noun | she, him, herself, this, who |
| Adjective | describes or modifies a noun or pronoun | green, linen, canvas, white |
| Verb | shows action, links, or helps another verb | bought, is, has been, feels |
| Adverb | describes a verb, adjective, or adverb | quickly, very, beautifully |
| Preposition | relates a noun or pronoun to another word | by, for, to, of |
| Conjunction | joins words or groups of words | FANBOYS, after, since |
| Interjection | expresses emotion | Gosh! Ouch! |

## EXERCISE

*To parse* means to break a sentence down by describing each word according to form, function, and syntax. In the blanks, name the part of speech of each word in the sentence—noun, pronoun, adjective, verb, adverb, preposition, conjunction, or interjection.

Example: The janitor washed the floor.

The      adjective

janitor      noun

washed      verb

the      adjective

floor      noun

1. Mary and her brother really enjoyed their lunch at the café.

Mary      _____

and      _____

her      _____

brother      _____

really      _____

enjoyed      _____

their              _____

lunch              _____

at                 _____

the                _____

café               _____

2. Wow! There are so many clothing stores in New York.

Wow!               _____

There              _____

are                _____

so                 _____

many               _____

clothing           _____

stores             _____

in                 _____

New York           _____

## EXERCISE

With a classmate, take a paragraph from one of your recent in-class or out-of-class writing assignments. Above each word in that paragraph, name the part of speech. When you have finished, trade papers with your partner to see if each of you has parsed the paragraph correctly.

## CHAPTER 15

# Sentence Patterns

An understanding of basic sentence patterns is essential to guide you in your understanding of our language and how it works. English uses four kinds of sentences: simple, compound, complex, and compound-complex.

## SIMPLE SENTENCES

A *simple sentence* contains a subject, a verb, and a complete thought, and that's all.

John scored the winning touchdown.

Simple sentences are also known as main or *independent clauses*; they can stand alone. (In other words, they make sense by themselves.) Sometimes you might be confused if you see a sentence beginning with a pronoun that refers to a sentence that came before it. For example:

John ran 30 yards. He scored the winning touchdown.

Although the second sentence needs the first sentence for context—you have to read the first sentence in order to know who *He* is—the sentence has a subject, a verb, and a complete thought.

## EXERCISE

Write a paragraph about a subject of your choice that includes at least five simple sentences.

_____

_____

_____

_____

_____

# COMPOUND SENTENCES

A *compound sentence* contains two or more independent clauses. In other words, a compound sentence is composed of two simple sentences joined together with a *coordinating conjunction* (FANBOYS).

> John ran 30 yards, and he scored the winning touchdown.

> John ran 30 yards and scored the winning touchdown.

The second sentence is not a compound sentence. It is an independent clause with a compound verb. We discuss punctuation later, but for now, note that two simple sentences joined together with a coordinating conjunction (FANBOYS) include a comma *before* the conjunction. There is no comma in the simple sentence.

Another way to join two independent clauses (or simple sentences) is to use a semicolon (;). A semicolon replaces a comma and any of the FANBOYS, but its use makes the connections between the two independent clauses more direct. Note the difference in tone between these two sentences:

> John ran 30 yards, and he scored the winning touchdown.

> John ran 30 yards; he scored the winning touchdown.

The first sentence adds a second idea to the first idea. The second sentence connects the two ideas and implies a direct relationship between the two ideas.

*Conjunctive adverbs*, which can be used with semicolons, emphasize the relationship between the two ideas.

> John ran 30 yards; moreover, he scored the winning touchdown.

Here are the common conjunctive adverbs:

## Conjunctive Adverbs

| | | |
|---|---|---|
| accordingly | however | nonetheless |
| also | incidentally | otherwise |
| anyway | indeed | similarly |
| besides | instead | specifically |
| certainly | likewise | still |
| consequently | meanwhile | subsequently |
| conversely | moreover | then |
| finally | nevertheless | therefore |
| furthermore | next | thus |
| hence | | |

When you use a conjunctive adverb after a semicolon, you *must* place a comma after the adverb.

## EXERCISE

Take the paragraph you just wrote in the last exercise, and see how many simple sentences you can combine with either FANBOYS or conjunctive adverbs. Remember how to punctuate those sentences.

# COMPLEX SENTENCES

A *complex sentence* contains an independent or main clause and at least one *subordinate* or *dependent clause*. Remember that an independent clause, a simple sentence, has a subject, a verb, and a complete thought; the sentence can stand alone. A subordinate or dependent clause contains a subject and a verb, but it does not contain a complete thought; this clause cannot stand alone (it makes no sense by itself); it depends on another independent clause to make sense.

Remember the weasel words, the *subordinating conjunctions?* See what happens to this sentence when I start playing around with subordinating conjunctions:

John ran 30 yards.

This sentence is a simple sentence, an independent clause. It can stand alone; it makes sense by itself. But look what happens when I add a subordinating conjunction, a weasel word.

After John ran 30 yards.   (fragment)

You should be saying, "So what happened? Finish the sentence." This dependent clause cannot stand alone and has just become a fragment. It depends on or must be connected to an independent or main clause in order to make sense.

After John ran 30 yards, he scored a touchdown.   (correct)

This sentence is a complex sentence because it contains an independent clause and a subordinate clause.

## EXERCISE

Take the paragraph you originally wrote and see how many sentences you can combine through subordination, making complex sentences with an independent and a dependent clause.

# COMPOUND-COMPLEX SENTENCES

As its name suggests, a *compound-complex sentence* contains at least two independent clauses and one dependent clause.

> After John caught the football, he ran 30 yards, and he scored the winning touchdown.

## EXERCISE

Now take three of your simple sentences and turn them into a compound-complex sentence.

### Summary

| | | |
|---|---|---|
| Simple sentence | one independent clause | John ran 30 yards. |
| Compound sentence | two independent clauses | John ran 30 yards, and he scored a touchdown. |
| Coordinating conjunctions | words that connect two independent clauses | For, And, Nor, But, Or, Yet, So (FANBOYS) |
| Subordinate clause | a dependent clause containing a subject and a verb that does *not* express a complete thought | After John ran 30 yards |
| Complex sentence | one independent and one or more dependent clauses | After John ran 30 yards, he scored a touchdown. |
| Subordinating conjunctions | words that connect dependent clauses to independent clauses | after, although, as, because, before, how, if, in order that, inasmuch as, provided, since, than, that, though, unless, until, when, where, while |
| Conjunctive adverbs | words used with a semicolon to emphasize the relationship between two ideas | accordingly, besides, certainly, consequently, finally, furthermore, hence, however, incidentally, indeed, likewise, meanwhile, moreover, nevertheless, |

| | | next, nonetheless, otherwise, similarly, specifically, still, subsequently, then, therefore, thus |
|---|---|---|
| Compound-complex sentence | two independent clauses and at least one dependent clause | Before John scored a touchdown, he caught a pass, and he ran 30 yards. |

## EXERCISE

Label the following sentences S (simple), CD (compound), CX (complex), or CC (compound-complex).

Willy Jack told her it was a stupid idea, but he had taken her picture when they crossed into Arkansas because he had seen a bar called the Razorback just across the highway and he wanted a beer (     ). They were twenty miles down the road when Novalee missed the camera and discovered [that] Willy Jack had left it in the bar (     ). She begged him to go back for it and he did, but only because he wanted another beer (     ). . . . Novalee felt warm and sticky (     ). She rolled down her window[,] and [she] let the hot outside air blast her in the face (     ).

From Billie Letts, *Where the Heart Is*

## EXERCISE

Take a paragraph from one of your written in-class or out-of-class essays and label the sentences according to their structure. If you find you are writing only one kind of sentence, see if you can rewrite your paragraph to include a variety of sentence structures.

# CHAPTER 16

# Pronoun Problems

## AGREEMENT

You learned in Chapter 14 that pronouns rename nouns. That seems simple enough, but, in fact, pronouns present challenges in terms of correct agreement and correct reference. The pronoun must agree either with its antecedent (the noun for which it stands) or with the verb.

Everybody went to their rooms after the fire drill.   (incorrect)

Is anything wrong with the sentence? Your teacher would tell you there is a pronoun agreement problem and write *agr* in the margin of your paper. Why? *Everybody* is a singular indefinite pronoun and the pronoun that follows it must also be singular. Thus the sentence should read:

Everybody went to his or her room after the fire drill.

Or, in order to simplify the his/her awkwardness:

The students went to their rooms after the fire drill.

Which sentence is correct?

Neither the coach nor the players are in the gym.

Neither the players nor the coach is in the gym.

Strangely enough, both are. When using *or, nor, either . . . or,* or *neither . . . nor,* the verb agrees with the noun closest to it. In the first sentence, because the noun, *players,* directly precedes the verb, the verb is plural whereas in the second sentence *coach* directly precedes the verb, so the verb is singular.

Each of those boys has a Mohawk haircut. They must be on the hockey team.

Here you have an example of a prepositional phrase (*of those boys*) following an indefinite singular pronoun (*each*). Do you remember the rule about prepositional phrases? A prepositional phrase can *never* function as the subject of a sentence. Thus *each* is the subject, and *has*, the verb, must agree with the subject.

> The soccer team has won every game this season.

> The soccer team have voted seven to three for Jim Larsen for their captain.

Both examples are correct. *Team* is called a collective noun and it can be considered either singular or plural. If you, the writer, are thinking of the individual members, you will use a plural verb; if you are thinking of the team as a unit, you will use a singular verb. The easiest way to deal with collective nouns is to always add the word *members*, which will then force you to use the plural verb. The following words are collective nouns: *army, audience, class, club, committee, crowd, faculty, group, jury, orchestra, team, troop.*

# REFERENCE

Here is a sentence I received from a friend of mine who is a movie producer. Do you see a problem here?

> More stars and studios alike love to be involved with projects like this, and they rarely come around.   (unclear)

Who or what does *they* refer to? Stars and studios? Or projects? I couldn't tell. My friend had a reference (*ref*) problem with the sentence that she needed to clarify.

> This weekend I planted dozens of daffodil bulbs and it strained my back. (unclear)

What strained my back? The bulbs? Probably not! What does *it* refer to? This sentence exemplifies an unclear reference and should be rewritten so the reader knows what *it* refers to.

# PRONOUN CASE

This example shows incorrect pronoun case:

> Who am I speaking to?   (incorrect)

The wrong form of the pronoun, *who*, is being used. The pronoun is the object of the preposition *to*, so it must be in the objective case. Thus the sentence should read,

> Whom am I speaking to?

or, to be absolutely correct,

> To whom am I speaking?   (correct)

# CASE

Pronouns function according to their position in the sentence; they can be in the *nominative case*, the *objective case*, or the *possessive case*. Nominative case pronouns function as subjects—*I* ran to the store—or subject complements (nouns or pronouns that follow linking verbs):

> Because I could not see the man's face, I was not sure *it was he* who knocked on my door.

Objective case pronouns function as objects, both objects of verbs:

> John caught the ball and *threw it* to Henry.

and most importantly, as objects of prepositions:

> Sarah sat *behind Nat and me* at the movies.

And possessive case pronouns show possession:

> That is my hat you're wearing.

Here is a review of the personal pronouns by case:

## Personal Pronouns

|  | *Nominative* | *Objective* | *Possessive* |
|---|---|---|---|
| first-person singular | I | me | my, mine |
| second-person singular | You | you | your, yours |
| third-person singular | He, she, it | him, her, it | his, her, hers, its |
| first-person plural | We | us | our, ours |
| second-person plural | You | you | your, yours |
| third-person plural | They | them | their, theirs |

Here, again, is the list of indefinite pronouns, those words that do not refer to specific nouns. Remember that some are singular and others are plural. Pronouns referring to them must agree.

## Indefinite Pronouns

| *Singular* | *Plural* | *Either* |
|---|---|---|
| another | both | all |
| anybody | few | any |
| anyone | many | some |

| Singular | Plural | Either |
|----------|--------|--------|
| each | several | none |
| either | | |
| everybody | | |
| everyone | | |
| neither | | |
| nobody | | |
| no one | | |
| one | | |
| somebody | | |
| someone | | |

## EXERCISE

Fill in the proper pronoun to agree with its antecedent.

1. Each of the women combed _____ hair before returning to the table.

2. Anybody should be allowed to express _____ opinion.

3. Neither of the students had the correct response to question 10 on _____ paper.

4. Does anyone here not know the combination to _____ locker?

5. Everybody has to have _____ books by tomorrow's class.

6. Either the players or the coach forgot to bring _____ whistle to the game.

7. Did somebody leave _____ high heels in the lounge?

8. Everyone on the boys' hockey team has _____ own workout.

9. One of the men brought _____ children to the museum.

10. Neither of the cars comes with _____ gas tank filled.

## EXERCISE

This exercise covers both pronoun-antecedent and subject-verb agreement. Fill in the blanks with the proper pronouns or verbs.

1. The number of murders in this state _____ been shocking.

2. Each of the terrorists _____ captured within 24 hours.

3. Not one of the PBS nature programs _____ shown dolphins on _____ program.

4. _____ everyone eaten _____ lunch?

5. Everyone on the team _____ been given _____ new uniform.

6. All of my sisters and my mom _____ going shopping on Saturday.

7. Neither Jeremy nor Bert _____ happy today.

8. Either my brothers or my sister _____ late every day.

9. Screeching down the street _____ two Mazda Miatas.

10. Each of the artists _____ _____ own show.

## EXERCISE

Choose the correct pronouns.

1. Do you know (who, whom) _____ made the team?

2. Joanie and (she, her) _____ took all the books back to the library.

3. We were the students (who, whom) _____ Mr. Babson chose to teach the class on manners.

4. (She, Her) _____ and (I, me) _____ studied together for the exam.

5. The match between Mark and (he, him) _____ will take place this afternoon at 1 P.M.

6. I haven't read as many history books as _____.

7. The class report was assigned to Bonnie and _____.

8. The school is famous because of _____ soccer players.

9. Mom was happy at _____ getting all A's this term.

10. That hat looks much better on you than _____.

# CHAPTER 17

# Punctuation

Punctuation clarifies meaning and allows writing to take on conversational tones. A *period* signifies a full stop—end of thought! A *semicolon* tells the reader to stop but understand that a closely related idea follows. Aside from the generally known uses of a *colon*, between the hour and the minute when writing time, between chapter and verse in the Bible, and after the greeting in business letters, a colon also tells the reader to "take note! A list follows." A *comma* tells the reader to pause, and *question marks* and *exclamation points* tell the reader how to inflect or read the sentence.

Consider the following:

A woman without her man is lost.

A woman, without her man, is lost.

A woman: without her, man is lost.

A woman without her man is lost?

A woman. Without her, man is lost!

Can you see how the punctuation changes the intention of the writer? Commas, apostrophes, and quotation marks seem to give students the most difficulty when they are editing their papers, so the rest of this chapter reviews the rules governing these punctuation marks.

## COMMAS

Commas are the cause of the most flagrant errors in writing—comma splices and run-on or fused sentences. A comma splice occurs when the writer puts a comma instead of a period, semicolon, or coordinating conjunction (remember the FANBOYS) between two complete thoughts. A run-on or fused sentence occurs when the writer neglects to put *any* punctuation between two complete thoughts.

For example,

My nose is running, I have a terrible cold;    [comma splice] or,

My nose is running I have a terrible cold.   [run-on]

Each sentence contains two complete thoughts or two independent clauses—my nose is running—and—I have a terrible cold. These two examples may be corrected in one of three ways: a period (My nose is running. I have a terrible cold.); a semicolon (My nose is running; I have a terrible cold.); or a coordinating conjunction (My nose is running, and I have a terrible cold.)

Note that when two complete sentences are joined by a coordinating conjunction, a comma must precede the conjunction. The comma marks the difference between a compound sentence—one that contains two complete thoughts—and a sentence with a compound verb. Note the following:

I love dancing, and I love socializing with friends.

This sentence contains two complete thoughts. But

I love dancing and socializing with friends

has one subject and two verbs. The first sentence is a compound sentence; the second sentence is a simple sentence with a compound verb and requires *no* comma.

Restrictive and nonrestrictive clauses have always been problematic. A restrictive clause is essential to the meaning of the sentence and, therefore, cannot be set off from the rest of the sentence by commas:

Cars that were built before 1970 do not have emission controls.

The clause, *that were built before 1970,* is essential to the meaning of this sentence and must not be set off with commas; otherwise the sentence would read *Cars do not have emission controls.*

In contrast,

Subarus, which are my favorite cars, have all-wheel drive

includes a nonessential clause and must, therefore, be set off with commas. The clause *which are my favorite cars* is not essential to the meaning of the sentence, so it is enclosed in commas to tell the reader it may be taken out of the sentence without hurting the meaning. Can you tell the difference in meaning between the following two sentences?

My sister who lives on Pine Island has lots of fruit trees on her property.

My sister, who lives on Pine Island, has lots of fruit trees on her property.

The other rules are quite simple and self-explanatory. Use commas to separate items in a series:

I have traveled to the Caribbean, Europe, South America, and Australia.

Your instructor may tell you that the last comma is unnecessary. Some of us use it; some of us do not.

Use commas following certain introductory elements like *as such, well,* and *yes* when they begin a sentence:

Well, no one ever told me!

after a succession of introductory prepositional phrases:

Under the stairs, behind the closet door, Dad had hidden our Christmas presents.

after an introductory adverb clause (but *not* when a clause follows an independent clause):

When I awoke this morning, the power was off because of the storm last night.

But:

The power was off when I awoke this morning because of the storm last night.

Use commas to set off an expression that interrupts the flow of the sentence:

My professor, a noted authority on George Bernard Shaw, bores me with his stories. I am, therefore, doing my homework in his class.

And, finally, use commas to separate items in dates and addresses, after the salutation of a friendly letter, and after the closing of any letter.

# EXERCISE

Add commas where needed or remove extra commas. No sentence is correct as written.

1. After I got up this morning I ran five miles.

2. Students, who study hard, will pass the test.

3. My mom however didn't believe me.

4. Most dorm residents know that they aren't supposed to have candles but they do anyway.

5. The girl, standing over in the corner, is the one who hit me. (There are many girls in the area.)

6. Last night Hugo ate pizza ice cream strawberries nachos and fudge.

7. Mom who is 55 years old still likes to snowboard.

8. Billy lives at, 23 Cherry Hill Lane, Salem, Massachusetts.

9. Mary Jones who is an English major flunked Freshman Composition.

10. My tedious boring ugly conceited date wants to see me again!

11. Mom said, that we should not stay out too late.

12. As a matter of fact I want to live in the same apartment next year as my freshman roommate.

13. Plants, which don't need much water, live in the desert.

14. I really like math so I'm going to take two math classes in summer school this year.

15. Dad said "When you get home please take the dog for a walk."

16. Basketball players, who score a lot of points, will be given an award.

17. Shiraz my favorite wine comes from Australia.

18. The comma test on Monday March 16 was too easy for me.

19. Milk that is my daughter's favorite drink has lots of calcium.

20. My cat tangled with a skunk, and then climbed a tree in fright.

# APOSTROPHES

Apostrophes to form possession seem to cause students problems, but the rule is really quite simple if you can remember this: Form the word; then add the apostrophe! That's all you need to remember.

**Look at that horses tail!**   [incorrect]

Form the word first; then add the apostrophe. In the sample sentence, the word *tail* signals there is only one horse. Thus form the word first—*horse*—and then add the apostrophe.

**Look at that horse's tail!**   [correct]

**Look at those horses tails!**   [incorrect]

In this sentence, *those* and *tails* signal there are several horses. So form the word first—*horses*—and then add the apostrophe.

**Look at those horses' tails!**   [correct]

What do you do with women and men and children? The same rule applies: Form the word first; then add the apostrophe.

**Shirley went to the mens department to buy her daughter some boxer shorts.**   [incorrect]

Remember that the plural of *man* is *men*, so the word is already formed; therefore, form the word and then add the apostrophe.

> Shirley went to the men's department to buy her daughter some boxer shorts.  [correct]

Personal pronouns in the possessive case (*his, hers, its, ours, yours,* and *theirs*) are already in the possessive case and do not require apostrophes.

Remember that *it's* can mean only one thing—*it is*. Any time you are tempted to use an apostrophe with *its*, ask yourself if you mean *it is*; if not, then do not use an apostrophe. Apostrophes are also used to show where letters have been omitted in a contraction, so put them in the proper place (*don't, can't, they're, you're*). Finally, use an apostrophe and the letter *s* to form the plural of numbers and letters when they are referred to as words:

> I got two C's on my report card.
>
> I don't know my 9's table.

## EXERCISE

Correct the apostrophe errors in the following sentences.

1. Yesterday I broke my roommates favorite mug.

2. It was a present from her summer job; she cooks at a womens and childrens center.

3. Now, its handle is in pieces.

4. I promised to buy her a new one at one of the store's in the mall.

5. She was'nt satisfied because she thinks all the stores mugs are dumb.

# QUOTATION MARKS

Quotation marks are used to enclose direct quotations, those exact words spoken by someone. Do not use quotation marks to enclose indirect quotations, those words that are *not* exactly quoted:

> My brother told me he was going to the show tonight. He wanted to know if I wanted to go too.

A direct quotation is set off from the rest of the sentence by a comma:

> Mary asked, "Are you going to the movies with Marc?"

Always place commas and periods *inside* the closing quotation marks:

> "I'm not sure," I answered. "I have to finish my homework first."

Always put semicolons, colons, question marks, or exclamation marks *outside* the closing quotation marks:

"Mom," I yelled, "I've finished my homework"; then I hid my assignment sheet under my pillow.

Finally, use only one punctuation mark at the end of a quotation:

Did you ever find out who first asked, "Is the moon made of cheese?"

## EXERCISE

Correct errors in quotation mark usage in the following sentences.

1. I was angry when my sister said that "she didn't like my new outfit."

2. I paid a lot for these clothes! I said.

3. She said, You got cheated!

4. I told her that "she didn't know what she was talking about."

5. Why don't you see if you can do any better? I finally said as I walked out of the room.

# CHAPTER 18

# Sentence Problems

## FRAGMENTS

Along with spelling, punctuation, and pronoun problems, fragments and comma splices cause student writers incredible grief. We explained comma splices and how to correct them in Chapter 17 when we discussed comma rules. In Chapter 15 we talked about independent and dependent clauses. Remember, a dependent clause, a group of words containing a subject and a verb but *no* complete thought, cannot stand alone. In other words, it cannot function as a sentence. If you should write a sentence that is, in fact, a dependent clause, it is called a fragment, and your instructor will emblazon your paper with a big red "frag" beside your grievous error.

I will wait patiently by the telephone. Until I hear from you.   [fragment]

*Until I hear from you*, although it contains a subject, *I*, and a verb, *hear*, is dependent; it cannot stand alone. If I were to walk into your classroom and greet you with "Until I hear from you," you'd shake your head, look at your neighbor, and wonder, "Is she crazy?"

How do you correct a fragment? Just connect it to the idea it depends on; in this case, add it on to the preceding independent clause:

I will wait patiently by the telephone until I hear from you.

Another common cause of fragments is misusing an *-ing* word:

I sat patiently by the telephone. Waiting for your phone call.   [fragment]

Again, the simple way to correct this fragment is to attach it to the sentence that precedes it:

I sat patiently by the telephone waiting for your phone call.

Just remember the definition of a sentence: a group of words containing a subject, a verb, and a complete thought. If a group of words appears in your writing that does not contain a complete thought, it is probably a fragment. Connect it to the sentence which it belongs to.

# SPLICED AND FUSED SENTENCES

Remember, comma splices occur when you connect two independent clauses together with a comma instead of using a period. Go back and review the comma rules if you are unsure about how to correct spliced or fused sentences (a fused or run-on sentence contains two independent clauses with *no* punctuation separating them).

## EXERCISE

Circle the dependent clause in the following sentences.

1. John drank a six-pack of Coke while he read the novel.

2. Since she had no homework, Elizabeth went to bed early.

3. Mom told me I couldn't go.

4. My best friend, who lives in Illinois, is coming to visit.

5. If you don't know the answer, you can look at the answer key.

## EXERCISE

Change the following fragments into complete sentences.

1. When I come home

2. The girl eating pizza while she talked

3. Before I got home with all my homework

4. Driving into the parking lot following a green Mercedes

5. Because the U.S. Coast Guard keeps a lookout for icebergs

## EXERCISE

Correct the following sentences using one of the three methods given for correcting comma spliced and fused sentences.

1. I like murder mysteries, they're my favorite kind of novel.

2. Freshman Comp is my favorite course I'm doing very well in it.

3. I like Texas but I miss my home state.

4. My dad never went to college, he was drafted out of high school.

5. I have a cat, her name is Zoey.

6. We ate scallops for dinner last night the whole family got sick.

7. My paper was awesome I got an "A" on it.

8. I really wish I hadn't studied so hard for this math test it's easier than I expected.

9. When I got up this morning my daughter was sleeping on her floor she must have fallen out of bed.

10. There are four people at work who really like me they follow me everywhere.

# CHAPTER 19

# Homonyms and Other Commonly Confused Words

Some words, called *homonyms*, are commonly confused because they have the same sounds but different meanings. Other words are nonstandard, words not acceptable in written work.

**accept** (to receive; verb)
**except** (but, exclude, leave out; preposition)

**advice** (suggestion about what to do; noun)
**advise** (to recommend or suggest; verb)

**affect** (to influence; verb. As a noun, it means a feeling or emotion)
**effect** (to bring about or to cause to happen; verb. As a noun, it means result)

**all ready** (completely prepared; adjective)
**already** (before now, previously; adverb)

**all right** (satisfactory; adverb)
**alright** (nonstandard, considered a misspelling)

**all together** (in a group; adjective and adverb)
**altogether** (completely, entirely; adverb)

**allusion** (indirect reference; noun)
**illusion** (incorrect idea or appearance; noun)

**a lot** (*always* two words, *never* alot; noun)
**allot** (to distribute or allocate; verb)

**altar** (sacred table; noun)
**alter** (change; verb)

**amount** (quantity that cannot be counted; noun)
**number** (items that can be counted; noun)

**bare** (uncovered, to uncover; adjective or verb)
**bear** (animal, to carry; noun or verb)

**being as, being that** (nonstandard use for *because* or *since*)

**beside** (next to; preposition)
**besides** (except or in addition to; preposition or adverb)

**brake** (pedal used to stop, to stop; noun or verb)
**break** (fracture, to crack into pieces; noun or verb)

**buy** (purchase; noun or verb)
**by** (beside, near; preposition)

**can** (is able to; verb)
**may** (has permission to; verb)

**capital** (principal city or uppercase letter; noun)
**capitol** (government building [the *o* indicates the dome]; noun)

**censor** (to suppress objectionable material, a person who suppresses; verb or noun)
**censure** (to criticize severely; verb)

**cite** (to refer to, to quote; verb)
**sight** (the ability to see; noun)
**site** (location; noun)

**coarse** (rough or crude; adjective)
**course** (plan, unit of curriculum, path; noun)

**complement** (to complete or supplement, something that completes; verb or noun)
**compliment** (praise, or to praise, noun or verb)

**conscience** (one's sense of right and wrong, moral sense; noun)
**conscious** (alert to or aware of; verb)

**could of, should of, would of** (These are incorrect and totally unacceptable forms of *could have, should have, would have*; verb and preposition rather than verb)

**desert** (arid, sandy area or abandon; noun or verb)
**dessert** (sweet food served at end of meal)

**elicit** (evoke or draw forth; verb)
**illicit** (illegal, adjective)

**emigrate** (leave a country to settle elsewhere, travel from; verb)
**immigrate** (enter another country to settle, travel to; verb)

**eminent** (distinguished; adjective)
**imminent** (about to happen, adjective)

**every day** (each day; adjective and noun)
**everyday** (commonplace, ordinary; adjective)

**farther** (refers to distance; adverb)
**further** (refers to quantity or degree; adverb)

**forth** (forward; adverb)
**fourth** (number between third and fifth; noun and adjective)

**good** (adjective)
**well** (adverb)

**hanged** (refers to people; verb)
**hung** (refers to things that can be suspended; verb)

**hear** (perceive with the ears; verb)
**here** (in this place; adverb)

**imply** (to state indirectly or to suggest; verb)
**infer** (to come to a conclusion based on evidence; verb)

**irregardless** (no such word) regardless is the correct word

**its** (possessive pronoun)
**it's** (it is; pronoun and verb)

**know** (understand; verb)
**no** (not so; adverb)

**later** (after the expected time; adjective)
**latter** (the second of two named people or objects; noun)

**lay** (to put or place *and* the past tense of *lie*; verb)
**lie** (to rest or recline; verb)

**lead** (a gray metal, to go before; noun or verb)
**led** (past tense of *to lead*; verb)

**loose** (unrestrained, not tight; adjective)
**lose** (to fail to win, to misplace; verb)

**may be** (might be; verb)
**maybe** (perhaps; adverb)

**media, medium** (media is the plural of medium; noun)

**passed** (overtook, didn't fail; verb)
**past** (events that have already taken place; noun or adjective)

**patience** (quality of being patient; noun)
**patients** (people being cared for by doctors; noun)

**personal** (private; adjective)
**personnel** (employees; noun)

**precede** (to come before; verb)
**proceed** (to go forward, to move on; verb)

**prejudice** (a noun)
**prejudiced** (adjective)

**presence** (condition of being; noun)
**presents** (gifts, gives; noun, verb)

**principal** (most important, capital sum, head of school (pal);
    adjective or noun)
**principle** (rule, fundamental truth; noun)

**rain** (watery precipitation; noun)
**reign** (period of rule, to rule; noun or verb)
**rein** (strap, to control; noun or verb)

**right** (correct, opposite of left; noun)
**rite** (ceremony; noun)
**write** (put words on paper; verb)

**sometime** (at an indefinite time; noun)
**some time** (adjective modifying time)
**sometimes** (now and then; adverb)

**stationary** (still, not moving; adjective)
**stationery** (writing paper; noun)

**supposed to, used to** (note the -*d* at the end of these two phrases)

**than** (used with comparisons; conjunction)
**then** (at that time; adverb)

**their** (belonging to them, possessive pronoun)
**there** (in that place; adverb)
**they're** (they are; contraction)

**thorough** (complete; adjective)
**threw** (past tense of throw; verb)
**through** (into, by means of; preposition)

**to** (part of infinitive [to be]; preposition, verb
**too** (overly, in addition; adverb)
**two** (number; noun)

**unique** (distinctly characteristic. Unique is an absolute that cannot be modified by *very* or *most*. It stands alone; adjective)

**waist** (middle of the body; noun)
**waste** (trash, to squander; noun or verb)

**weak** (not strong; adjective)
**week** (seven days; noun)

**weather** (atmospheric conditions; noun)
**whether** (possibility of choice; conjunction)

**which** (used to refer to things; pronoun)
**who** (used to refer to people; pronoun)
**that** (some grammarians say *that* can refer to people or objects. Check your instructor's preference; pronoun)

**Who's** (who is or who has; contraction)
**Whose** (possessive form of who; possessive pronoun)

**witch** (woman with supernatural powers; noun)
**which** (what; that; pronoun)

**your** (possessive form of you; possessive pronoun)
**you're** (you are; contraction)

# CHAPTER 20

# Editing Checklist

When we are teaching editing to our students, we often begin by asking them to bring colored pencils to class. We then give them a list of tasks they should perform, using a different colored pencil for each task. You may want to try this until you feel proficient at proofreading your work. We also suggest you do each task separately; in other words, read your work all the way through for each error you may need to correct.

1. Check each sentence to ensure it is a complete sentence, not a fragment or a comma splice or a run-on. Does each sentence have a subject, a verb, and contain a complete thought? Hint: To find the subject of a sentence remember the following:

   * Find the verb (the action word). Ask Who? or What? performed the action.

     While playing catch in their backyard, John and Greg broke the dining room window.

     Remember: -*ing* words without a helping verb are *not* verbs. What is the verb in this sentence? Who performed the action? *John and Greg* are the compound subject.

   * If you cannot find a subject, the sentence is probably a command or request and the subject is *you* even if it does not appear in the sentence:

     Hand me that pen, please.

     (You) hand me that pen, please.

   * When you are trying to find the subject of a question, simply turn the question into a statement, and you'll find the subject:

     Have you had dinner yet?

     You have had dinner.

- *Here* or *there* at the beginning of a sentence are *not* subjects. They are adverbs, and the noun following the verb is the subject.

Here is the pen you requested.

The pen you requested is here.

Do you have any sentences that contain two independent clauses separated by a comma or not separated at all? Do you remember how to correct fused and comma spliced sentences?

2. Check each sentence to ensure it has proper punctuation.

3. Check each sentence to ensure it begins with a capital letter and all proper nouns and appropriate proper adjectives are capitalized.

4. Check all nouns that end in -*s* with an apostrophe to ensure they show possession. Be sure you have placed the apostrophe in the correct place. Check all contractions to ensure the apostrophe is placed correctly.

5. Check each sentence for correct comma use. Check each sentence to see if it opens with an introductory element that should be separated from the main part of the sentence by a comma. Check each sentence that contains any of the FANBOYS (*for, and, nor, but, or, yet,* and *so*). If independent clauses appear before and after the FANBOYS, you have a compound sentence and you must place a comma before the conjunction. Be sure each word in a series is followed by a comma. Remember that restrictive clauses (those clauses essential to the meaning of the sentence) are *not* enclosed in commas, but nonrestrictive clauses are set off by commas.

6. Check each sentence to ensure that each verb agrees with its subject. Remember, prepositional phrases cannot function as subjects of sentences. Check for correct verb forms and tenses.

7. Check each sentence to ensure correct pronoun use. Be sure the subject and object forms of personal pronouns are used correctly. Remember that the subjective case is used after forms of the verb *to be*. When using two pronouns (for example, "He and I went to the movies") together, be sure pronouns are in the same case they would be if they were being used alone. Be sure all your pronouns agree in number and in gender with their antecedents (those words they stand for). And be sure all your pronouns refer to a specific word. If they don't or if you can't find the word they refer to, rewrite the sentence.

8. Are all words spelled correctly? If you are using a computerized spell checker, look up any word the computer highlights if you are not absolutely sure of the correct spelling. Remember, spell checkers do not recognize homonyms. We strongly advise you to keep your own spelling list of those words you commonly misspell.

# CHAPTER 21

# Notes for ESL Writers*

## AGREEMENT OF SUBJECT AND VERB

1. A verb must agree with the subject in number and person.

   He is late for his appointment.

   (Third-person singular subject *he* with third-person singular verb *is*.)

   The boys are in the garage.

   (Third-person plural *boys* with third-person plural verb *are*.)

   a. Although *s* added to a *noun* indicates the plural form, *s* added to a verb indicates the third-person singular.

      He *agrees* with Juan.

      They *agree* with Monsieur Girard.

   b. A plural verb is always required after *you*, even when the pronoun, *you*, is singular.

      *You are* the first guest to arrive.

2. Words or phrases between the subject and the verb do not affect the number of the verb.

   The *box* of manila envelopes *is* almost empty.

3. Singular subjects joined by *and* or by *both . . . and* require a plural verb.

   *Both* the letter *and* the envelope need to be retyped.

4. a. When two subjects are joined by *and* and preceded by *each, every, many a*, or *many an*, a singular verb should be used.

      *Every* name and address on that list *is* correct.

---

*Many of these notes are appropriate for non-ESL writers as well.

b. *Each, every, either, neither, one*, and *another* are always singular. When they are used as subjects or as adjectives modifying subjects, a singular verb is required.

*Neither* of the girls *is* ready to leave.

5. Singular subjects joined by *or, nor, either . . . or, neither . . . nor, not only . . . but also* require a singular verb. However, when there is more than one subject and one of the subjects is plural, the verb should agree with the subject immediately preceding it.

Mary *or* John *is* working at the typewriter.

*Neither* the teacher *nor* the students *are* happy about the change.

6. Within the sentence, parenthetical expressions introduced by *as well as, in addition to, together with, including, rather than*, and so on, do not affect the number of the verb.

The *secretaries*, as well as the supervisor, *are* to have new desks.

The *report*, including the statistical data, *is* to be typed as soon as possible.

7. a. Even though the verb may precede the subject, it must agree with the subject.

Enclosed *is* my résumé.

b. When a sentence begins with *there is, here is*, or *here are*, the verb must agree with the real subject, which follows the verb.

*There are* many *members* who cannot attend the meeting.

8. a. *One of* or *One of the* should be followed by a singular verb; the verb agrees with the subject *one*.

Every *one of* the children's plates *is* empty.

b. The phrases *one of those who* and *one of the things that* should be followed by plural verbs because the verbs refer to *those* or *things*.

North Dakota is *one of the states* that *border* Canada.

9. a. Use a singular verb when a noun that expresses *quantity, a period of time*, or an amount of *money* represents a total amount; however, when these nouns represent a number of individual units, use a plural verb.

That *20 cents* on the table *is* for the stamps you gave me.

b. After *one-half of, part of, three-fourths of, most of, some of, all of*, use a singular verb if a singular noun follows *of* and use a plural verb if a plural noun follows *of*.

*One-half* of the books *have* been moved to the new building.

10. a. Some nouns that are plural in form are always singular in meaning (*news*, *summons*, *works*) and require a singular verb.

    The *news* on the radio *was* alarming.

    b. Other nouns that are plural in form require a plural verb even when they are singular in meaning (*headquarters*, *premises* [*a building*], *proceeds*, *remains*, *riches*, *valuables*, *wages*.)

    My *scissors are* lost. (*Scissors* are always plural.)

    c. Some nouns have the same form in both singular and plural (*corps*, *gross*, *series*); the verb must agree with the meaning intended.

    The *moose were* plentiful last season.

    This *moose was* shot by my uncle.

    d. Some nouns ending in *ics* may be used in either a singular or a plural. A singular verb is used when the noun refers to a course of study or science. A plural verb is used when the noun refers to activities or qualities.

    *Economics is* a required course in my major.

    *Statistics are* easier to grasp in tabular forms.

11. Collective nouns are considered singular when they refer to the group as a unit and as plural when the numbers of the group are thought of as acting separately.

    The *committee is* preparing its report.

    The *committee* (members) *are* all capable people.

# PRONOUNS

1. A personal pronoun must agree with its antecedent (the word for which it stands) in person, number, and gender.

    All *students* are to report at 9 A.M. for *their* examinations.

    *Luis* plans to take *his* car to the picnic.

    *You* may need *your* raincoat on this trip.

2. a. Use a singular pronoun when the antecedent is a singular indefinite pronoun, such as *anyone, each, every, everyone, everybody, anybody, either, neither, no one, nobody, one, another, something*.

    *Everyone* is expected to bring *his* own lunch.

    b. Use a plural pronoun when the antecedent is a plural indefinite pronoun, such as *both, few, many, others, several*.

    *Several* said *they* would come early to help with the preparations.

    c. The following indefinite pronouns may be singular or plural, depending on the noun to which they refer: *all, any, more, most, none, some.*

       *None* of the *girls* are planning to bring *their* cars.

       *None* of the *money* has been deposited, but *it* is ready to be taken to the bank.

    d. Because indefinite pronouns express the third person, pronouns referring to these antecedents should also be in the third person (*he, she, it, they*).

       If *anyone* wants a copy of this report, *he* should let me know at the end of the meeting.

       *Most* of the employees want *their* checks before Christmas.

3. The *nominative* form of a personal pronoun (*I, we, you, she, he, they, it*) is required when the pronoun is the subject of a verb or when the pronoun follows a linking verb.

    *He will* not *have* any difficulty if *he follows* the instructions in his textbook.

    It *was she* who called you earlier this evening.

4. Use the objective form of a personal pronoun (*me, us, you, her, him, them*) when the pronoun is the object of a verb or a preposition.

    They *told me* to *meet them* here.

    Jean said she would take the message *to them.*

5. Compound personal pronouns ending in *self* or *selves* are used to emphasize a pronoun or a noun already expressed or to reflect the action of the verb back to the subject. They *must not* be used in place of simple personal pronouns. (The noun or pronoun to which the compound personal pronoun refers must be expressed in the same sentence.)

    I will do the work *myself.*

    She found *herself* too ill to make this trip.

    The gifts are for Lotte and *me. (not* myself)

6. When a pronoun follows *as* or *than* in a comparison that is not a complete clause, the correct form of the pronoun can be determined by mentally supplying the missing words.

    Tomas says he can type faster than *I.* (than *I can*)

    Maria's jingly bracelet annoys Miss Allen as much as *me.* (as much as *the jingly bracelet annoys me*)

7. When a compound subject or object contains a pronoun, the correct form can be determined by reading the sentence and omitting everything in the compound but the pronoun.

Paul and (me, I) will be at the door to meet you. (Omit *Paul and*, and you must say, "I will be . . .")

Jim told Dave and (I, me) to open the box of books. (Omit *Dave and*, and you must say, "Jim told me to open . . .")

8. a. Who and whom may be used as interrogative or relative pronouns and may be either singular or plural in meaning. *Who* (or *whoever*) is the nominative form; *whom* (*whomever*) is the objective form.

   Marie is the girl *who* is sitting near the door.

   To *whom* shall I give this package?

   b. When a parenthetical expression such as *he thinks* or *we believe* occurs within a relative clause, disregard the parenthetical expression when deciding which form of the pronoun to use.

   *Who* do you think are going to receive awards?

9. The relative pronoun *who* is used when referring to persons; *which* and *that* are used when referring to places, objects, and animals.

   He is the boy *who* is wearing a red tie.

   She is the type *who* can always be dependable.

   The banner *which* is on the wall belongs to our club.

   The horse *that* won the race yesterday is expected to win again today.

# ADJECTIVES AND ADVERBS

1. When the word following a verb describes the subject of the sentence, that word should be an adjective. Verbs of the senses (*taste, smell, look, sound, feel*) and linking verbs (forms of *appear, be, become, seem*) are usually followed by adjectives. Some other verbs (such as *come, get, grow, prove*) are sometimes followed by adjectives.

   The lemonade tastes *bitter*.

   He appeared *angry*.

2. Words referring to the action of the verb are adverbs. Adverbs tell *when, where, how,* and *how much*. Sometimes verbs of the senses and linking verbs are used as verbs of action. When the modifier refers to the action of the verb (and does not describe the subject), the modifier must be an adverb.

   He walked *unsteadily* across the room.

   She looked *carefully* before crossing the street.

3. An adverb should be placed as near as possible to the word it modifies. Adverbs such as *only, almost, nearly, scarcely, ever, merely, too,* and *also*

require special care. These examples show how the placement of *only* may change the meaning of the sentence.

*Only* Suzette wanted Michel to go.

Suzette *only* wanted Michel to go.

Suzette wanted *only* Michel to go.

4. a. To compare two persons, places, or things, use the *comparative* degree. Form the comparative degree of one-syllable adjectives and adverbs by adding *er* to the positive form. Form the comparative degree of two-syllable (or more) adjectives and adverbs by adding *er* to the positive form or by inserting *more* or *less* before the positive form.

He is the *bigger* of the two players.

Paco is *more* likely to be late than Francisco.

b. To compare more than two persons, places, or things, use the *superlative* degree. Form the superlative degree of one-syllable adjectives and adverbs by adding *est* to the positive form. Form the superlative degree of some two-syllable adjectives and adverbs by adding *est* to the positive form; of others by inserting *most* or *least* before the positive form.

Gary took the *largest* doughnut from the box.

He was the *least* fearful of the group.

c. To form the superlative form of three-syllable (or more) adjectives and adverbs, insert *most* or *least* before the positive form.

Nancy is the *most* attractive of the three sisters.

5. When comparing one person or thing *within* the group to which is belongs, use the superlative form. However, when the person or thing is compared with individual members of its own group, use the comparative form, along with the words *other* or *else*.

Linda was the *most* talented of the contestants.

There are *more* boys in my homeroom than in any *other* homeroom in this school.

Pierre's face is *dirtier* than *anyone else's* in the gang.

6. By their very meaning, some adjectives and adverbs cannot be compared. Among these are *always, completely, correct, perfect, appropriate, square, round, never, dead, unique.* However, they may be modified by such words as *almost, nearly, hardly, scarcely, more,* and *less* to suggest an approach to the absolute.

His *almost* perfect score is not surprising.

Her vacation plans were *nearly* complete.

Ricardo's behavior was *less* appropriate than Sam's.

# PREPOSITIONS

1. Certain words should be followed by specific prepositions, and certain words may be followed by different prepositions depending on meaning.

   a. Agree *with* a person, *to* a plan, *on* or *upon* an approach or point of view.

      I do not agree *with* Marianna.

      Did you agree *to* make the trip?

      They do not agree *on* the method of scoring the game.

   b. Argue *with* a person, *about* something.

      Did you argue *with* Kai about the money?

      What will they argue *about* next?

   c. Apply *for* a position, *to* someone or something.

      Ralph plans to apply *for* that job at the motel.

      If you would apply yourself *to* your work, it would soon be done.

   d. *Convenient for* a purpose or use, *convenient to* a place.

      Will it be *convenient for* you to come tomorrow?

      Our new house is *convenient to* the school.

   e. *Discrepancy in* one thing, *between* two things.

      There are some *discrepancies in* his statement.

      There is a *discrepancy between* my figures and yours.

   f. *Proceed to* a place, *with* an action or a plan.

      You may *proceed to* the head of the line.

      You may *proceed with* the typing of the report.

   g. *Speak* or *talk to* (tell something to) someone, *speak* or *talk with* (discuss with) someone.

      I shall have to *speak to* him about this error.

      He would like to *talk with* you about your plans.

h. *All* or *both* are followed by *of* only when a pronoun follows.

*Both* robins found the same worm.

*All of* us are going on the bus.

i. *Inside* or *outside* should not be followed by *of*. When referring to time, use *within*, not *inside of*.

You may set the box just *inside* the door.

He will return *within* a month.

j. *Different from* (not *than*) something else.

This book is *different from* the one you have.

k. Identical *with* (not *to*) the other one.

Her dress is identical *with* mine.

2. It is important to know how to choose correctly among prepositions to express different meanings.

a. *Between* is used when referring to two items; *among* is used when referring to more than two.

Divide the work *between* the two groups.

The money can be divided equally *among* the four of you.

b. *Besides* means "in addition to," *beside* means "by the side of."

You will need this book *besides* those you already have.

Your little girl asked to sit *beside* me.

c. *At* and *in* denote position; *to* and *into* indicate movement toward. When *in to* are two separate words, *in* is used as an adverb, *to* as a preposition.

John is working *in* the library, but he will go *to* his English class next period.

Please take this report *in to* Mrs. Smith.

d. *From* is used when referring to persons; *off* is used when referring to things. Do *not* use *of* or *from* after *off*.

I received this gift *from* Marie.

Mary took my coat *off* the chair.

e. When *except* is a preposition, use the objective form of a pronoun that follows.

Because of the storm, everyone was late to class *except* Bill and *me*.

f. Instead of *in regard to*, use *with regard to*, or *as regards*.

*With regard to* our conversation, please send me a memo.

*As regards* our conversation, please send me a memo.

# PLURALS

1. The plural of most nouns is formed by adding s to the singular form. If the singular form ends in *s*, *ch*, *sh*, *z*, or *x*, however, the plural is usually formed by adding *es*. Singular nouns ending in silent *s* remain the same in the plural.

   book    books        dash    dashes        corps (silent *s*)

2. When a singular noun ends in *y* preceded by a vowel, the plural is formed by adding *s* to the singular. If the final *y* is *preceded by a consonant*, however, the plural is formed by changing the *y* to *i* and adding *es* to the singular.

   holiday    holidays        inventory    inventories

3. Plurals of singular nouns ending in *o preceded by a vowel* are formed by adding *s* to the singular. Some nouns ending in *o preceded by a consonant* also form their plurals by adding *s*. This is particularly true of nouns related to music. Other nouns ending in *o preceded by a consonant* form their plurals by adding *es*. When in doubt, consult the dictionary.

   studio    studios        solo    solos        potato    potatoes

4. The plurals of most singular nouns ending in *f*, *fe*, or *ff* are formed by adding *s* to the singular. However, the plurals of some nouns in this category are formed by changing the *f* or *fe* to *ve* and adding *s*. To be sure, refer to the dictionary.

   chief    chiefs        life    lives        half    halves

5. The plurals of some nouns are formed by changing letters within the word or the ending of the word.

   man    men        foot    feet        child    children

6. When a compound noun is written as one word, pluralize the final elements as if it stood alone. Plurals of hyphenated or spaced compounds are formed by adding *s* to the chief element of the compound. When a hyphenated compound does not contain a noun, however, simply add *s* to the final element.

   layoff    layoffs            runner-up    runners-up
   chairman    chairmen        shut-in    shut-ins

# POSSESSIVES

1. To form the possessive of a singular noun not ending in *s* or in an *s sound*, add an apostrophe followed by an *s*.

   the president's gavel      Helen's coat

2. a. If a singular noun ends in *s* or an *s sound*, add an apostrophe and an *s* if a new syllable is formed in the pronunciation of the possessive.

   The boss's briefcase      Mr. Norris's report

   b. If the addition of *s* would make an *s-ending* word hard to pronounce, add the apostrophe only.

   Mrs. Davies' party      Mr. Andrews' order

   Note: Form the plural of a noun first; then apply rule 3 or 4 to form the possessive, as appropriate.

3. The possessive of regular plural nouns is formed by adding only the apostrophe after the *s*.

| Singular | Singular Possessive | Plural | Plural Possessive |
|----------|---------------------|--------|-------------------|
| boy | boy's | boys | boys' |
| typist | typist's | typists | typists' |

4. The possessive of irregular plurals is formed by adding the apostrophe followed by *s*.

| Singular | Singular Possessive | Plural | Plural Possessive |
|----------|---------------------|--------|-------------------|
| child | child's | children | children's |
| man | man's | men | men's |

   Note: Form the plural of a noun first; then apply rule 3 or 4 to form the possessive, as appropriate.

5. To form the possessive of a compound noun (whether solid, spaced, or hyphenated), add an apostrophe plus *s* to the last element of the compound.

   grandson's      switchboard operator's      clerk-typist's

6. An unhyphenated possessive expression and a hyphenated compound adjective provide alternative ways of expressing the same thought.

   A two week's trip or a two-week trip

7. A noun or a pronoun that modifies a gerund (the *-ing*-ending form of a verb used as a noun) should be in the possessive case.

   I appreciated his carrying my books.

   Roger's leaving early disrupted the class.

8. Possessive personal pronouns *do not* require an apostrophe.

| | | |
|---|---|---|
| he, his | she, her, hers | they, their, theirs |
| it, its | you, you, yours | we, our, ours |

Note: Do not confuse personal pronouns with contractions that sound like the possessive pronouns.

| | |
|---|---|
| its (possessive) | it's (it is, it has) |
| your (possessive) | you're (you are) |
| their (possessive) | they're (they are) |
| theirs (possessive) | there's (there is, there has) |

# Glossary

**Analytical level**   Level of reading that includes the skills of recognizing an author's rhetorical modes (organization patterns), questioning content, text marking, annotating, outlining, mapping, and summarizing.

**Annotating**   A prewriting technique where you make notes in the margin of a piece of writing to help you remember as you prepare to write about that piece.

**Aside**   Comment made that departs or digresses from the topic at hand. In writing, an aside is written within parentheses.

**Audience**   That group of people a piece of writing is directed toward. Thus a writer should try to determine the readers' knowledge of the subject, their biases, and their interests before choosing level of language and tone.

**Brainstorming**   A prewriting technique where you list, as ideas come to you, anything that you can connect to a topic you want to write about.

**Clustering**   See *mapping.*

**Coherence**   Relationship between all the parts of an essay that make the essay easy to read. The use of transitional phrases, repetition of key terms, and parallelism all ensure a tight connection of ideas.

**Colloquial language**   Language appropriate in conversation but considered nonstandard usage in college or professional writing. Examples include expressions like *dorm* for dormitory, *kind of, you know, flunk* the exam, and *wrinkles* for parents.

**Connotation**   Meanings associated with a word that are not the dictionary definitions but may have emotional or experiential connections.

Animals often carry strong connotations: what do you think of when you hear *swine, skunk, toad*? See *Denotation.*

**Context**   Situation or circumstances in which a word is used or an idea is developed.

**Creative level**   Level of reading that serves as a bridge between the first four levels of reading and the writing process. This level requires you to go beyond the words on a page, to take some kind of action.

**Critical level**   Level of reading that introduces the *Socratic method* (the use of questions). You also learn to separate fact and opinion by recognizing support (called evidence in argumentative writing).

**Critical thinking**   Ability to analyze and assess what we read, hear, and write by examining and questioning.

**Deduction**   Beginning an argument with a generalization and then applying that generalization to a specific case. Paragraphs that begin with topic sentences and are supported by evidence are examples of deductive reasoning. See *Induction.*

**Denotation**   Literal or dictionary definition of a word. See *Connotation.*

**Diction**   Choice of words the author uses to achieve a certain purpose and audience. See *Standard usage* and *Nonstandard usage, Formal English* and *Informal English.*

**Ethos**   Ethical appeal used in argumentative and persuasive writing determined by the reasonableness of the argument based on evidence and tone. See *Logos* and *Pathos.*

**Fact**   Something that has been objectively verified; that which cannot be argued. See *Opinion.*

**Formal English**   Language of all serious writing, which should be used in formal essays, essay answers, research papers, and scholarly writing. See *Informal English.*

**Induction**   Reasoning that moves from the particular to the general. A paragraph that begins with examples and leads to a generalization that serves as a topic sentence at the end of the paragraph is an example of inductive reasoning. See *Deduction.*

**Informal English**   Language most of us use most of the time. The language of general magazines, newspapers, and books. See *Formal language.*

**Interpretive level**   Level of reading that involves understanding what an author really means. Includes the skills of recognizing an author's purpose, style, and tone.

**Journal**   As a prewriting technique, a place to freewrite, keep notes, respond to readings and record ideas about potential topics.

**Literal level**   Level of reading that deals with what an author says. It means comprehending the message on the page—being able to identify the general topic, the author's thesis or main idea, and the supporting evidence.

**Logos**   Logic or rationale an author uses to appeal to an audience by using induction, deduction, and strong supporting evidence. See *Ethos* and *Pathos.*

**Mapping**   A prewriting technique where you visually arrange ideas on paper to organize and relate ideas about a topic. Also called *clustering.*

**Metaphor**   Figure of speech that compares two unlike things without using "like" or "as." *She is an elephant!* See *Simile.*

**Nonstandard usage**   Language using dialect (the language that typifies a particular region), colloquialism (the language of conversation), and slang (trendy words that appear and disappear from everyday use).

**Opinion**   This word has two quite different meanings. We offer both denotations, but for the purpose of writing thesis statements the second definition is required. An opinion can be a belief that is not substantiated, or it can be a judgment based on knowledge or expertise. Many opinions are held based on prejudice, or peer belief, or parental belief without consideration. Base your opinions on the result of your study, inquiry, or research.

**Outlining**   Arranging ideas in outline form to focus paper. From the outline, you can freewrite about the topics listed. Outlines can also be used as an organizational check after you've written your first draft.

**Paragraph**   The basic unit of writing, a paragraph is a mini-essay. It is composed of a topic sentence and related sentences that together develop a main idea.

**Parallel structure**   Words, phrases, sentences, and ideas put into the same grammatical form.

**Pathos**   Emotional appeal an author uses by addressing the audience's feelings and values.

**Prewriting**   That period of time when a writer considers the assignment, considers purpose and audience, uses the methods of invention—freewriting, brainstorming, mapping, or writing in a journal—and then formulates a thesis and direction for the essay.

**Process**   Repetitive (recursive) actions of prewriting or planning, writing or drafting, and rewriting or revising that occur as a writer works toward a final product.

**Purpose**   This word has two meanings with regard to writing. The first is the reason the writer is producing an essay—to inform, to amuse, to teach, to direct, to analyze, or to persuade. The second meaning relates to the author's purpose for the essay—the author's interest in the topic, the author's ideas, the author's "itch."

**Rewriting**   Action that occurs after the first draft when an author revises or "re-sees" the draft, looking at fundamental elements of organization, coherence, and unity.

**Rhetorical modes**   Organizational patterns that serve as ways to develop a piece of writing. These patterns can be used alone or in combination in an essay.

**Sight vocabulary**   Words that are recognized when seen in print. These words may or may not be part of your speaking vocabulary, but you know their meaning when you are reading.

**Simile**   Comparison of two dissimilar things using "like" or "as." *He is as big as an elephant.* See *Metaphor.*

**Slang**   Inappropriate language for college writing, but typical vocabulary used in informal speech and often associated with a particular group of people.

**Socratic method**   Method of teaching that uses questions to draw information from students rather than lecturing.

**Standard usage**   Written language of educated native English speakers seen in college and professional writing.

**Style**   The *way* something is written rather than *what* is written, style refers to the author's voice. A writer's style may be formal or informal, depending on the purpose and audience, but a reader will recognize the author's voice in either instance.

**Text marking**   Underlining, annotating, and otherwise studying a piece of reading by annotating the page.

**Thesis**   The essay's main idea. A *thesis statement* usually includes the author's purpose and should imply the direction of the writing.

**Tone**   The author's attitude toward the subject, usually transmitted through diction.

**Topic**   General assignment or subject about which a writer chooses a specific area to discuss.

**Topic sentence**   Thesis of a paragraph.

**Transitional words**   Words or phrases that link sentences, paragraphs, and ideas in a piece of writing to achieve coherence.

**Unity**   Evidence that all sentences in a paragraph relate to the topic sentence and all paragraphs relate to the thesis statement.

# Works Cited

Adler, Mortimer. "How To Mark a Book." *How To Read a Book: The Art of Getting a Liberal Education.* 1940 (revised 1972).

"Analyze," *American Heritage Dictionary.* 1982 ed.

Angelou, Maya. *I Know Why the Caged Bird Sings.* New York: Random House, 1997.

Bain, Alexander. *English Composition and Rhetoric.* 2ᵈ ed. Boston: Houghton Mifflin, 1982.

"Bob and Warren." Unpublished student essay, 1990.

Bookman, Ann. "Family Leave Act, Five Years Later," *Boston Globe,* August 3, 1998.

Brady, Judy. "I Want a Wife." *Ms.,* Vol. 1, No. 1, December 31, 1971.

Carson, Rachel. *The Sea Around Us.* New York: Oxford University Press, 1951.

Chamblee, Cynthia M. "Bringing Life to Reading and Writing for At-Risk Students." *Journal of Adolescent and Adult Literacy,* Vol. 41. 532–537.

D'Angelo, Frank. "The Topic Sentence Revisited." *College English,* 37, 1986.

Del Castillo, Rose. "Americanization Is Tough on 'Macho'." 1989.

Dickens, Charles. *Hard Times.* New York: W. W. Norton.

Ehrenreich, Barbara. "In Defense of Splitting Up." *Time.* April 6, 1996.

Elbow, Peter. *Writing Without Teachers.* New York: Oxford University Press, 1973.

"Elephant," *American Heritage Dictionary,* 1982 ed.

Emig, Janet. "Writing as a Mode of Learning," *College Composition and Communication,* 28, 1977.

Espen, Hal. "The Woodstock Wars." *Windows on Writing.* Eds. Laurie G. Kirszner and Stephen Mandell. St. Martin's Press, 1996. 39.

"Essay," *American Heritage Dictionary,* 1982 ed.

"Expository," *American Heritage Dictionary,* 1982 ed.

Fleeger, John. "Why Isn't Pete Rose in the Hall of Fame?" *Windows on Writing,* New York: Bedford, St. Martin's, 1995.

Francis, Robert. "Catch," *The Orb Weaver.* Middletown, Connecticut: Wesleyan University Press, 1960.

Gansburg, Martin. "Thirty-Eight Who Saw Murder Didn't Call the Police," *New York Times,* March 27, 1964.

George, Nelson. "Rare Jordan." *Essence.* November, 1996.

Golden, Michael. "Don't Rewrite the Bible," *Newsweek,* November 7, 1983.

Goodman, Ellen. "In the New Wave of Chick Flicks, A New Kind of Man," 117–118.

Goodman, Ellen. "Self-Serving Society," *Boston Globe,* October 19, 1996.

Gorman, James. "What the Nose Knows." 1986.

Greene, Bob. "It Took This Night to Make Us Know," *Johnny Deadline: Reporter.* Chicago: Nelson-Hall, 1976.

Grinna, Ilene. "A Civility Lesson for Students." Unpublished essay, 1998.

Highet, Gilbert. "The Subway Station," *Talents and Geniuses.* New York: Curtis Brown, 1957.

Jacoby, Jeff. "Kennedy's Destructive Hate Crimes Bill," *Boston Globe,* July 20, 1998.

Jacoby, Jeff. "Seventy-Five Years of Underestimating Calvin Coolidge," *Boston Globe,* August 6, 1998.

Kean, Thomas. "The Crisis Coming to Campus," *Washington Post,* May 1, 1995.

King, Martin Luther, Jr. "I Have a Dream." New York: Writer's House, 1963.

King, Martin Luther, Jr. "Three Types of Resistance to Oppression." New York: Writer's House, 1963.

Lam, Andrew. "They Shut My Grandmother's Room Door." San Francisco: Pacific News Service, 1989.

Lave, Tamara Rice, "Equal Before the Law." *Newsweek* 13 July 1998. 14.

Markoe, Merrill. "Men, Women, and Conversation." *Windows on Writing*. Eds. Laurie G. Kirszner and Stephen R. Mandell. St. Martin's Press, Inc. 1996. 58.

McClain, Leanita, "The Middle-Class Black's Burden," *A Foot in Each World: Essays and Articles by Leanita McClain*. Evanston, Illinois: Northwestern University Press, 1986.

McCusick, Donna. "Integrated Reading and Writing: Theory to Research to Practice." From selected conference papers: National Association for Developmental Education, Vol. 3. 30–32.

Mikulski, Barbara. "A Polish American Speaks Up: The Myth of the Melting Pot," *Poles in America: 1608-1972*. Dobbs Ferry, New York: Oceana, 1973.

Montville, Leigh. "Requiem for a Super Featherweight," *Sports Illustrated*. May 29, 1955.

Moon, William Least Heat. "Arizona 87," *Blue Highways: A Journey into America*. New York: Little, Brown & Co., 1986.

Morgan, Thomas L. and William Barlow. "From Cakewalks to Concert Halls."

Mori, Toshio. "The Woman Who Makes Swell Doughnuts," *Yokohama, California*. Caldwell, Idaho: The Caxton Printers, Ltd., 1949.

Mushnick, Phil. "The Hall of Fame Is Now Ready for Rose." *TV Guide*, August 29, 1998.

Naylor, Gloria. "The Meanings of a Word." *New York Times*. February 20, 1986.

Nelson, Mariah Burton. "Who Wins? Who Cares?" *Women's Sports and Fitness*, July/August, 1990.

Nyhan, David. "The Prison Population Is Rising—Politicians Must Be Very Proud." *Boston Globe*. August 5, 1998.

Nyhan, David. "Turn Off the TV Before It Ruins Us." *Boston Globe*. September 16, 1996.

Orwell, George. "Poverty." *Down and Out in Paris and London*. Orlando, Florida: Harcourt, Inc., 1933.

Osborne, Charles. *Applied Imagination*. New York: Scribner, 1957.

"Paragraph," *American Heritage Dictionary*, 1982 ed.

Parker-Pope, Tara. "Custom Made." *Wall Street Journal*. September 30, 1996.

Quinn, Carin C. "The Jeaning of America—and the World." *American Heritage*. Vol. 30/3, 1978.

_____ "Rationality About the Mentally Ill." *Boston Globe*. 3 August 1998. A:10.

Rosen, Mike. "People of the Ruined Hills."

Rudolfsky, Bernard. "The Fashionable Body." *Horizon*. Autumn 1971.

Samuelson, Robert J. "Can America Assimilate?" *Newsweek*. April, 2001.

Sanders, Scott Russell. "Women and Men." *Women and Men*. 1987.

Schlesinger, Arthur, Jr. "What If RFK Had Survived?" *Newsweek*. 8 June 1998. 55.

Seyler, Dorothy. "Active Reader's Outline." *The Reading Context*. New York: Allyn and Bacon, 1997.

Staples, Brent. "Role Models, Bogus and Real." *New York Times*. June 24, 1994.

Tennies, Arthur C. "In Defense of Deer Hunting and Killing." *National Observer*. January 19, 1975.

Vander Voort, Danielle. "Take Me to Your Leader." Unpublished student essay. 1997.

Vidal, Gore. "Drugs." *Homage to Daniel Shays: Collected Essays*. 1972.

Viorst, Judith. "Friends, Good Friends—and Such Good Friends." *Redbook*. 1977.

"The Voyage Continues." *Boston Sunday Globe*. January 4, 1998.

Wells, H. G. "The Potwell Inn." *Writing Prose*. Eds. Thomas S. Kane and Leonard J. Peters. New York: Oxford University Press, 1959. 107–108.

White, E. B. "The Three New Yorks." *Here Is New York*. New York: Harper Collins, 1949.

White, Tim. "Save the Cape from Overdevelopment." *Boston Globe*. 4 August 1998.

Whitehead, Kristin. "Street Smart." Unpublished student essay. *Windows on Writing*. Eds. Laurie G. Kirszner and Stephen R. Mandell. St. Martin's Press, 1996. 585–586.

Will, George F. "The Case of Phillip Becker." The Washington Post Writers' Group, 1980.

Williams, Randall. "Daddy Tucked the Blanket." *New York Times*. June 10, 1975.

"Write," *American Heritage Dictionary*. 1982 ed.

Malcolm X. "Learning to Read." *The Autobiography of Malcolm X*. New York: Random House, 1964

Zimring, Franklin E. "Confessions of a Former Smoker." (Original Title – "Hot Boxes for Ex-Smokers.") *Newsweek*. 20 April 1987.

Zinsser, William. *On Writing Well*. 3$^d$ ed. New York: Harper & Row, 1976.

# Credits

**Drawings:** Pages 104 and 125, by Dottye Yakovakis.

**Photos:** Pages 38, 56, 136, and 177 by Karen Ruzicka; page 108, © Duomo/CORBIS; page 144, © AFP/CORBIS; page 156, © Wally McNamee/CORBIS; page 180, © Bettmann/CORBIS.

# Index

LIBRARY
ST. LOUIS COMMUNITY COLLEGE
AT FLORISSANT VALLEY